SEPARATION-INDIVIDUATION:

Theory and Application

Gardner Press Series in Clinical Social Work

Edited by Mary L. Gottesfeld

Separation-Individuation: Theory and Application

By Joyce Edward, Nathene Ruskin, Patsy Turrini

Existential Psychotherapy

By David G. Edwards

Separation–
Individuation:

Theory
and
Application

By
Joyce Edward, M.S.S.A.
Nathene Ruskin, M.S.S.
Patsy Turrini, M.S.S.

GARDNER PRESS, INC.
New York

Gardner Press, Inc.
19 Union Square West
New York 10003

Library of Congress Cataloging in Publication Data

Edward, Joyce., Ruskin, Nathene., Turrini, Patsy.
  Separation-individuation: Theory and Application.

  Bibliography: p.
  Includes index.
  1. Separation-inidviduation. 2. Mahler, Margaret S.
3. Child psychology. 4. Psychotherapy. I. Ruskin,
Nathene. II. Turrini, Patsy. III. Title. [DNLM:
1. Child development. 2. Personality development.
3. Object attachment. 4. Anxiety, Separation.
5. Psychoanalysis—In infancy and childhood. WS 350.5 E25s]
RC489.S45E38   155.4'18   81-4249
ISBN 0-89876-018-6   AACR2

Printed in the United States of America

Dedicated to our Teachers, Colleagues, and Friends

Gertrude and Rubin Blanck

Contents

Acknowledgments

We wish to express our deep appreciation to Dr. Margaret M. Mahler. Her lifelong efforts have greatly extended the psychoanalytic understanding of normal and pathological development. While we describe our own understanding and application of her theoretical concepts, it is her work that has served as a guide and inspiration for our endeavors.

We also wish to acknowledge the help of Mary L. Gottesfeld, who encouraged us to undertake this work and whose advice and support have been most valuable.

We thank Judy Mishne, who read the book and provided excellent suggestions, and Mary Fletcher, our typist, whose patience and organizational ideas were most helpful.

Finally, we express our gratitude to our clients. Our therapeutic collaboration has given life to the concepts we describe and has helped to shape our translation of the theory into clinical practice.

Introduction

The purpose of this book is to summarize, for mental health practitioners, the contributions of Margaret Mahler to contemporary psychoanalytic developmental theory and to share with others our particular applications of her concepts to clinical practice. Mahler and her colleagues have devoted the last thirty years to the study of disturbed and normal children, employing psychoanalysis as an investigative tool, in the tradition of Freud, Hartmann, Spitz, and others. Through systematic observational studies of children and their parents, utilizing "free-floating psychoanalytic observation" and a predetermined experimental design, Mahler has detailed a complex developmental sequence to which she has given the name *separation-individuation*. Her work affirms Freud's recognition of the significance of infantile experiences for later development. Her identification of nodal developmental points, during the preoedipal period of life, supports Spitz's findings that critical organizers occur long before the oedipal negotiation. Separation-individuation theory broadens psychoanalytic theory significantly, helping to move psychoanalysis further in the direction of becoming a general developmental psychology, a goal envisioned by Hartmann some forty years ago (1939, p. 8).

Separation-individuation involves progression along two tracks. Separation refers to the child's movement from fusion with the mother; individuation consists of those steps that lead to the development of an individual's own personal and unique characteristics. Moving from autism to symbiosis, through four subphases of separation-individuation, namely differentiation, practicing, rapprochement, and a fourth open-ended subphase, the child advances toward a position of on-the-way to object constancy. This signals the genesis of the ability to retain an internal representation or image of "important others," as distinct from a representation of the self, and makes it possible for the child to retain a connection in the mind with significant persons, whether they are absent or present, frustrating or gratifying. At the same time, this progression leads to a position of on-the-way to self constancy, which represents a beginning sense of the self as separate from others, continuous in time and space. This process, in turn, encompasses an increasing capacity to retain an on-going sense of sameness, despite fluctuations in emotions, and bodily feelings, or external surroundings. The use of the phrase *on-the-way* acknowledges that the process is lifelong. While the principal achievements occur from the third or fourth month to the thirtieth or thirty-sixth month of life, the process is never completed. New derivatives of the earlier processes are manifest in new phases throughout the life cycle.

Favorable negotiation of the separation–individuation sequence leads to psychological birth and helps to promote the structuralization of the mental apparatus, the development of adaptive capacity, the acquisition of identity, and the resources for mutuality in human relationships. Both healthy narcissism and the ability to form meaningful social relationships develop in correlation. Out of the significant exchange between infant and family during the earliest years, the qualities of attachment, trust, empathy, and compassion are slowly acquired. It is the achievement of self and object constancy that, over time, enables human beings to experience themselves as members of the family of humankind, and, at the same time, makes it possible for them to endure and adapt to the inevitable experiences of aloneness, both of which form a part of the human condition.

The developmental accomplishments associated with this progression depend, first and foremost, upon the intactness of the infant's inborn ego apparatuses. The critical role of constitutional endowment in determining the developmental outcome is emphasized by Mahler. Her studies show the remarkable capacity of the child who has average endowment, to extract needed supplies, even under somewhat less than optimal circumstances. On the other hand the studies show that deficiencies in the innate givens may seriously limit an infant's ability to take full advantage of available nurturing. To the extent that constitutional strengths are dependent upon favorable prenatal and neonatal experiences, Mahler's work provides added impetus to a committment to ameliorate those conditions, such as poverty, discrimination, maternal illness, etc. which have long been recognized as deleterious to the infant's development in utero. Indeed, preparation for psychological birth, like preparation for physical birth, is best made before conception.

Mahler's work also affirms and gives specificity to the role of "nurture" in the developmental outcome. The relationship between child and family, is critical for the negotiation of separation and individuation. The nature of the exchange alters, over time, in accordance with the changing needs of the child. It is an early attuned, symbiotic relationship between infant and mother, or her substitute, that provides the firm foundation for all that follows. The physical and libidinal availability of "ordinarily devoted" parents fosters the child's growing capacity for separateness, and affords the child those opportunities for identification and learning that are essential for individuation. The continuing, though changing, bond between child and parents for the long duration of childhood also leads to maturing concepts of others. From valuing the mother as a need-gratifier to valuing her love, the child comes to appreciate her as a person in her own right. The abilities to share, to love, to care for another, to temporarily put another's needs ahead of one's own, and to tolerate anger toward another out of love that also exists evolve slowly over time. This capacity for mutuality in human relatedness extends gradually to other family members, and at adolescence, extends beyond the family.

It is not desirable for the child to separate too rapidly or too early. While parental support and encouragement of the child's forward strivings are essential, parents must not abandon their roles as developmental partners at too early a point in the child's growth. The sustained bond with the parents is generally promoted by the child's prolonged dependency. In addition, however, tolerable degrees of separation anxiety, as well as the child's keenly felt need to share his or her accomplishments at certain points during the progression, serve to ensure the necessary continuation of the requisite libidinal connection.

Mahler's affirmation of the vital role played by the parents, particularly the mother, in the earliest phases adds support to efforts to strengthen family life. This includes social planning and legislation, community organization, and direct service to clients, either individually, in families, or in groups.

We regret that time does not permit a fuller elabloration of the preventative implications of Mahler's work. Indeed we regard that subject as worthy of another book, since the potential for prevention may prove in the long run to be of greatest significance for society as a whole. The detailed view of the slow progression from dependency to independence provides an additional perspective for examining some of the critical social and emotional problems confronting us today. By further documenting the developmental needs of the growing child, Mahler's work may be drawn upon for purposes of

broad social planning and the more specific elaboration of preventative and early interventive efforts. In so far as parent education
may enhance child care capacities, her work may be utilized for that
purpose. Louise Kaplan has already translated Mahler's concepts in
a way that makes them highly useful for parents. (1978) The
Mother's Center Program, which now includes 10 centers throughout
the country has based their child care program largely upon Mahler's findings and has included a summary for parents of her work
in their Manual. (Mother's Center, 1980).

The processes that Mahler has delineated may have their coun-
terparts at physical and cellular levels of life. In *The Lives of a Cell*
Lewis Thomas (1974) has focused on the tendency of cells to pool resources and to join together. He sees this fusion as accounting for
the progressive enrichment and complexity of living things. However, even in the microbial world deviant symbiotic negotiations,
that are "an overstepping of the line by one side or the other, a biological misinterpretation of the borders" (p. 89), usually result in dis-
ease. Symbiosis must be regulated and modulated at the cellular
level. Thomas notes that it is the immune reactions, referred to as
the genes for the "chemical marking of self," as well as "reflective
response of aggression and defense," that keep the force toward fusion from getting out of hand (p. 33). The parallels between cellular
and psychological processes are striking.

There are implications for society as a whole in the theory of human separation and inidviduation. Anthropologist Edward T. Hall
(1977) has noted that the world of human beings divides into cul-
tures whose members either "cut the apron strings" or do not (p.
225). Referring to life as a "continuous process of consolidation and
detachment," Hall has noted the significant differences between
those societies in which children grow up but not apart from their
parents and those where the young in growing up move toward intrapsychic separateness.

Today, there appears to be a pressing need for the human being
who has achieved both self and object constancy, possessing resources for independent functioning and for identifying with and
joining others. The decline of tradition, of the authority of religion,
and the general weakening of the supports provided by family and
community, require a greater degree of individual inner strength,
self-esteem, and self-regulation and direction. At the same time, the
fragility of nature's balance on the planet, the limitations of resources once thought infinite, and the realization that, in some way,
our individual well-being has become increasingly dependent upon

the well-being of persons who are far removed from us geographically and culturally, force upon us an increased sense of ourselves as members of a human fellowship. Indeed, we are compelled, for purposes of survival, to extend feelings of concern to people we shall never see or know, and to begin to share with them more equitably in the utilization and conservation of the earth's resources. In the final analysis, our capacity to adapt as human beings at this juncture in history may well depend upon the degree to which we have achieved psychological birth and our ability to care for our children in a way that fosters the acquisition of those qualities that lead to independence and capacities for interdependence.

In what follows, we shall summarize Mahler's contributions to the understanding of normal and pathological development. For uniformity, we employ the language of psychoanalysis, the language used by Mahler in her original writings. We include a glossary presenting Mahler's definitions of terms wherever possible and draw from other resources when necessary. In Part Two case studies are presented to illustrate application of the theory, as we have understood it, to the treatment of clients who manifest a range of social and psychological problems. We convey the way in which the theory has served as a guide to practice, expanding the capacity to listen, to observe, and to understand our clients more empathetically.

Our efforts are intended to stimulate the reader to explore Mahler's writings in depth. No summary could substitute for the original contributions. We share our experiences in the hope that others will be encouraged to draw from this theory in their unique fashion. Mahler has, herself, built her work on the contributions of theorists who have preceded her. As a "carrier of the psychoanalytic tradition" (Bergmann, 1976 p. xii) she is now stimulating the technical and creative efforts of another generation of practitioners and theorists.

Part

One

THEORY

CHAPTER 1

Forerunners of Separation-Individuation: Autism and Symbiosis

Separation–individuation refers to the developmental sequence through which the human infant moves from the twilight state of neonatal life to a tuning in to the world of reality and the achievement of a sense of separate individual entity.

The term *separation* signifies the intrapsychic developmental track of differentiation, distancing, boundary-formation, and disengagement from the mother. *Individuation* denotes the evolution of intrapsychic autonomy, that is, the development of psychic structure and personality characteristics. Normally, the infant is physiologically equipped for these developmental tasks with reflexes that serve adaptation, a powerful innate drive for individuation, and a capacity to use the essential maternal ministrations. The libidinal availability and nurturance of the maternal caretaker is vital.

There are universal trends in this progression as well as a wide range of individual variations related to both innate and external factors. Clearly demarcated stages have been identified during which certain behavioral indicators are observable, certain specific needs become manifest, and particular developmental achievements take place. The accomplishments of one stage pave the way for the development of the next. Gains accumulate and are consolidated, over time culminating in structural developments that equip the child for the negotiation of subsequent developmental tasks, particularly those associated with the next major organizer, the oedipus complex. (Rangell, 1972).

While psychological birth is the outcome of four specific subphases of the separation–individuation progression to be delineated in the following chapter, the negotiation of those subphases is significantly influenced by the foundation established during the earliest periods of neonatal life. In recognition of the developmental import of the earliest months of life, Mahler has preceded her delineation of the separation–individuation subphases with a detailed elaboration of the periods of normal autism and symbiosis that follow birth and are regarded by her, as the forerunners of separation–individuation.

NORMAL AUTISM

At the beginning of life the normal infant sleeps most of the time, arousing under the pressure of need, particularly under the impact of hunger. Ordinarily the infant at this time manifests only fleeting states of alert activity. There are, of course, wide variations in neonatal behavior that have significant implications for subsequent development, which we will address ourselves to later. At this period of life, inside or outside self and object are not differentiated. This is an objectless period. Need satisfaction appears to derive from an inner omnipotent orbit and the infant is described as being in a state of primitive hallucinatory disorientation. Mahler refers to this as a stage of absolute primary narcissism when there is no awareness of another or of an outside. It is as if the infant experiences himself or herself as the source of his or her own satisfaction, self-sufficient and omnipotent. In this state, the infant does not differentiate between self and caretaker, between self and the reliever of tension.

Biological Homeostasis

At this stage, the infant is almost purely a biological organism. Equipped with rudimentary ego apparatuses (Hartmann, 1939) that serve the purposes of adaptation, such as the rooting, sucking, and clinging reflexes, the newborn's life centers around physiological activity. The central task of the normal autistic phase is the establishment of physiological homeostasis. To the degree that a state of well-being associated with a feeling of internal stability (homeostasis) is achieved, both physiological and psychological development are favored. Indeed, it is at this very early state of being that feelings about oneself begin to crystallize.

Homeostasis is fostered in the infant not only by the intactness of overall congenital equipment and the adequacy of maternal care, but also by the existence of an inborn stimulus barrier that protects against the intrusion of excessive outer stimuli. While this protective shield guards against the infant becoming overwhelmed by exterior stimuli, it must be stressed that it does not protect against excessive inner stimuli.

Coenesthetic Reception

During the period of normal autism, experiences are mediated through coenesthetic reception. (Spitz, 1965). Perception takes place at a level of deep sensibility and in a total kind of way. For example, when experiencing pain in one part of the body, the infant is likely to experience the entire body as in pain. In accordance with the rules of the coenesthetic organization of the central nervous system, a reaction to any stimulus that surpasses the threshold of reception is "global, diffuse, syncretic—reminiscent of fetal life" (Mahler, 1975, p. 43). Perception through the sensorium, known as diacritic perception, does not yet operate. The kinds of signs and signals that reach and are received by the infant at the stage of coenesthetic reception are those generated in relation to equilibrium, tension (muscular or otherwise), posture, temperature, vibration, skin and body contact, rhythm, tempo, pitch, tone, resonance, clang, and so on (Spitz, 1965). Mahler notes that the infant initially familiarizes himself or herself with the mother through coenesthetic receptivity (1975). Before a mother becomes recognized as a need-statisfying mother, she is experienced coenesthetically. We presume that because coenesthetic receptivity operates from the beginning of life, during the autistic phase the child requires the nascent beginnings of this "feel."

Inner stimuli are experienced by proprioceptors such as the muscles, subcutaneous tissues, tendons, and joints, and by enteroceptors that receive sensations emanating from the stomach and the intestines. Over time, these are recorded in the mind and lead to a beginning awareness or cathexis of the inside of the body (Mahler, 1975). These early inner body experiences contribute, ultimately, to the development of the body ego and the body-self, forming the very core of the self. They remain the crystallization point of the "feelings of self" around which a "sense of identity" will become established (Mahler, 1968, p. 11).

Just as the child is, in part, innately equipped for the beginnings of self-discovery, the infant is also equipped, to some degree, for the slow discovery of the object. From early on, the grasping and rooting reflexes are directed toward the human object and affirm a capacity to discriminate animate from inanimate. From early on the infant is more responsive to the human voice, smell, face, and so on than to nonhuman stimuli. The capacity to turn the head toward the breast enables the infant to initiate perceptual contact, utilizing vision in the service of pleasure and, at the same time, promoting contact with the mother.

While the autistic phase is characterized by a relative unawareness of external stimuli, this does not mean that there is no responsiveness. It is the fleeting quality of the responsivity to external stimuli that makes for continuity between the normal autistic phase and the phases to follow (Mahler, 1975).

SYMBIOSIS

From the second month on, a dim awareness of the need-gratifying mother appears to take place and marks the beginning of the phase of normal symbiosis in which the infant and mother form a dual unity within a common boundary. Mahler has referred to the beginning phase of symbiosis as a stage of primary narcissism (in contrast to the autistic stage of absolute primary narcissism). The distinction is made by virtue of the fact that now the infant appears to be dimly cognizant that need-satisfaction cannot be provided by oneself but comes from somewhere outside.

The term *symbiosis* describes a state of undifferentiation, of psychic fusion between infant and mother, in which the infant's sense of "I" is not distinct from the "not I." This "delusional somatopsychic *omnipotent* fusion with the representation of the mother and, in particular, the delusion of a common boundary between two physically separate individuals" (Mahler, 1975, p. 45) is the soil from which all other human relationships ultimately form. Yet, it can also be the point to which a pathological ego may regress in cases of severe disturbance of individuation, as in psychoses (Mahler, 1968).

Coenesthetic Sensing and Need-Gratification

During the early part of symbiosis that merges with the autistic phase, coenesthetic receptivity still operates, and there appears to be an overlapping between the coenesthetic sensing of the mother as "the symbiotic half of the self" and the dim awareness of her function as need-gratifier and, therefore, somewhat "out there." Mahler has noted that we can still observe in the adult intense longings for the symbiotic mother—not just the need-satisfying one but the still coenesthetically remembered part of the self, with whom one experienced the harmony of the dual unity stage (1971). We can sometimes see this clearly in our work with clients.

The value of the worker's familiarity with the coenesthetic form of reception lies in the help it may provide in understanding a client. There are clients, for instance, who in speaking of the death of a mother, or even a person who has represented an early aspect of mothering to them, note a feeling in their bodies as if they have lost some vague aspect of the bodily self.

Smiling Response

A behavioral indicator of the significant developmental shift at symbiosis is the unspecific smiling response (Spitz, 1959), which heralds the entrance into the stage of the need-satisfying object relationship, the beginning of perceptual, emotional, "social" activities of humans.

At the peak of symbiosis, roughly 4 to 5 months of age, when the infant has become more familiar with the mothering half of the symbiotic self, the smile becomes a specific response to the infant's particular mother, in contrast to the earlier smile, which could have been elicited by the sight of any human face. The specific smile attests to a special bond between mother and infant (Mahler, 1975), and constitutes a milestone in the progression toward the capacity for human relatedness. It marks the inception of the infant's ability to invest in, relate to, and ultimately care about one special person.

The Cracking of the Autistic Shell

It must be noted that at the inception of the symbiotic phase, the stimulus barrier or the autistic shell that protected against external stimuli, begins to crack. The normal infant shows an increase in fussiness, crying, and signs of discomfort after the stimulus barrier has ceased to serve its protective function. This marked increase in overall sensitivity to external stimuli has been confirmed by electroencephalographic studies (Benjamin, 1961). Now the mother must begin to serve as the protective shield. The fused "mother-infant membrane" replaces the inborn stimulus barrier.

Indeed, we can look upon development up to this point as having provided a transitional phase from intrauterine life to the world of reality. Both the normal infant and the ordinary devoted mother have during the autistic phase, a certain period of respite. The infant, protected by his or her own resources to some degree, is free to proceed with essential tasks related to physical growth.

Maternal Partnering

The mother's holding behavior, her feeding, smiling, talking, supporting, cradling and the countless ministrations that the "good enough mother" provides for her infant are regarded, by Mahler, as the "symbiotic organizers of psychological birth" (Mahler, 1975, p. 49). It is the emotional rapport of the mother's nursing care, her provision of the nutrients needed by the infant, the social symbiosis between them, and her protection against excessive stimuli that serve as the organizer of psychological birth.

Optimal physical closeness between mother and infant as well as eye-to-eye contact promote an obligatory sense of oneness. The mother's support of the baby's body, the assured cradling, patting, and rocking are among the actions that constitute the holding behavior of the mother and promote comfort, safety, a sense of union, and "safe anchorage." Breast feeding, incidentally, was not found by Mahler to be a necessary requirement for optimal symbiosis. As might be expected, mothers who breast fed uneasily did not provide optimal holding, while mothers who bottle fed comfortably did. Eye-to-eye contact also serves as a stimulus that draws the child's attention to the outside.

Protection against excessive stress traumata is now the responsibility of the mother. An overload of stress may tax the infant's limited resources, leading to affectomotor storm rage reaction, in which affect and movement overwhelm the infant. Organismic distress is the extreme reaction to excessive stress. A forerunner of anxiety, it is akin to panic reaction. The occurrence of organismic distress in both the autistic and symbiotic phases requires the mother's assistance in the maintenance of the infant's homeostasis. Neurobiological patterning processes may be thrown out of kilter if such assistance is either not forthcoming, or, for some reason, not successful (Mahler, 1968).

Drive Differentiation

Balanced drive differentiation also depends upon an optimal level of homeostasis. The differentiation between pleasurable, good experiences attendant to gratification and comfort, and painful, bad quality experiences attendant to frustration and dysequilibrium takes place over time. Gradually, these become associated with part aspects of self and the object—that is, frustrating, bad experiences come to be associated with bad aspects of self or object, and good, satisfying experiences to good aspects of self or object. According to Mahler, libido and aggression differentiate out in accord with such differentiated "good" and "bad" scattered part images of mother and self. Thus, a predominance of bad, frustrating, overwhelming experiences ultimately threatens a drive differentiation where the balance is likely to be on the side of aggression. Since the infant is initially protected, in part, from an overload of noxious stimuli by the capacity to eject them, too much bad tends to foster excessive expelling maneuvers, leading to pathological consequences that we shall take up in subsequent chapters.

The Role of the Infant

Critical to the developmental outcome of this period are the mother's availability and her capacity to offer nurturance and relief. Equally important, however, is the child's capacity to perceive and accept the "mothering agent" (Mahler, 1968, p. 43). Furthermore, successful partnering on the part of the mother is partially dependent on the infant's capacity to stimulate her activities and to guide her attunement. Both the infant's smiles and the infant's cries are powerful stimulators of the mother's capacities. Mahler has repeatedly noted the importance of the child's capacity to extract needed supplies from the mother. Mahler has gone so far as to propose that the "lion's part of adaptation must come from the pliable, unformed infant" (Mahler, 1975, p. 63). However, she does not mean that mothers do not need to follow the child's needs through the various phases, and notes that there must be some measure of adaptation on the mother's part as well (1975).

Developmental Achievements

While the specific bond with the mother is considered to be the principle psychological accomplishment of the symbiotic phase, additional developmental phenomena of critical import take place. The negotiation of this phase fosters the establishment of confident expectation, the promotion of a degree of identity, an enhancement of narcissism, the expansion of certain ego functions, as well as contributing to the formation of the body image.

Confident Expectation

In response to the mother's consistent, reliable, and attuned need-gratification, a state of confident expectation (Benedek, 1938) is promoted in the child. This expectation that needs will be met and human assistance will be available, develops out of countless experiences, and facilitates the child's venturing forth. It serves as a resource that the child may draw upon when faced with the stresses attendant to developmental tasks and conflicts that lie ahead. A sufficient degree of confident expectation enables the infant, from the third or fourth month on, to keep disruptive impulses towards immediate tension discharge in abeyance—a prerequisite for the formation of the ego (Mahler, 1961). Accordingly, the ego functions of frustration tolerance and anticipatory thought are advanced. The expectation that one's needs will be met transforms the feeling of an objectless state of tension to a state of longing for the person who is associated with the relief of tension. This, according to Schur (1966), marks the important point when the human organism develops from a biological to a psychological organization. The wish has replaced purely physiological need.

Identity Formation

Certain patterns of motor activity and drive discharge which emerge during this phase in response to the mother's particular style of care may carry over into later phases, thereby contributing ultimately to the child's unique identity formation (Mahler, 1975, pp. 49–51).

Body Image

Demarcations of representations of the body ego, within the symbiotic matrix, take place in accordance with the experience of pleasure and pain. "The body ego contains two types of representations: an inner core with a boundary that is turned towards the inside of the body and divides it from the ego; and an outer layer of senoriperceptive engrams" that contribute to the "body-self" boundaries (Mahler, 1975; p. 46, c.f. Bergmann, 1963). We have already noted that the infant's inner sensations form the core of the self. The "rind" of the body ego, so to speak, which marks the periphery of the body depends upon a shift having taken place to a sensoriperceptive cathexis of the outer body, as compared to the earlier proprioceptive-enteroceptive cathexis associated with the internal body. The demarcation of the body is further aided by the tendency on the part of the infant to eject, by way of projection, destructive unneutralized energy beyond the body-self boundaries (Mahler, 1968). Added to these sensing experiences of the infant, of course, are the effects of the mother's bodily care of the infant, which contribute to a libidinization of the body, as well as to whatever sensations derive in relation to the psychosexual erotogenic zones. All of these experiences ultimately contribute to representations that are deposited in the mind, so to speak, and, over time, amalgamate in a way that contributes to the formation of the body image. The experiences of this early period create a foundation for what is to come.

Narcissism

We have already noted that the autistic phase is considered by Mahler as a period of absolute primary narcissism, a period of hallucinatory omnipotence. The symbiotic phase, in which some dim awareness of an outside source of gratification has begun to develop, is considered the period of primary narcissism and of conditional hallucinatory omnipotence. During symbiosis, when the infant takes the mother's love as the center of experience and she becomes incorporated into the personal experiences and inner perceptions of the infant, it is considered that the infant has moved into a period of secondary narcissism. This occurs at about 4 months and connotes a perception of the self-mother. "I" and the "not I" are not yet differentiated. Optimal secondary narcissism within the optimal symbiotic orbit, in which the harmony of the mother-infant unit is perceived, must prevail for a long enough period to become integrated into the mind. This positive psychic state has been called "oneness" (Kaplan, 1978), though, at this point, "oneness" means "we." It carries with it an experiential feel that we might liken to the perception of being on a winning team: "We together will win." Although omnipotence remains firm, it has changed from objectless omnipotence to self-mother omnipotence.

Residues of these experiences contribute significantly to the development of sound secondary narcissism in which the child, drawing on the original sense of omnipotence and then on the shared grandeur with mother, takes into the self the accretions of narcissism that will be added to and transformed and will ultimately form the base for a realistic, positively toned sense of self.

We have long known that the ego ideal draws from this original reservoir of early narcissism and omnipotence. In the Introductory Lectures (1916-1917, p. 429), Freud proposed that the ego ideal was created by man for himself in the course of his development in order to recover the self-satisfaction which was associated with primary infantile narcissism and which, since then, "has suffered so many disturbances and mortifications." Many years later Jacobson (1964) noted that the ego ideal that is "forged from ideal concepts of the self and from idealized features of the love objects" (p. 96), gratifies the infantile longing, never fully relinquished, to be one with the mother. Thus, the ultimate construction of this guiding structure, the ego ideal, is dependent upon this early mother-infant symbiotic experience.

Mahler's work affirms the notion of narcissism as a normal aspect of the human personality. Healthy narcissism may be thought of as self-love, self-pride, bodily-love, self-regard. It is an essential dynamic generating an ongoing flow of feelings of self-worth and positive self-esteem. The development of sound secondary narcissism is a ground level building block that serves to support the developing personality as one confronts the challenges of ongoing developmental tasks, and provides the cornerstone for the establishment of an independent sense of self.

Additional Ego Functions

In addition to those ego capacities already noted, including anticipation, frustration tolerance, and delay, we should like to emphasize that, at symbiosis, there begins the slow process of the formation of representations of mother, contributing to an "idea of mother" or mothering that, in time, comes to serve as an inner resource, a step on the way toward object constancy.

As the infant acquires recognition that the loved object brings help and gratification, as he or she begins to derive comfort from even hearing the sounds and calls of mother in a nearby room, the capacity to use the image or the idea of a mother to delay gratification develops. There is a growing sense that help, aid, and comfort will become available, provided the child is not required to wait too long. Longing replaces craving and is now accompanied by hope. This inner idea of mother begins to provide a soothing function in the mind, leading over time to greater ability to control inner moods through anticipation of future satisfaction. Eventually, it is out of this "taken in" experience of mother's soothing that the infant acquires some capacity to calm itself and mitigate anxiety. The countless minute internalizations of the mother's functions contribute over time, as Tolpin (1971) has pointed out, to the child's achievement of a degree of self-soothing capacity. It is also the mother's responses to the infant's signals of distress that ultimately foster the infant's capacity to utilize affects for signal purposes. While the actual formation of these capacities for both self-soothing and signal anxiety takes place after the infant is "hatched" from symbiosis, the achievement of the "idea of mother" as a result of good enough early experiences prepares the way.

SUMMARY

We have summarized the way in which the normally endowed infant in an "average expectable environment," (Hartman, 1939) that is, in the care of a "good enough mother," moves from the objectless period of autism to an increasing awareness of the self and other within a common boundary. These early experiences, when favorable, equip the child for the gradual and complicated move away from mother, affording the child a sufficient measure of individual development and a sufficient measure of trust in others to venture forth.

CHAPTER 2

The Psychological Birth of the Human Infant: Normal Development

The separation–individuation sequence proper follows the autistic and symbiotic phases described earlier. The four subphases are: (1) differentiation, (2) practicing, (3) rapprochement, and (4) consolidation of individuality and the beginnings of emotional object constancy. The establishment of the fourth phase marks, as its delineation implies, the intrapsychic achievement of a sense of separateness. With this development, the child attains psychological birth, having gained a sense of self as a human being separate from mother.

DIFFERENTIATION (5-10 months)

In differentiation, the first subphase, there is a turn to the "other-than-mother" (Mahler, 1975) world. Up to now mother has been perceived of as the "need-satisfier" within a dependent relationship. Now the infant begins to sort himself or herself out from mother, and to develop some of his or her own attributes. This outward movement can take place successfully when the symbiotic phase has been fully savored and inner pleasure continues, while attention is turned to the outside world as the result of stimulation of hearing, listening, looking, and seeing. Thus, expansion beyond the symbiotic orbit can occur within the safety of the continued emotional availability of the mothering person. Interest in what is external is facilitated by the evolution of "a more permanently alert conscious system." Mahler and coworkers observed "a certain new look of

15

alertness" in infants at this stage, and use the term "hatched" for this behavioral manifestation (Mahler, 1975, p. 54).

What follows are, in general, hypotheses as to the state of the psychic organization of the developing infant. These general, phase-related developments with highly individualized variations are dependent upon relationship to the mother, the innate endowment, and the specific history of the infant.

As soon as signs of differentiation appear, the behavioral data of the preverbal periods become easier to translate into psychological terms. What is observed becomes easier to understand because we can watch how the baby behaves when the mother is present, as compared with when mother is absent.

Between the fifth and seventh months of life the infant feels the mother's face with the hands, as well as looks closely with the eyes. He or she becomes interested in objects worn by the mother—eyeglasses, jewelry—and checks what is mother, what smells and feels like mother, and what is not mother. As the infant actively keeps track of mother's comings and goings, the child seems to form the first human memories. The child is comparing "mother" with "other," the familiar with the unfamiliar, and starts to discriminate between mother and all that is different. This visual pattern of "checking back to mother" is the most important regularly occurring sign of cognitive and emotional development. The maturation of the locomotor function that allows the baby to pull away from the mother's body facilitates this.

While remaining close to mother, the infant creeps, climbs, and stands upright; coordination of hand, eye, and mouth begins. Peek-a-boo games, initiated by the mother, are taken over by the child and indicate that he or she has some idea of separateness. Although a specific relationship with the father begins during the symbiotic phase with the smiling response, response to father is later than toward mother or siblings. Attachment increases throughout the differentiation subphase. Contact with father is, from the first, an exciting experience of "the other," and serves to attract the infant out of the symbiotic orbit.

Stranger Anxiety and Stranger Reactions

The group of behavioral phenomena known as "stranger reactions" and "stranger anxiety" is described as occurring at this development phase. The individual differences, variations in timing, and type of reactions are great. Once the infant has reached the degree of individuation at which mother's face can be recognized and the child is familiar with mother's general mood and feel as a symbiotic partner, he or she turns to a prolonged exploration and study of the faces and configuration of others, studying them from a distance or close by. The child appears to be comparing the stranger's face and mother's face, not only externally but with whatever internal image the youngster has, at that stage, of "mother." As their current observation shows, Mahler and coworkers have observed that in those children for whom the symbiotic phase has been optimal, with prevailing concomitant "confident expectation," "curiosity and wonderment" is the predominant valence of their inspection of strangers. Conversely, children in whom basic trust is less than optimal tend to show varying degrees of anxiety when confronted with those who are not familiar to them. In a wider context, this reaction to strangers is thought to indicate that the infant is now sufficiently individuated to know the difference between the face of mother and "others." The stranger is studied from close by, or from afar, in what seems to be the attempt to compare the inner image of mother with the features of the stranger's face. This same checking back to mother occurs in relation to other interesting experiences. Mahler regards this as a first step towards object constancy and an aspect of evaluation of the love object.

IDENTITY FORMATION

During this subphase, identity formation is further fostered by mutual reflection. Infants present a large variety of cues to indicate needs, tension, and pleasure. In a complex manner, the mother tends to respond selectively to only certain cues. The infant gradually appears then to alter his or her behavior in relation to the mother's selective response (Mahler, 1968). Out of this interaction emerge behavior patterns that express certain overall qualities of the child's personality. Out of the infant's infinite potentialities and in keeping with his or her innate limitations, the mother responds to her unconscious needs and fosters those particular attributes that create, for her, "the child" who reflects her unique and personal needs. The infant begins to emerge as an individual and as the unique child of his or her own mother (Lichtenstein, 1964).

Developmental Achievements of Differentiation

In summary, six to seven months is the peak of manual, tactile, and visual exploration of the mother's face and exposed body parts. This activity develops into the cognitive function of checking the unfamiliar against the already familiar. Recognition that the stranger is not the same as the by now familiar mother appears to raise the first threat of object loss as indicated by the observable stranger anxiety of the five to six month old. By age 8 to 9 months, greater cognitive development brings with it a clearer threat of loss as the mother is no longer always available at the infant's will. This threat is evidenced by the phenomenon of separation anxiety. The specific memory of mother becomes more highly organized with the child's repeated checking of mother's comings and goings. The mother's continued loving care of the infant's body helps build "normal narcissism."

As already stated, external behavior reflects internal development. Growth is smoothest when autonomous ego functions such as cognition, perception, and memory go along together with the awareness of bodily separation from the mother.

PRACTICING (10-15 MONTHS)

The differentiation subphase overlaps the second subphase—practicing. Mahler divides this into early and late periods. As the child begins to creep or crawl, while still holding on, and is able to move away physically from the mother, the early period is initiated. The late, or "practicing period proper," depends upon the child's free, upright movement and the vastly different view this gives him or her of the world. This subphase is characterized by the infant's joy in movement, investment in practicing motor skills, and exploration of the environment that has now been greatly expanded for him or her by this mobility.

Early Practicing

The infant's interest in inanimate objects grows at this time. At first, it is in those articles brought by mother—a blanket, diapers, toys, bottle. It is noteworthy that the youngster may choose one of these objects as a transitional object—to be discussed later.

With mother as an anchor, the fixed point in what becomes an exciting though frightening, now always-changing world, wider exploration becomes possible. As long as mother is within sight or sound of voice, ensuring "distance contact," there is pleasure in these early explorations. Throughout the entire practicing period, the child returns to mother for brief periods of "emotional refueling." It is as if some brief contact with mother reassures and comforts, and provides the emotional energy for further daring missions. Such contact can be from a distance, a meeting of the eyes across a room, or the physical contact of lifting, hugging, and brief holding.

Late Practicing

When the child starts to walk, a giant step is taken towards becoming his or her own person (individuation). The different view this gives of the world, the vast possibilities it opens up are staggering to contemplate. During this beginning period, between the ages of about 10 and 18 months, and spread out over the whole second year, the child's world expands gloriously in all directions.

The child practices his or her motor capabilities and is exhilarated by the mastery of the "other-than-mother" environment. The predominant moods are elation, exhilaration, and joy in the experience of the "feel" of using muscles and the whole vibrant body. The knocks, the bumps, the falls are part of the adventure and the infant does not seem to mind them. In fact, there is confirmation of the outlines of the body-self as the child knocks against the solidity of the floor or table edge. The child notably does not cry when this occurs. He or she lifts and carries objects of all shapes and sizes, and perfects control of his or her body. It seems likely that the anxiety involved in each new step "away" is compensated for by the "elation" of escape from engulfment by the mother. This is attested to by the toddler's running away from mother with the expectation of being chased and caught; the fear of reengulfment is being turned from passive to active. It is instructive to note that the child's first steps are in a direction away from mother, not toward her.

Self Image and Self-Esteem

Mothers ordinarily react to these new accomplishments with pleasure. The child's feeling of safety in moving away depends in some measure upon the parent's emotional support and interest. Autonomy and self esteem are thereby encouraged. The admiration, expecially of the "ordinary devoted mother" (Winnicott, 1962) increases the child's healthy love of self. The toddler wll soon deliberately behave in such a way as to evoke the admiration that makes him or her feel such exaltation. Greenacre's term "love affair with the world" has been used to convey the affective coloration of the practicing phase toddler. (Greenacre, 1957). The child is experiencing a phase-appropriate grandiose self image.

Gender Identity

With regard to gender identity, the boy who has discovered pleasure associated with his penis a few weeks earlier can now see it because he is upright, from many different angles and touch it more easily, with the result that there is greater cathexis of this sensuous pleasure-giving organ. The reaction in the female to awareness of anatomical difference will be discussed under gender identity, as it unfolds in the rapprochment subphase.

Role of the Father

It is during this subphase that attachment to father gains greatest momentum. In contrast with mother, who is relied upon as solid "home base" for refueling, father becomes the representative of "out there"—the space that, at this subphase, is most valued by the child. Father comes to be associated with the upright position, the quality of intensity and elation of this period. He is the "other," the "different" parent, not just the secondary mothering person.

Mood

Although there is relative obliviousness to or forgetfulness of mother's presence, a state of "low-keyedness" exists in her absence. At such times, there is often a slowing down of activity and some loss of interest in the formerly stimulating surroundings. Interest, in fact, seems to have turned inward and is conjuring an inner world of mother-self experience. This special "state of self," from which is inferred that there is "imaging" of the mother, has been likened to a miniature depression. The child seems to be trying to hold on to a precarious emotional balance. It is as if there is a "dawning aware-ness that the symbiotic mothering half of the self was missed" (Mah-ler, 1975, p. 75).

At times like this, it becomes more apparent that the actual pres-ence of the mother has been needed to produce and maintain the toddler's mood of elation. The child does not continue to behave as before, nor does he or she become very obviously anxious. The be-havior indicates that the youngster is now strong enough to long for what he or she misses, without falling apart, and with some self-comforting. It seems that the delight in mobility, and the exploration that allows, together with "emotional refueling," effectively counter-acts any lowering of mood.

Self-Soothing

Among the developmental achievements of the separa-tion–individuation progression are the child's acquisition of the ca-pacities for self-soothing and the development of signal anxiety. Uti-lizing Mahler's theoretical findings and recommendations regarding the need for the "minute study" of this early developmental period, Marian Tolpin (1972) has focused intensively on the way in which these two capacities are developed in conjunction with the processes of separation–individuation. Tolpin has proposed that the infant ac-quires the abilities to soothe and calm himself or herself, and to deal with anxiety experiences through the slow internalization of those maternal functions that originally served to soothe, calm, and regu-late anxiety. Using Heinz Kohut's concept of "transmuting inter-nalizations," Tolpin has elaborated the steps by which the infant be-gins to internalize these maternal functions—functions that in turn, contribute to the building up of the ego "bit-by-bit."

Transitional Object

The capacity for self-soothing is achieved in two steps. At a time when the "good enough mother" can no longer provide the full mea-sure of symbiosis that at an earlier stage served to calm and soothe, the infant creates a transitional object out of a blanket or other inanimate object that has the smell or feel of mother. This is in-vested with the mother's tension-relieving and soothing functions and represents, for the child, that blissful state connected with symbiotic unity. Tolpin adds that the transitional object is created at the point at which it becomes increasingly impossible and undesirable to achieve the symbiotic experience of the early months in even the most adequate partnership. The child, at the second half of the first year, is simply becoming too active and too big for the mother to enfold and calm as she did earlier.

The transitional object represents a way station and will finally be decathected, which is to say, it will lose its importance when the child can begin to perform soothing operations for itself without the need for an illusory external soother. The tension-reducing effects of the mother as the soother of symbiosis that were first invested in the blanket undergo transmuting internalization and are preserved as a part of the child's own capacity "to calm down." The transitional object is not mourned because its soothing functions "go inside" as mental structure, and it is no longer needed.

Signal Anxiety

The processes by which anxiety becomes signal anxiety also involve transmuting internalization, according to Tolpin (1972). In this line of development, Tolpin postulates that with an advance in self-object discrimination or differentiation, the infant becomes increasingly able to perceive the various aspects of the mother's activities, including her function as a reliever of anxiety (Tolpin, 1972, p. 337). Furthermore, the infant comes to recognize a relationship between expressing the signal of anxiety and the relief of anxiety. Tolpin suggests that "repeated experiences of small amounts of distress, which is promptly relieved, lead to the infant's perception of beginning distress as the forerunner of activities that bring relief" (p. 340). The infant has to be capable of retaining the idea of a relationship between his or her own signal of distress and the anxiety-reducing activity of the mother before this erstwhile maternal function can be internalized. The mother's relieving function must be reduced in phase-approriate doses so that the degree of anxiety, which has to be handled, does not overwhelm the infant. Then the child's pysche acquires the responses to the signal of anxiety via internalization.

Further Developmental Achievements of Practicing Subphase

Primary motor and cognitive skills are exercised in the service of the beginnings of autonomy. These autonomous achievements are the main source of narcissistic enhancement from within. Most infant-toddlers show three contributories to sound secondary narcissism—self-love, primitive valuation of their accomplishments, and omnipotence (Mahler and Kaplan, 1977, p. 73).

Motoric feats are themselves of primary importance because they are the means through which distance and closeness are actively determined by the child himself or herself. It is through body movement that contact is made with expanding reality.

RAPPROCHEMENT (15-22 MONTHS)

As the junior toddler (12-15 months) grows into the senior toddler (up to 24 months), important emotional changes occur. During the early part of this phase as the perceptual and cognitive faculties grow, evidence of the separateness of the self from object becomes more apparent to the child. The implications of physical separateness become clearer. The mother, who up to now has not been fully recognized as a discrete person in her own right, takes on a new significance. The relative obliviousness to mother's presence, which pertained in the previous subphase, gives way to constant concern with her whereabouts. The child finds, more and more, that his or her wishes do not always dovetail with those of mother or father. An increased need, a wish for mother to share every activity, becomes evident. Mother's emotional availability becomes vital. This is not so easy for her to understand and provide. There is puzzling contradiction for her in the fact that the recently independent toddler has, once more, become very demanding and dependent. Thus, renewed interest in mother is the result of the child's growing perception, as an internal event, of the mother's separate existence. The child actively "woos" her into sharing activities by bringing toys to her, by trying to get her interest and attention, by trying to get her to share with him or her. When the toddler succeeds and mother responds, the frightening realization of separateness is temporarily staved off.

Rapprochement Crisis

Within a short time, the wooing behavior is replaced by coercive types of behavior aimed at the reestablishment of the mother infant dual unity. The child actively resists separation from the mother.

However, no matter how much the toddler insistently tries to coerce the mother, they can no longer function effectively as a dual unit. The child can no longer participate in or maintain the delusion of parental omnipotence. Verbal communication becomes more and more necessary. Gestural coercion by the toddler, or preverbal empathy between mother and child can no longer afford the earlier satisfaction.

The child gradually realizes that the parents are separate persons with their own interests. The child's delusion of grandeur must be gradually given up. This is a painful process, frequently involving dramatic fights with mother—less so, according to Mahler, with father. This "crossroad" in development has been termed the "rapprochement crisis." (Mahler, 1972).

Mother needs to be unobtrusively available and ready to share some of the toddler's activities while, at the same time, able to let go and give a gentle push to encourage further individuation and independence.

Conflict arises out of the child's wish to have mother magically fulfill needs, yet allow him or her to be unaware that help is actually coming from the outside. The child will, for example, use mother's hand as if it were an extension of himself or herself, and then rage if mother acts as if she understands the needs and allows her hand to become part of the child—her very understanding reminds the toddler of his or her helplessness!

There is both a deliberate search for and avoidance of intimate bodily contact. The wish for reunion and fear of engulfment are characterized by "shadowing" of mother (watching her every move) and "darting away" with the expectation of being chased and caught. This behavioral manifestation of wanting to push mother away, and hold on to her at the same time, is called "ambitendency" and is typical of the two-way feelings of this phase. It will later develop into true ambivalence.

This is a period during which indecision is typical. The symbolization of conflicting wishes was demonstrated in the Mahler group's observations of the child who stands undecided on the threshold of the toddler room, while mother is in the infant room with a younger sibling. The conflict is to enter the toddler world, away from mother, or remain with her in the infant room. There is growing awareness of the existence of other children and social interaction begins. However, play is parallel rather than interpersonal, and is on the level of wanting what other children have, or wanting to do what they do.

Specific anger and hostility accompany frustration because frustration has, by now, become bound up with awareness of helplessness and powerlessness. The child's self-esteem is involved. It is this factor of self-awareness that underlies the child's endless saying of "no." The mother's "no" is experienced by the child as evidence of her power and the child's lack of power. Thus, the youngster's frequent repetition of "no" during one phase of rapprochement represents an identification with the aggressor. The struggle involves conflict, engendered by the child's continued need and sense of helplessness that propels him or her to reengage with mother while at the same time actively moving away. Temper tantrums are set off by humiliation and fear, and the sense of aloneness of this period of development. They also provide an avenue for discharge of accumulated tension.

In many toddlers, there is a resurgence of stranger reaction often referred to as "shyness." The whole range of affective experience becomes greater and more differentiated. For example, sadness, anger, and disappointment are experienced either in mother or as a result of the realization of the helplessness of limited power.

Role of Father

The father plays a vital role in the life of the child at rapprochement. He is seen as belonging in a category of "love object" that is very different from that of the mother. His image is less distorted by virtue of the way in which it has been formed. The image of the mother evolves by being differentiated from within the symbiotic dual unit of mother and child, and is then separated out from that. In this process, there is strong and fluctuating libidinal and aggressive cathexis of the maternal image. The image of the father is less "contaminated," and, therefore, closer to external reality than is the image of the mother. This is of basic importance at rapprochement when splitting of the mother, not father, image may occur. The father acts as a vital support against the child's backward pull to the symbiotic relationship, representing as he does external reality. Some youngsters seem to turn exclusively to father to evade the regressive pull, while others are so ambivalently enmeshed with their mothers that they do not have time for their fathers. The "out there" space of the father does not refer to his role in the world of work outside the family, but to his position outside of the symbiotic orbit of the mother-child unit. His is more intersting mainly in that sense.

TRIANGULATION:

Out of the experience with the father, an object representation of father that is distinct from that of mother, is formed. The rapprochement child becomes increasingly aware of mother and father's special relationship to one another, and their relationship as a couple, to the child. This process referred to as triangulation (Abelin, 1971) promotes the child's capacity for triadic relationship. It also fosters new identifications, including an identification with the rival. Stimulated by an intrapsychic understanding of the relationship between two loved objects, mother and father, the child begins to identify with the parent who like himself or herself, wants the mother. To quote Abelin (1971) "There must be an I, like him wanting her." (p. 233). This process of triangulation not only contributes to the formation of the self-image by way of identification with the rival, but paves the way for subsequent negotiation of the oedipus complex. Attachments are thus consolidated to both mother and father. In Jacobson's view (1964, p. 116) the child relinquishes the incestuous and patricidal wishes associated with the oedipus complex out of love for the parents.

Psychoanalytic understanding of the contribution of the father to preoedipal development is rapidly expanding, and a comprehensive review is beyond the scope of this book. The attention of the reader is drawn to the work of the panel on the role of the father in the preoedipal years at the 1977 meeting of the American Psychoanalytic Association (Prall, 1978). The conclusions of the panelists underlined the importance of the father as an object for identification, as part of the ego ideal and a precursor to superego development. He serves to shift the child's object relations from diadic to triadic, to mitigate a too close relationship between mother and child, and is instrumental in the formation of sexual identity.

Discovery of Sexual Differences

The child discovers anatomical sexual differences between the sixteenth and twenty-first months. We have stated that the boy discovers his penis and its involuntary erection and detumescence earlier as a result of the upright position of walking. Seeing and touching has led to greater pleasurable cathexis. In contrast, by the beginning of the third year, the penis is often clutched at, as if for reassurance. Although the discovery of anatomical sexual differences takes different forms in different children, the girl's discovery of the penis confronts her with something she is lacking and, thus, with narcissistic injury. A range of behaviors, including anger, defiance, anxiety, and the wish to undo the difference, is evident. The tendency is to blame the mother, to turn back to her, demand from her, but be disappointed in her, which fosters the ambivalent tie to her. This enmeshment makes becoming a separate individual more difficult for the girl. Boys turn to the outside world or their own bodies more easily. Identification with father helps them cope later with their castration anxiety.

Thus, the differences in development between boys and girls become rather significant from this point on; that is, the boys disengage and turn to the wider world more easily, while the girls hang on angrily and are less independent. It seems possible that the ambivalence in girls slows down differentiation between self and object and heightens fear of loss of the object's love. Here a type of projection is involved in the form of, "Is she angry with me because I am angry with her?"

Coping Mechanisms

The acute rapprochement crisis necessitates the institution of coping mechanisms. Although the child, by now, is able to understand that if mother leaves the room she is somewhere else (that is, object permanence in Piaget's sense), this does not take care of the child's feelings of missing the mother.

Initial reaction to mother's leaving may be clinging, followed by depressive mood and inability to play. Bursts of motor activity are unfocused and scattered, designed to avoid sadness, as contrasted with the low-keyed conjuring of her presence in the previous period of elation. Another adult in the room may be used as a "kind of symbiotic mother substitute," an extension of the self, not another love object. This activity could also be viewed as a defensive "splitting" mechanism with the struggle seen with many variations. The "good" mother is longed for but only in fantasy, because when she returns she will be greeted usually with negative reactions. Even if the observer becomes the "good mother of symbiosis," the actual mother, on her return, will be treated with ambivalence, as if to avoid further disappointment.

Other mechanisms, or "transitional phenomena," for coping with the anxiety generated by separation during the rapprochement crisis include attachment to inanimate objects that are connected with the absent mother, substitute satisfaction through eating or drinking, and being read to (which, interestingly enough, can serve to provide closeness to the reader, combined with the distancing of the wider world as it is depicted in the story).

At this stage, the children do better if they can be active in the leave taking—acting, rather than being acted upon. A relationship with a teacher provides a new connection rather than a mother substitute, especially if the new adult provides alternative satisfactions and encourages interest in the outside world.

Although the temper tantrums of this period express undifferentiated affect, the range and differentiation of affects do broaden. Many different kinds of behavior are used to deal with sadness, anger, disappointment, and helplessness. There is also some attempt to suppress expression of feelings. Empathy for others is often demonstrated. There are signs of true identification with the attitudes of others, especially the parents.

By about 21 months, there is a diminution in the rapprochement struggle. The extreme alternation of demand for closeness and autonomy levels off. What is the optimal distance from mother is clearer for each child within the context of their specific makeup. Children at this stage can no longer be grouped in accordance with phase-specificity, but are individually distinct and different from each other.

Those factors that help the child to function when the mother is absent include 1) language development, which means that objects can be named so that desires can be made known and greater control over the environment is thus exercised; 2) internalization via identification with a "good" providing mother and father; 3) progress in use of play for mastery and the ability to express wishes and fantasies through symbolic play.

CONSOLIDATION OF INDIVIDUALITY AND THE BEGINNINGS OF EMOTIONAL OBJECT CONSTANCY

The fourth subphase of the separation–individuation process is not a subphase in the same sense as the first three, since it is open-ended. The observed changes reach no single definite terminal point. The main tasks of this phase are, according to Mahler (1975, p. 109) "the achievement of a definite, in certain aspects lifelong, individuality, and 2) the attainment of a certain degree of object constancy."

From the neonate at birth with no awareness of self and object, through the omnipotent self-object unit of the symbiotic phase, through the gradual dawning awareness of separateness in the differentiation and practicing subphases and the abrupt shock of awareness in the rapprochement crisis, emerges the intrapsychic sense of a whole self and a whole object.

This slow establishment of emotional object constancy involves all aspects of psychic development. It implies the unification of the "good" and "bad" object into one whole mental representation, which, in turn, fosters fusion of the libidinal and aggressive drives. It is only with this fusion that hatred for the object can be tempered when the to-be-expected aggression is intense. Although this fusion is still a fluid and uncertain achievement, it is sufficient in the normally developing 3-year-old to allow some independent functioning without the physical presence of the mother.

The separation–individuation process culminates in the child's sense that mother is available and dependable, even when she is physically absent, when the child is very angry with her, or when she is not providing satisfaction. This internal sense comes about as a result of the building of stable and enduring internal images of the primary love object, who is usually the mother. This must be achieved in both intellectual and emotional terms, and remain reliable irrespective of the state of need or inner discomfort.

The Significance of Object Constancy for the Child

There is general agreement that object constancy refers to both the libidinal and cognitive aspects of the young child's attachment to mother, and that it presupposes a certain degree of neutralization of aggression as well as of libidinal energy. With object constancy there is a primarily libidinal cathexis of the maternal representation. The mother is perceived as good, gratifying, and helpful (Mahler, 1966;). The "good" and "bad" aspects of the mother are integrated into one unified representation and the defense mechanism of "splitting" of the object representation is no longer needed. The stable mental representation of the mother is no longer subject to easy regression. The quality of the maternal representation is such that it produces in the child a sense of security and comfort, just as the actual mother has in the past.

However, it must be noted that the degree to which this early developmental achievement holds firm may be dependent upon the overall balance of inner and outer forces impinging upon the child at any given time. If the child is physically ill, for example, the former equilibrium may be temporarily lost. Nonetheless, under normal circumstances, the level of constancy reached during this first round of separation–individuation does make it possible for the child to participate in, sustain, and enjoy experiences beyond those involving primarily the mother. The broader world of family, friends, nursery school, or play group offers enrichment to the child. The stable mental representation of the object supports the ego in its regulatory operations and in the capacity to tolerate the frustration caused by delay of gratification (Fleming, 1975). An idea can bring relief, soothe, and mitigate feelings of unpleasantness and frustration. The child has begun to have some degree of confidence in the capacity to tolerate discomfort, difficulty, and anxiety without being overwhelmed.

Significance of Object Constancy for the Adult

At least a minimal level of object constancy is required to enable the adult to adapt independently. Throughout the life-cycle, some degree of separation anxiety can be anticipated in reaction to life events that promote a new level of separated development. The child who goes to camp, the adolescent who takes a hostelling trip, the adult who enters college or employment are all confronted with a new level of separation. Unconsciously, perhaps consciously at times, these changes are eased by drawing on all that has become associated in the mind with the "idea of mother."

We consider certain events of everyday life with the purpose of noting how adaptive, independent functioning is facilitated by the state of object constancy. There is no conscious script, of course.

Mr. Rose, a young worker on his first job, is angrily reprimanded by his employer for some failure. If the mother's regard for the little boy Mr. Rose once was is firmly incorporated, that mental representation provides a continuous silent flow of the feeling of being loveable. His self-esteem does not plummet. This sustains the young man in the face of negative attack. It is then as if the now adult Mr. Rose can say to himself, "You, employer, do not appreciate me or my efforts, but my mother did, and so I know I am worthwhile. I can tolerate your criticism, unfair though it may be, and try to learn the job better."

Ms. Zinn, a 40-year-old mother, goes for the first time to a meeting of the political group she plans to join in the suburb to which she and her family have recently moved. She knows no one, whereas she had many friends in the group to which she belonged previously. She feels herself becoming anxious and is about to leave, but instead thinks, "I feel quite alone here but there must be many friendly people among all these strangers. I will try to make contact. If that is not possible and I am still uncomfortable, I can always leave then." It is the attribute of object constancy that serves to restore her equilibrium and modulates her level of need tension.

Mr. and Mrs. Harris are amicable marriage partners. Their arguments about some matters can become intense but are eventually resolved without residual bitterness. Mrs. Harris has learned to recognize the hotness, even violence of her temper at times. She thinks to herself during an argument, "If I did not love you, I would throw this plate at you! I hate this feeling of hating you, but I do, right now. But when we resolve this argument, we will both feel better and I will be glad that I restrained myself." Her rage toward her husband is tempered by the memory of her love for him and this regulates her attitude. She can maintain the connection to him during severe frustration by fused good-bad images.

Mr. Bell takes his 14-year-old son skating. It is a very cold day and his own clothing reflects his intolerance of the cold. His son seems to him to be underdressed but the youngster does not complain of being cold. Mr. Bell silently congratulates himself on having resisted the temptation to criticize his son's choice of clothing. He experiences himself as separate from his son in personal need, feeling, and preference. His state of object constancy precludes confusion of the self-representation with the object-representation.

Self Constancy

Mahler describes self constancy as an enduring individuality consisting of the attainment of two levels of the sense of identity, which are awareness of being a separate and individual entity, and awareness of a gender-defined self-entity. By this we have understood that self constancy represents a state in which the child has begun to acquire an experiental feel of himself or herself as continuous and discrete in time, space, and state.

We quote from Lichtenberg on this subject since he frequently cites Mahler's work, and his suggestions lend clarity to a subject that is currently receiving much attention. He has expressed the feeling of self constancy in the following way:

> I am the same me—the same member of my family—whether it is a time when I am alone and stroking my body before sleep—or when I am with mother, agreeing or opposing, or when I am showing off my skills and it brings delight or a tempered calming-down. The continuity in time is paralleled by a continuity in space: my body—my mind—my name are all "self"-contained (the self as place); and by a continuity in state: active or passive, asleep or awake. Cohesion of the self is the experiential sum of these continuities in time, space, and state (Lichenberg, 1975, pp. 472-73).

Lichtenberg further states his belief that although self constancy and object constancy are interdependent, a cohesive sense of self precedes the image of the "whole mother" in Mahler's sense. He emphasizes that within the cohesion there is flexibility and variability.

CHAPTER 3

Vicissitudes of Autism and Symbiosis

In their sensitive, precise, and rich delineation of the complex steps through which the human infant progresses from autism to symbiosis and then through the separation–individuation subphases to a position of on-the-way to object constancy, Mahler and her coworkers have conveyed the intricate challenge that development poses for human young and their families, as well as the impressive capacities that the ordinarily endowed infant and ordinarily concerned parents possess for the tasks at hand. Nonetheless, favorable human development is not assured and early processes are subject to vicissitudes. Severe disruptions during the first phases of human life, the vulnerable periods of autism and symbiosis, are particularly threatening. In the extreme, they may lead to psychosis, to malformations in psychic structure that predispose to psychosis at subsequent stressful junctures during the life cycle, or to psychosomatic disorders (Spitz, 1965). This is in keeping with a genetic principle drawn from embryology that injury incurred during the early period of gestation is likely to result in major anatomical deformities, whereas similar trauma occurring at a later developmental point has less consequence.

MOTHER-INFANT UNIT

Mahler stresses that the vicissitudes of early development must be considered in terms of the mother-infant unit. This is in keeping with her findings that developmental advances in the infant must be catalyzed by maternal partnering as well as maturational achievements. The infant is, in fact, absolutely dependent upon the mother in early life, not only for physical survival but for assistance in the development of that separate structure, the ego, which in time must assume the task of self-preservation. Inadequacies of a severe nature in either of the partners, or disharmonies of serious proportions, in their exchange, may compromise future achievements.

INNATE FACTORS IN CHILDHOOD PSYCHOSES

During the period of autism, the infant is ordinarily well endowed and well protected so that the requisite degree of physiological homeostasis is assured. Mahler has concluded that the most profound deviations associated with this early period, the childhood schizophrenias, are in most instances related to some severe constitutional defects in the child. Contrasting the extreme pathology of psychotic children with those severely traumatized but not psychotic children, studied by Freud and Dann (1943) and Goldfarb (1945), Mahler has been led to believe that there is an essential innate difference between those children who become schizophrenic and those other severely traumatized youngsters. Freud and Dann studied concentration camp children who had lost their mothers under brutal conditions and were exposed to extreme maternal deprivation, being cared for by ever-changing objects who, themselves, were under profound stress. Though their tragic experiences profoundly effected the children's development, they nonetheless achieved strong ties with one another and were able to integrate whatever meager substitute maternal care was available, probably utilizing the autoerotic resources of their own bodies, and, perhaps, transitional objects to the utmost (Winnicott, 1953), thereby averting psychosis.

The babies studied by Goldfarb were moved from foster home to foster home during their early years. They, too, seemed able to extract substitutions for their loss of mothering so that, though they may have paid a price in terms of neurotic disorders, character distortions, and psychopathic difficulties, they retained their sense of reality. In some way the rudimentary egos of these infants were able to sustain some kind of memory trace of earlier need-satisfaction from an external source and to create, therefore, a "nondehumanized narcissistic orbit for themselves" (Mahler, 1968, p. 51). This is in keeping with Mahler's view that the normally endowed infant possesses capacities for extracting "every drop of human stimulus, of environmental nutrient, every bit of human contact available" and manifests "striking powers of recovery" (Mahler, 1968, p. 50). The psychotic children studied, whose histories on the whole failed to reveal a profound degree of environmental trauma, seemed unable to move toward the world of reality because of some innate feature within themselves.

INFANTILE AUTISM

Childhood autism is the most profound disturbance of the earliest developmental period. It is a pathological condition in which there are no signs of affective awareness on the part of the child of other human beings. The psychotic child remains at the most primitive level of human existence. The child's self, including the bodily self, seems not be distinguished from the inanimate objects of the environment, and there is an innate lack or loss of differentiation between living and lifeless matter (Mahler, 1968). Behavior that could indicate the child's capacities to perceive need-gratification as coming from the mother is absent. Because of a "primary defect," the autistic child cannot utilize the mother as a "beacon of orientation" in the world of reality. In the histories of autistic children one finds descriptions of early behavior that indicate that there was no anticipatory posturing at nursing, no reaching out features, and no specific smiling response. Mothers comment: "My baby never smiled at me"; "Our child never greeted us when we entered a room"; "He or she never cried, and never noticed when I left the room." These early symptoms of primary autism often go unnoticed as pathological signs at the time, or may be confused with indications of possible deafness or retardation.

Later, as the outside inevitably begins to impinge upon the child, symptoms are developed that represent defensive efforts to shut out the intrusive, irritating world of reality. The children tend to create a small, restricted world of their own. They manifest an obsessive desire for the preservation of sameness and a stereotyped preoccupation with a few inanimate objects or actions. They appear contented and seemingly self-sufficient, provided they are left alone, and are likely to be completely mute, or if they do speak, their language is not used for functional communication (Mahler, 1968). Mahler has considered that autism may occur when a constitutionally fairly sturdy infant is exposed to pervasive severe trauma during the vulnerable early period of life. However, she regards it as more likely that psychosis is related to an inborn, defective tension-regulating apparatus that probably cannot be adequately complemented even by quantitatively or qualitatively efficient mothering. Such infants appear to manifest an inherent ego deficiency that from the start—that is, beginning at the undifferentiated phase—predisposes them to remain or become alienated from reality (Mahler, 1952, p. 289).

Other Deviations at the Autistic Phase

Failure to achieve physiological homeostasis during the autistic period, though of lesser severity than in the case of the psychoses, may also have critical impact on future development. Instability in the normal body states of the infant tends to interefere with, among other things, the early "hallucinatory sense of omnipotence" that derives from a feeling of well-being. This paves the way for the "confident expectation" to be established during symbiosis in relation to the self-object unit, and is a step toward the ultimate formation of confidence in both the self and the object, and more broadly probably plays a role in fostering a basic optimism with regard to life itself. Further, where excessive frustration and pain prevailed during the first weeks, drive differentiation may be adversely affected. Under the impact of unusually negative experiences there is the danger that the aggressive drive will predominate over the libidinal drive (Mahler, 1968). We are reminded of Loewald's (1972) view that the drives are organized through interactions in the early exchange between mother and child, and that since the organization of the drives is "very early business in the course of psychic development" (p. 243), interference with this differentiation is of profound consequence.

Less than optimal homeostasis may be the result of defects in the infant's inborn ego aparatuses, either in the sucking, grasping, or other reflexes, in the capacity to summon the mother through affectomotor reactions such as crying, deficiencies in the protective shield, or in the motor sensory apparatuses. Congenital handicaps or serious accidents or illnesses developing after birth would constitute further sources of interference with the infant's well-being and, concomitantly, impede the most adequate mother's capacities for caring for and comforting her baby.

While Mahler accords the newborn's congenital equipment a high priority in determining the outcome of the autistic phase, severe inadequacies in the maternal partnering may prove ominous. We are reminded that it is the mother's manifold ministrations to the neonate that slowly summon the infant, by way of herself, to the outside world. It is the mother's day-in-and-day-out touching, tending, and holding behaviors that contribute to the gradual unfolding sense "that I am" that constitutes the earliest step in the process of identity formation (Mahler, 1975). This accords with Ribble's (1943) view that the young infant is brought out of an innate tendency toward vegetative, splanchnic regression and into increased sensory awareness of a contact with the environment by way of mothering. Spitz (1965) has observed along the same lines that the mother must "quicken" the infant's innate equipment. According to Spitz, "the vital spark has to be conferred on the equipment through exchanges with another human being, with a partner, with the mother" (1965, p. 95). Similarly, Lichtenstein (1977), drawing directly on Mahler's work, notes that the emotional conviction "that I am" must be "teased out" by some human interaction. It is not assured by ego development but depends, first and foremost, on the mother's early affirmation of the child's being.

There is evidence that neurobiological patterning may be adversely affected by unattuned maternal care during the first weeks of life. James (1960) has traced the tenseness, precocious degree of alertness, and jumpiness of an infant girl to inadequate nourishment during the first 6 weeks of life. Though the child grew physically, the normal stimulus barrier seemed impaired as a result of the slight hunger she experienced, the result of a failure in the need-gratifying function of the nurse who tended her after birth. At two weeks the infant could be roused from sleep by a dog's bark, or by noise from a distant airplane. She became hyperreactive and hypersensitive and, though not psychotic, her development was atypical, requiring early intervention.

Mahler (1968) has herself noted that failure on the mother's part to reduce the infant's "organismic distress" (p. 13), the forerunner of anxiety proper, during the autistic and the symbiotic phases may result in distortions of the neurobiological patterning processes. Somatic memory traces are created that combine with later experiences and may thereby increase later psychological pressures (Greenacre, 1958).

Greenacre (1941) has further proposed that unfavorable conditions in the neonatal period and in the prenatal and natal period as well may, if severe, frequently repeated, and sustained, contribute to increased reactivity in the infant that, in turn, may heighten the baby's susceptibility to and the intensity of later anxiety reactions. A "predisposition to anxiety" may ensue.

Finally, we briefly refer to the work of Benjamin (1961) whose electroencehpahlographic studies and observations bear out Mahler's observations that there is a marked increase in overall sensitivity to external stimulation around 3 to 4 weeks. This coincides with the transition from the autistic to the symbiotic phase (Mahler, 1968). Benjamin notes that this is a point of "maturational crisis." If the mother fails to assume the role of "organizer" in the face of the diminishing protective shield, the infant may become overwhelmed by stimuli. Aggressive drive energies may be induced that tend to have a disorganizing effect on the budding ego, leading to ego distortions.

Maternal failure may stem from a variety of factors, including the mother's intrapsychic conflicts as well as illness on her part, or to limitations imposed on her mothering such as those experienced with poverty. As clinicians, we are all too familiar with the restrictions a poor mother faces in the provision of adequate nutrition, health care, housing, heat, and so forth, on behalf of her infant.

An illustration of how inadequacies during the autistic phase, in the fit between infant and mother, may be reflected in deficiencies in secondary narcissism, can be seen in Mary a 15 year old depressed adolescent. Mary showed among other features, a profoundly lowered sense of self-esteem, a pessimistic attitude toward life in general and her own future in particular, and a puzzling quality of unusual physical discomfort. She felt as if she never "fit in her body." She could not find a comfortable sitting or sleeping position, was ill at ease in her clothing and, in general, felt that she had never achieved a comfortable feel of her body. Mary's mother had contracted severe rheumotoid arthritis during her pregnancy with Mary, had been in severe pain, and was generally restricted in her movement during the first weeks after Mary's birth and afterward. Separated from her husband and unable to afford assistance, she had done as best she could, assisted by Mary's 5-year-old brother. While there was evidence that, in part, Mary's discomfort served as an identification with her crippled mother, we postulated that the mother's ministrations to Mary must have been difficult and uncomfortable for both mother and infant. When an explanation of this was offered to Mary she experienced some relief. She noted that at least it made some sense out of feelings that she could not understand and made her feel that her discomfort was not all in her "imagination." She added that she had always welcomed real illnesses for they gave a reason to her chronic discomfort.

SYMBIOSIS

Symbiotic Psychoses

Childhood psychosis, or a predisposition to psychosis, is the ominous outcome of severe problems in the symbiotic phase as well as the autistic period. Symbiotic psychosis, however, represents a fixation at, or a regression to a more differentiated stage, namely, to the stage of the need-satisfying part object.

Ordinarily, the clinical symptoms of this disorder do not become apparent before 3 to 5 years of age. When they do become manifest, they are much more complex and variable than those of infantile autism. Children of the symbiotic group rarely show conspicuously disturbed behavior during the first year, except possibly sleep disturbances (Mahler, Furer, and Settlage, 1959). Their mothers may describe them as having been oversensitive infants. Disturbances become apparent either gradually or fulminantly at points in development at which maturational functions of the ego usually affect separation from the mother. It appears that the inborn ego apparatuses of such children develop discordantly with the capacities for separation. Either the apparatuses of primary autonomy develop prematurely or the capacity to tolerate separation lags behind the phase-appropriate maturation of the ego apparatuses. Thus, the capacity to move away is out of phase with maturational achievements, and while this discrepancy affects ego formation from the start, the discrepancy between maturation and development increases over time. Certain subsequent maturational achievements may then lead to overwhelming anxiety in an impaired ego. Independent locomotion is one of the functions that may challenge such children beyond their capacities if they are propelled to move away, physically, before they are emotionally ready to do so. Sexual and aggressive impulses proceeding toward maturation, and involving the child's increasing preoccupation with his or her own bodily sensations, may draw the child away from mother to a degree beyond his or her capacity. Indeed, masturbation, ordinarily viewed as promoting separation in that children are able to provide themselves with pleasure, may, in psychotically prone children, be experienced as creating too great a feeling of separateness. Similarly, the shift to the triad, particularly at the oedipal phase, may trigger separation anxiety in that the child is drawn to the other parent and away from the symbiotic orbit. The reaction to these experiences of perceived separation in the psychotically prone toddler is bewilderment and panic. According to Mahler, it takes only a slight additional frustration or trauma to set off ego fragmentation. The acute break with reality is usually ushered in by some event that induces separation and annihilation panic, such as hospitalization with separation from the mother, the birth of a sibling, or enrollment in nursery school.

The clinical picture that may, as we noted, vary much more than in the case of those children suffering from primary autism, is characterized by "agitated catatoniclike temper tantrums and panic-stricken behavior." This is followed by bizarrely distorted and often feverishly increased reality testing and hallucinatory attempts at restitution. Such children attempt to restore and to perpetuate the delusional omnipotence phase of the mother-infant fusion—a period in which the mother was experienced as an ever-ready extension of the self, always at the service and command of the infant. Stereotyped speech productions point to a predominance of hallucinatory soliloquy with an introjected object. Mahler points out that the symbiotic psychotic syndrome is aimed at restoring the symbiotic-parasitic delusion of oneness with the mother, and thus serves a function just the opposite of that served by the autistic mechanisms. However, since constant panic is unbearable, the primarily symbiotic syndrome may, and often does, give way to a regressive yet stabilizing secondary regression to autism. This results in a break with reality and loss of identity, which are the major symptoms of psychosis. "The mother in the flesh," and outside reality, have slipped away. (Mahler, et al., 1959, p. 827). The regression in the case of the symbiotic psychotic child may be so insidious that the prolonged prepsychotic phase may remain undiagnosed until school age.

Again, Mahler considers that innate factors are ordinarily paramount in this severe disorder. In the developmental histories of the children Mahler studied, unusual sensitivities as well as unevenness in growth patterns were evident and the children showed a striking vulnerability to minor frustration. They appeared to have manifested extreme reactions to small failures that normally occur during the practicing of partial ego functions. Such children might give up an activity in which they had failed or hurt themselves. While, as we have noted, the vulnerabilities appear to be related to increased separateness, Mahler does trace the predisposition of the child to the rigidly fused representations of self and object during symbiosis. The permanently fixed fusion of the symbiotic phase does not appear to allow for progress toward individuation (Mahler,

1961). While the emphasis is on the constitutional vulnerability and oversensitivity of those infants with a predisposition to psychoses, Mahler considers that a disturbance in the mother-child relationship may contribute. A parasitic, infantilizing mother may prevent the child from experiencing those requisite slow dosages of separateness in symbiosis, or a "hitherto overly doting" mother, who abandons the differentiating but still symbiotic infant, may traumatize the infant. However, Mahler (1968) warns it is very often the defect in the child that initiates the vicious circle of the pathogenic mother-child relationship by stimulating the mother to react to the child in ways that are deleterious to the child's attempts to separate and individuate.

Adolescent and Adult Psychoses

To our knowledge, Mahler has not specifically studied the relationship between early developmental impairments and adolescent or adult psychoses. However, the work of Burnham, Gladstone, and Gibson (1969) and Ping-Nie Pao (1979) with adolescent and adult schizophrenics accords well with Mahler's findings. Burnham and associates note that faults in differentiation and integration emanating from early developmental vicissitudes may render a person vulnerable to schizophrenic disorganization under specific conditions. Lacking a stable, relatively autonomous inner structure, the poorly differentiated individual is dependent upon and easily influenced by external structure. If customary supportive structure is lost, or there is confrontation by unfamiliar adaptational demands, disorganization is possible. These investigators see normal social role transitions as likely to constitute crises leading to schizophrenic disorganization and, in their writings, offer evidence of such potential in transitions to the roles of college student, soldier, spouse, parent, and so forth.

Pao (1979) has proposed that adolescent and adult schizophrenia represents the outcome of severe failure in the development of object constancy and in the achievement of anxiety tolerance and instinctual drive tolerance during the earliest years. Under pressure of drives or external stress, the schizophrenic structure is likely to become inundated with anxiety, which is experienced at the level of organismic distress, and the integrative function of the ego becomes temporarily paralyzed. Other ego functions then become temporarily suspended as well, with a loss of self continuity. The profound organismic panic leads to efforts to achieve the best possible means for restoring a feeling of safety. This may mean the employment of those maintenance mechanisms which precede the use of primitive defense mechanisms, that is deanimation, dedifferentiation, deneutralization, in addition to primitive defenses such as denial, introjection and projection. The symptoms of adult shizophrenia are consequently "the best possible solution the person can come up with at a given moment." (Pao, 1979, p. 225)

Less Than Optimum Symbiosis

An optimum symbiosis provides a sound base for all subsequent development. While severe early failures lead to psychosis under complex circumstances as we have delineated, less serious deprivation or a prolonging of symbiosis beyond the phase specific point also tends to distort organization. The child's capacity to maintain needed ongoing ties with the object, and to weather the failures and frustrations attendant to the separation–individuation progression, depends upon the achievement of a sufficient degree of "confident expectation" during the symbiotic phase. The gradual formation of sound secondary narcissism draws importantly from that shared sense of omnipotence associated with an attuned, satisfactory union of mother and infant. The feelings of "safe anchorage" that facilitate the child's turn to the other-than-mother world are the outcome of an optimal symbiotic exchange. Thus, deficiencies in symbiosis deprive the child of the requisite foundation for later developmental tasks. Moreover, where symbiotic gratification has been insufficient, an intensified longing for what has been missed may be carried over into the subphases. Symbiotic needs may encroach upon subphase adequate needs. At the practicing phase such toddlers may remain preoccupied with a need for mother that either precludes or dampens the "love affair with the world." At rapprochement, when there is an inevitable pull toward a return to the symbiotic orbit, this may be so overwhelming as to heighten ambitendency well beyond the norm. The impact of symbiotic problems may vary from moderate to severe, depending upon whether subsequent conditions afford an opportunity for reparation and compensation. The likelihood is that early severe deprivations leave some mark even when a favorable turn in development favors progressive growth. Areas of vulnerability may remain as a residue of past failures. We think of certain individuals who appear to have achieved significant ego development and yet, throughout their lives, remain highly vulnerable to unattunement in their significant relationships and particularly vulnerable in the face of separations and losses.

The prolongation of symbiotic gratification beyond the phase specific time also endangers development. We have already considered briefly the noxious impact on the child of those mothers who regard their infants as part of themselves in what Mahler (1955) has termed a parasitic symbiosis. Such mothers may prevent their child's disengagement and individuation, fostering psychosis. Other mothers, unable to tolerate the child's separating efforts, may abruptly disengage themselves, leading to the abandonment experience that Masterson (1976) has considered an integral aspect of borderline development. Conversely, certain infants disengage themselves defensively to escape the enveloping attachment. This has pathological consequences.

Mrs. Ross was a client who had experienced a parasitic symbiosis. Born with a heart murmur, and treated by a physician who had apparently cautioned the mother against allowing her infant to cry for any undue length of time, Mrs. Ross had been overgratified and overprotected throughout her life. She experienced herself as the center of her mother's world. When seen for treatment, she exhibited multiple phobias along with severe depression. Among her many fears was one of eating at restaurants, which caused some marital discord because entertaining customers was important in her husband's business. Her fear was, in part, traced to her inability to wait for food. At home she ate frequently, whenever she pleased, and though she provided scheduled meals for her family, she herself ate while preparing the meals. She recalled that her mother had freed her from the family eating schedule and she had always had a snack available day or night. If she wished to study in bed on a weekend, mother would carry trays to her. Indeed, as a young adult, her mother actually hand fed her when she came home, fatigued from work. Mother had commented that even as a baby she had never put her on scheduled feedings. At times, she expressed resentment that her mother had not prepared her for the "real world" and yet she had a deep longing for those services that made her feel both loved and extremely important. She had also identified with her mother's view of her as a "damaged child" who needed unusual care lest she perish. She also feared experiencing frustration, expecting an accompanying degree of rage that would be life-threatening. Later in treatment, we came to understand that she also feared that her mother's own well-being would be threatened if she could do more for herself. She saw her mother as dependent upon their tie, as she was. Sadly, a month after she gave birth to her only child, her mother suffered a stroke. Mrs. Ross was convinced that her fears were justified. At a time when she needed mother less and was not preoccupied with her, feeling satisfied and complete with a baby within her, her mother lost her reason for existence. With her mother's death a year later, she went into a profound depression.

A further consequence of a parasitic symbiosis has been proposed by Stoller (1975). Tracing femininity in certain boys to excessively prolonged symbiotic experiences, Stoller concluded that these boys were unable to sense themselves as separate from their mother's female body. Thus, he has proposed that a parasitic symbiosis may interfere with the acquisition of gender identity. Incidentally, Stoller found the converse true in the case of certain little girls who displayed marked masculinity. In their cases, there had been a traumatic disruption of symbiosis (Stoller, 1976).

There are situations in which children have been infantilized, and overprotected long beyond the phase specific time, for reasons that seem unavoidable. Where a child is born handicapped, or becomes ill during the early years, extended attunement and care may be requisite for physical survival. Mothers in such cases are seriously challenged to balance the child's physical and psychological developmental needs. However, in the case of Mrs. Ross, certain features suggested that, while the heart murmur heightened the problem, her mother's needs were such that the mother-child relationship might well have been the same, even if she had been physically healthy.

SUMMARY

We have sought to highlight some of the vicissitudes of the autistic and symbiotic phases of human development. Critical to the outcome are the strength and adequacy of the "inborn ego apparatus" and the partnering of the "ordinary devoted" parents (Winnicott, 1949). Serious deficiencies in either may lead to childhood psychosis or may render an individual prone to psychotic breakdown at adolescence or adulthood. Mahler also draws attention to a variety of vicissitudes which may lead to less serious arrests and fixations. These findings provide additional support for the view that effective mental health prevention must be directed towards the prenatal, natal and postnatal periods of life. In terms of treatment, her work suggests some of the steps that may require retracing, in order for development to proceed. In addition her observations can serve to alert the clinician to derivatives or replications of phenomena derived from this early period in development, as they are apt to appear in the therapeutic encounter.

CHAPTER 4

Vicissitudes of Separation-Individuation

Healthful negotiation of the subphases of separation-individuation is favored when the foundation laid down during symbiosis and autism is firm, when maturation keeps pace with development, and when both parents are capable of providing the requisite partnering. However, development even under the most advantageous conditions does not proceed smoothly or in an orderly way. Internal stress and conflict are inherent aspects of growth, and the human condition is such that obstacles and adversities are, to a degree, "expectable." Whether conflict and adversity stimulate or impede development depends both upon the quality and quantity of the stress, and the strength of the organism at that particular time. Inevitably, however, as the child progresses through the subphases, he or she pays a price for advancement in terms of loss and pain. The longing for the early union between mother and infant parallels the thrust towards individuation, exerting a strong pull throughout life, particularly during the first years when partnering is so vital. In addition, the fact that individuation depends upon identification with those from whom the child is concomitantly differentiating adds to the potential for self-object confusion at a time before boundaries are firmly established (Pine, 1979). Mahler considers that "not even the most normally endowed child, with the most optimally available mother, is able to weather the separation-individuation process without crises, come out unscathed by the rapprochement struggle, and enter the oedipal phase without developmental difficulty" (Mahler, 1975, p. 227).

There are, however, certain experiences, intrinsic or extrinsic, occurring at nodal points during separation-individuation that are likely to place development in greater jeopardy. We say likely since we cannot make accurate developmental predictions. While it may be valid retrospectively to come to view a given client's difficulties as the outcome, in part, of specific subphase problems, we cannot assert that the reverse is true, that a given condition inevitably leads to specific pathological development. Nonetheless, to be alert to potential dangers places us in a position from which we may more effectively intervene on behalf of children "at risk," and broaden and improve those preventative strategies that are an integral aspect of mental health services. In addition we may more sensitively comprehend the genetic origins of some of the pathology that we seek to remediate.

DIFFERENTIATION VICISSITUDES

We have already noted the importance of an optimum symbiosis in fostering smooth hatching and the healthful negotiation of the subphases. In the absence of basic trust the child is ill-prepared for the cognitive discovery of the other-than-mother world. The turn outward also becomes more anxiety-ridden when there is insufficient individuation to support it. Experiences with the stranger, may under such circumstances arouse a pathological degree of anxiety or a prolonged period of mild stranger reaction, interfering with the pleasurable inspective response that ordinarily encourages the outward turn. Preoccupied still with securing what has been missed, and deprived of the accretions to structure that a favorable symbiosis fosters, such children are less adequately equipped to meet the subphase challenges. To the degree that symbiotic needs predominate, they overlap and alter each phase. The most serious developmental dangers at this point occur when the child fails to differentiate or, on the other hand, differentiates prematurely. The former leads to psychosis, as we have already considered, while the latter is apt to lead to borderline and/or narcissistic disorders as well as to the proclivity to depression.

Premature Differentiation

Premature differentiation, that is, before the child has derived the full measure from symbiosis, upsets the developmental balance. In order to progress, the child then must resort to some form of compensatory efforts to achieve equilibrium (Spitz, 1959). Such efforts, though they are sustaining at the time, tend eventually to distort development. Premature differentiation may be the result of a child's precipitous confrontation with the difference between mother and self, by the failure in attunement that precludes a feeling of symbiotic unity, or unpredictability in the mother's attachment and care. In some instances, the child himself or herself disengages prematurely in an effort to escape a parasitic symbiosis. Finally, a certain unusual precocity of the ego may foster too early differentiation, even when the mother has been favorably attuned (Mahler, 1975). Precocious development for example, of the sensory or perceptive functions may lead to visual hyperalertness, or hypersensitivity to touch that forces the child to confront the outside world precipitiously. In such circumstances, a mother is challenged to compensate by providing a particularly sensitive protective shield that must be withdrawn at the appropriate time in order to avoid hindering the individuating ego's gradual exercise of autonomy (Mahler, 1975).

Premature differentiation makes it more difficult for the child to guard against the fear of early object loss and fosters increased separation anxiety in children who must then find ways, on their own, to cope with such fears. In the face of such challenges, several types of compensatory arrangements have been noted that, over time, may lead to pathology of varying degrees of severity. Among such compensations are premature ego development, a tendency on the child's part to mother himself or herself, and the development of a "false self" (James, 1960).

Premature Ego Development

Where the congenital equipment lends itself, ego development is sometimes accelerated. While this increases the child's coping capacities, the prematurely formed ego is likely to prove fragile and its functions are frequently limited to those necessary for survival. Malone (1967) has described certain emotionally deprived, economically disadvantaged children who developed unusual ego capacities to compensate for deficiencies in their environmental experiences. They achieved unusual abilities to negotiate their often dangerous and demanding worlds. However, their early restricted ego development led to early closure and to the forfeiting of genuine mastery and flexible adaptability.

The False Self

Where differentiation has been forced to proceed ahead of the tolerance for separation and the achievement of sufficient individuation, certain children appear to exploit their premature ego capacities in the service of achieving a degree of self. They begin to take over attributes of others but these identifications differ from those selective identifications normally associated with the formation of a sound sense of self. They are actually imitations of a transient and global quality. Assuming the mannerisms, mode of speech, and other characteristics of those whom they are with, they remind us of those tiny chameleons that change color in accord with the surroundings. This adaptation leads to the formation of the "as if personality" (Deutsch, 1942), or what has been termed "the false self" (James, 1960), a personality constellation associated with borderline pathology. This adaptation is facilitated by an early reactivity to the environment and an unusual capacity for identification (James, 1960). It is not always clear whether the precocious ego capacities in such persons were the result of premature differentiation or whether the early differentiation was associated with precocious ego development.

Mrs. Walker was a client who, having apparently differentiated defensively and prematurely to escape an intrusive parasitic symbiosis, utilized her ego capacities to imitate attributes of others. In response to developmental necessity she had become, an actress who studied what she thought would be appropriate in a given situation and then proceeded, in an imitation of others whom she had observed performing under similar circumstances, to play a part.

Narcissistic Compensation

Mahler has pointed out that in some situations children may begin to take over their own mothering. It is as if the child becomes his or her own developmental partner. We recall Martha, a young adolescent client who, as a child, postured in front of her mirror, stroking her hair for long periods of time. The history revealed that, as an infant, she had banged her head against the crib at a time when her overwhelmed mother was preoccupied with the care of the father who had made a suicidal attempt. The head banging was understood as an attempt at securing some kind of stimulation and self-recognition, though unfortunately through aggressive means.

When family life improved and the mother sought to reconnect with the child, there was some reversal of development that appeared to have been moving in a psychotic direction. However, the mother's efforts were less than successful. Martha continued to have serious problems in the narcissistic realm. We came to undersand her experiences before the mirror as a way of providing herself with needed body libidinization and mirroring, reflecting incidentally a more healthful shift, at least toward a positive investment in the self. Nonetheless, the attempt was still to serve as her own developmental partner. Ordinarily the child's own motor, visual, tactile, and other activities contribute to body libidinization and to healthy narcissism via self-recognition and appreciation. However, development of sound secondary narcissism depends upon the participation of both mother and child. Where a child assumes too much of the task, narcissism is affected as well as the capacity for higher levels of object relations. Martha withdrew to herself and even when mother and later father became more libidinally available, she bypassed their offerings. What began as an effort at adaptation ultimately led to a pseudo-self-sufficiency, to a withdrawal from still vitally needed object related experiences and to a preference for grandiose fantasies over reality experiences. This may have resulted because even when the parental partnering was improved it was not adequate. However, such compensatory efforts, in themselves, interfere with the child's ongoing opportunities for individuation by way of identification. A closed unit is formed in which the child relies on fantasied nurturing and accomplishment. Martha spent hours imagining herself an accomplished pianist performing before appreciative audiences. However, she found it impossible to practice regularly for her weekly piano lessons.

Such arrangements preclude the opportunities for healthful identification. Only when the self, according to Mahler, can take in and absorb the mother's loving care, can the mother become an external object eligible for those identifications that contribute to ego and to later superego formation. This turn back to the self, though often successful in the short run, may lead the child to "give up" on the object world and continue to seek satisfaction from within.

Such an individual was Mrs. Small, whose mother had been hospitalized during the last quarter of Mrs. Small's first year. When the mother returned, Mrs. Small had already begun to turn to herself and was unresponsive, according to family reports, to mother's efforts to reengage her. The history, as it unfolded over time, suggested that the mother, in turn, distanced from the daughter. Many

years later, Mrs. Small expressed dismay at the fact that she had
been able to identify with so few of what she objectively regarded
as very positive qualities in her mother. While in part this might be
understood as a means of avoiding self-object merger in a patient
needing to defend against profound symbiotic wishes, we also came
to consider the patient's turning to herself at differentiation, and her
subsequent maintenance of a disengagement from mother as imped-
ing her opportunities for growth promoting identificatory experiences. It might be added that this arrangement led to borderline organization with narcissistic features.

An unfortunate feature of these compensatory efforts is that they
may appear to the parent, or other observers, as highly desirable.
The child's precocity, seeming independence, and mature characteristics may be valued and encouraged. It requires a particularly sensitive parent who can keep in mind a child's age-appropriate and
phase-specific needs in the face of prematurely developed capacities.
This is especially true in a society that more and more seems to be
seeking and promoting an ever-increasing acceleration in human development. However, unless these adaptations are understood as
compensatory in most instances, and as indicative of some developmental deviation calling for interventive efforts, such children stand
in danger of paying a heavy developmental price. Where a child
turns to himself or to herself for missed narcissistic supplies, a pattern may become established over time that renders such arrangements almost impervious to attempts at intervention.

THE PRACTICING SUBPHASE

Favorable negotiation of this subphase is also dependent upon
what has gone before. Where mother has been previously optimally
available, the child is free to venture forth from a vantage point of
"safe anchorage." If, however, the child has not had a full measure
of earlier closeness, then the negotiation of practicing may be jeopardized. In the absence of confident expectation the toddler remains overly preoccupied with mother and is unable to become en-
thusiastically involved in the pleasurable exploration and mastery of
the now expanding world of reality. The dampening of enthusiasm
due to concern over mother's availability may lead to transient and
abbreviated practicing experiences that lack the enthusiastic, narcis-
sistically enhancing features that are so necessary for promotion of a

positive sense of self. On the other hand, if mother has been too intrusive, and has interfered with the early distancing efforts, entrance into and subsequent negotiation of practicing may also be impeded.

Deficits in Partnering

Despite the practicing toddler's seeming obliviousness to mother, her partnering remains vital. Opportunities for "refueling" and "checking back" are essential. Without them, helplessness and bewilderment may prevail. The mother's capacity to "let go" of the child as well as her own object constancy is tested. She must keep the child "in mind" when he or she is "out of sight." Keeping in touch remains essential though now such contact is increasingly maintained through vision and speech. For those mothers who have difficulty in relating to their children when the youngsters move away, there may be either an effort to hold the children back, or, feeling that there is little more to gain from the children, the mother may seek to accelerate their growing up. Where efforts are on the side of pushing the child ahead, it would appear that the youngster begins to evidence greater need for closeness.

The mother is challenged to allow the child to individuate at his or her own pace, and to achieve an "optimal closeness" in relation to the toddler's unique needs. If the mother is too much there, the toddler's courage is likely to fade, and the mother's too great interference with the child's forward thrust may lead to a defensive, almost frantic effort to be free of mother. The consequent frustration stimulated by overcontrol may stimulate an excessive amount of aggression. On the other hand, if mother withdraws altogether, panic may ensue, or the child may become excessively preoccupied with securing mother's partnership to the detriment of sound practicing activities. It may be difficult for certain mothers to find the proper distance from which to provide a "refueling" base because they must seek contact primarily when they require it for themselves.

The mother's "mirroring admiration" of the toddler's pursuits reassures the child that he or she can make it in the wider world and at the same time contributes to the development of sound secondary narcissism. Where the mother is in some way threatened by the child's venturing forth because of her own need to hold on to the child or because she lacks sufficient confidence in the child's capacities (perhaps for realistic reasons such as might be the case where a child has a handicap), the accomplishments of practicing may be drained of some of the rich affective coloring provided by mother's acknowledgement.

A patient comes to mind whose history pointed to considerable discouragement by the mother of her growing daughter's widening activities. We came to note that when during the course of treatment she began to broaden her interests, her initial response was enthusiastic, but this quickly "fell flat." At times, we could discern a certain amount of anxiety that could be understood as the reflection of separation fears. However, this did not appear to explain her response adequately. At some point, this patient noted that she could recall her mother squelching her enthusiasm over a new accomplishment, such as riding a bike or learning to roller skate, with the explanation that it was "bad luck" to make too much of such experiences. This led to vivid recollections of mother's extensive superstitions that, among other things, served to inhibit the mother's acknowledgement of her children's accomplishments. It is difficult to identify to what degree this mother's fear and reluctance to see her daughter move away and absence of essential mirroring contributed to the difficulty this patient had in consolidating developmental gains. What was clear in the therapeutic situation, however, was that there was a strong conflict between the wish to acknowledge, enjoy, and share accomplishments and the fear that such acknowledgments might bring "bad luck."

Bodily Feelings

The child assumes increasing possession and control over his or her own body at the practicing subphase. Some mothers, however, seem to experience difficulty in relinquishing their control and may be observed picking the child up, restricting the child's movements, and in general continuing to retain the child's body as if it were their own possession. Derivatives of this early experience are sometimes noted in certain patients who, in their treatment, appear to give over the responsibility for their bodies to the worker. Such individuals may, for example, want to reduce their smoking or to lose weight. They behave as if the therapist should somehow be able to deal with these issues without really involving them in the task. It is, of course, difficult to ascertain without extensive material on a given case the degree to which a given patient's search for connection with the worker by way of the body may be an expression of instinctual aim-directed wishes or the extent to which it may be an indicator of a failure to have reached a level of separation and individuation at which the body is sensed as belonging to themselves.

We think of Mrs. Masters, who constantly looked to the therapist to direct her toward seeking needed medical care, and to devise ways to motivate her to diet successfully, even though she was of average weight. This young woman appeared to have failed to assume possession of her own body and to experience responsibility for it. Her mother, an intrusive, controlling, narcissistic woman, continued to phone weekly to check on her 30-year-old daughter's weight and health care. In the past, she had monitored her daughter's daily food intake in an effort to assure that she would have a very thin, "model's" body, admired by both parents. The patient was rewarded with small gifts for eating minimally and for maintaining the desired weight. In addition, both parents had strong ideas, again derived from the way in which models carried their bodies, and were from this patient's earliest years very much involved with her posture and walking. On one hand, Mrs. Masters resented her family's efforts to "shape" her body according to their ideals, yet she gained satisfaction from this connection with them. In treatment she complained that the worker showed no interest in her and was failing to offer the encouragement she needed to follow through on certain medical advice. She felt she was unable to take the initiative and needed "motivation" from the worker. When she developed the need to engage in a series of corrective exercises, she telephoned her mother, anticipating that mother would follow up to see if she were carrying out the regime. Her disappointment was deep when mother did not follow through, and she became depressed, neglecting the exercises completely. Although she began to understand that she treated her body as if it belonged to her mother, she continued to have great difficulty in assuming responsibility herself. We increasingly came to appreciate the degree to which taking over her body constituted an intolerable threat of separation.

Constitutional Considerations

The child's innate capacities and the rate and manner in which they unfold may be such as to disrupt the developmental balance at practicing. The toddler, for example, who walks very early, moving away from mother before the acquisition of sufficient capacity for intrapsychic separateness, may be in danger. A mother's sensitive awareness of this, and her ability to "be there," may be necessary to smooth out such disparities between maturation and development. On the other hand, unusual delays in motor maturation may diminish the elation of this subphase or may raise anxiety in the mother, interfering with her growth-promoting attitude of confidence in the child's capabilities.

Severe handicaps such as blindness and deafness of course pose special difficulties requiring unusual ingenuity and patience on the part of the developmental partners. Selma Fraiberg (1977) has described the creative efforts made by the parents of a blind child, Toni. Following Toni's healthy development in the preceding phases, she reached a "developmental impasse" at the practicing subphase. At a time when she could be expected to begin crawling and paddling, Toni withdrew to a passive and immobile state at times of nonstimulation. The mother finally gave her a "gentle push" by placing her in a walker, and in a short time Toni began to cruise about the house. Within three months, at age 13 months, she began to walk with support and to creep, showing the same elatedness in "getting into everything" ordinarily experienced by the sighted practicing child.

The Role of Aggression at Practicing

As during other subphases, the arousal of excessive aggression constitutes a developmental danger. The physical accomplishments of the practicing phase make optimum use of aggressive drive energies, but the active aggressive momentum of the individuation process must be neutralized. Where conditions lead to greater than average negativism, excessive temper tantrums, a tendency to passive-aggressive behavior, or the deflection of energy toward discharge activities, the utilization of aggression in the service of separating and individuating activities may be impeded.

SUMMARY

The maturation of the child's emerging ego functions may take place even under less than optimal practicing conditions. However, if there is too great a struggle during this period, there may be insufficient libidinal energy with which to cathect the body, the unfolding autonomous ego functions, and the other-than-mother world

(Mahler, 1975). Furthermore, where the pleasure of separate functioning is insufficient to compensate for the pain of object loss, the child may fail to overcome the separation anxiety attendant to that subphase, or may become disposed to a basically depressed mood (Mahler, 1966) or narcissistic vulnerability.

RAPPROCHEMENT SUBPHASE

If conditions are advantageous at this subphase, minor deviations related to previous developmental difficulties may be smoothed out or compensated for. On the other hand, earlier deficits may be exacerbated or new problems may arise as the result of particular stresses or trauma occurring at rapprochement. Borderline or narcissistic organization or certain deviations in the infantile neurosis are thought to have their origins in the vicissitudes of this developmental period.

Vulnerability is heightened in the third subphase by the convergence of three phase specific phenomena: the fear of object loss, greater awareness of bodily sensations as the child proceeds through the anal phase of psychosexual development, and the discovery of the anatomical differences. Fear of object loss is partly relieved by earlier internalizations, but becomes complicated because the introjection of parental demands introduces a new fear, the loss of the object's love (Mahler, 1975).

The child enters the rapprochement subphase in a subdued mood, increasingly aware of his or her immaturity and vulnerability. The exhilaration and heightened narcissism of the practicing phase, having made their developmental contributions, have waned. The exciting accomplishments of a short while ago have become part of the child and the novelty has worn off. The child turns back to the mother and actively seeks approval and love and her involvement in activities. Mother begins to be experienced as a person in her own right, someone who now must be "wooed" as contrasted to her just "being there." It is not long, however, before this reunion becomes conflictual and the "refueling" behavior of the practicing period is replaced by an active search for or avoidance of close body contact with mother. Shadowing and darting are the behavioral manifestations of the wish for reunion and the fear of reengulfment.

Difficulties between child and mother are probably inevitable during this subphase. At the Mother's Center Program, the mothers as a group expressed the feeling that somehow they had "failed" their toddlers, in the face of their children's seeming regression at this stage (Turrini, 1977). It is difficult to comprehend let alone deal with the child's insistent demands for attention that alternate with an insistence on independence, heightened by the "no" and the increased negativism characteristic of the anal phase. Both occur at a time when the child is realistically more capable than ever before, so that mothers may come to expect more than the child is actually ready to offer.

Development at rapprochement may be jeopardized by discrepancies between the progression along the separation track and that of the individuation track; by a continuation into that subphase of unsatisfied earlier needs; by a lack of requisite parental partnering; by a too rapid, traumaticlike deflation of self or object omnipotence, or by an encouragement of a prolonged continuation of a belief in that omnipotence; and lastly, by problems involving modulation of destructive aggression associated with the struggles of this subphase.

At a time when the stresses of rapprochement converge with the pressures of the psychosexual maturational sequence, whatever reservoir of "confident expectation" has been established is increasingly drawn upon. Where a deficit of emotional supplies from previous subphases has led to insufficient resources, the struggles of this phase may be depleting.

A diminution in confident expectation at this phase exacerbates the feelings of object loss, leading in some instances to a basic depressive affect, or a proclivity to depressive illness (Mahler, 1966).

Ensuing separation and grief reactions may give way to despair for a while, or to impotent resignation and surrender, sometimes bearing a masochistic coloring in certain children. In others, anger and discontentment may persist following a short period of grief and sadness. In all such cases, Mahler observed, there is an increased need for mother and an intensification of ambivalence that stand in the way of the development of object constancy.

Unmet Symbiotic Needs

Unmet symbiotic needs carried into rapprochement encroach on the subphase adequate relatedness to the parental partners. The phase-specific longing to regain the symbiotic closeness may be unduly heightened and lead to an excessive degree of coerciveness and clinging. This is then accompanied by a consequent fear of the longed-for but dreaded merger, leading, in turn, to increased distancing as a defense. Ambitendency is likely to be intensified beyond the norm. The dread of merging and the alternating fear of separation, characteristic of borderline pathology, may represent a distorted version of this conflict (Blum, 1974).

Still in search for missed symbiotic gratification, some children may turn to the father for nurturing instead of utilizing him for the unique contributions he ordinarily makes at this developmental point. This tends to interfere with the establishment of a distinct object representation of father different from that of mother, and, consequently, impedes the important achievement of triangulation and those developmental accomplishments associated with this advance in object relatedness. In turn, this is likely to have an impact on the subsequent oedipal negotiation and the organization of the infantile neurosis.

Deflation of Omnipotence

The child's beliefs in his or her own omnipotence and in the parental omnipotence in which the child partakes constitute the foundation of early infantile well-being and self-esteem, and must be gradually replaced by a realistic recognition, conviction, and enjoyment of the child's now developing individual autonomy. This will be further consolidated by the achievement of object constancy (Mahler, 1966). Circumstances that lead to a too abrupt deflation of the sense of their own and their shared omnipotence may foster an angry dependency upon and ambivalent feelings toward the parents. The result may be excessive reliance on splitting, and a turning of aggression against the self, leading to feelings of helplessness and a basic depressive affect.

Among the factors that may lead to an abrupt deflation of omnipotence as contrasted to a gradual "toning down" is a withdrawl on the part of the mother at a time when she remains vitally needed. Accidental factors may also play a role at this stage in confronting the child traumatically with his or her lack of omnipotence. We think of those children who sustain a serious injury or illness, or whose parents may become severely ill or die at that developmental point.

Mrs. Elliot for example, suffered recurrently from periods of agonizingly low self-esteem and self-depreciation that alternated with a more realistic appraisal of her considerable talents and achievements. There were times when she indeed overestimated those achievements but could reassess more accurately when gently prodded to do so.

She said that she had chosen the particular worker consulted because she wanted a woman like herself, married to the same type of man as her own spouse. She had made the effort to establish these external details about the worker. She then proceeded to overidealize the worker. This was later understood as a recurrent theme of her life. She had often overvalued friends, early sexual partners, her husband, and most important of all her mother. This 45-year-old client could be lifted from despair by a positive communication from her mother, or reduced to sadness and longing if she were ignored, as she frequently was.

In due time, client and therapist came to understand this search in the environment for boosting partners as the attempt to bolster a deficient sense of self-esteem. Aspects of her life history, which supported the hypothesis that her problems stemmed in some measure from too rapid a deflation in necessary belief and participation in the parental omnipotence, were forthcoming.

When she was about 2 years old, her father returned from naval service. She lost not only the familiar relatives they lived with, but her mother too, because mother became romantically too reinvolved with her refound husband to pay much attention to the little girl. To add to this deflation, Mrs. Elliot had undergone emergency surgery at the age of 2½ years. Her mother, absorbed in her new life, had been insufficiently available once more. Thus, the history of early, unavoidable illness and pain had been compounded by maternal inadequacy in partnering at a crucial phase of development. Both phenomena contributed to a precipitous deflation of omnipotence.

On the other hand, development may also be threatened where the parents act as if the child is, indeed, omnipotent, where they submit to the child's coercion or overvalue the child in unrealistic ways. This interferes with the acquisition of a more reality-based view of the self.

When 24-year-old Mr. Norge was fired from the third job he had held since college graduation, the need for self-investigation became evident. His self-opinionated and dogmatic stance was not compensated for by his real ability on the job. He was the youngest, by some eight years, in a family of four sons. He grew up as the showpiece of his conforming parents and siblings who found unconscious satisfaction in his early precocity. Under the rubric of not stifling his creativity, they did not help him to control his impulsive, self-indulgent behavior. His egocentricity had been tolerated at the private schools and small college he had attended. He was thus never made fully aware of the need for more modest and disciplined behavior until he entered employment.

Discrepancies between Development and Maturation

Discrepancies between maturation and development originating in earlier developmental phases are likely to continue to have an impact on the rapprochement experience. For example, the child who achieved precocious locomotor development interfering with a smooth practicing experience may at rapprochement show an unusual degree of "darting away" that interferes with the balance between engagement and disengagement. Further, the mother having considered her toddler "advanced" may find it difficult to assess the child's phase-specific requirement for her availability and be unable to assume an "optimal distance."

Mr. Fine, a client who attempted physical feats well beyond his experience, seemed at first to be exhibiting counterphobic behavior. He began his first ski venture on the expert slopes with the result that he broke his leg. In time, we began to recognize that, despite his good intellect, he had unusually poor judgment regarding his physical prowess.

We learned that Mr. Fine had begun walking at about nine months and his general precocious physical maturation was a source of considerable pride to his athletic father. As a little boy, he had been encouraged and rewarded for his daring. Neither parent was able to assess the discrepancy between his premature physical prowess and his age-appropriate lack of judgment. It appeared that as a child he had not been adequately protected nor guided in his activities. By the time he reached rapprochement, his heightened ambitendency apparently took on dangerous proportions, not understood or managed by his parents. He had been told that when he was about 2 he had jumped off a table and, hitting his head, had become unconscious. While his parents took adequate care of him following the accident, they had watched him climb on the table and had failed to restrain him, not wanting to interfere and assuming he would manage because of his unusual "independence." It was our impression that Mr. Fine's lack of caution was, among other things, rooted in the early discrepancy between maturation and development, and his parents' failure to accommodate to it.

Parental Partnering

The mother's acceptance of the child, her availability, and her active support are requisite at rapprochement. She must be willing to "let go" but not abandon the child. Where she is less than optimally available, the child may need to invest too much energy in wooing her, with the result that less libido and not enough neutralized aggression is available for the formation of the many developing ego functions that are in the process of formation at this time. If the converse is true and the mother shadows the child excessively, additional anxieties may be aroused with regard to whether the child is capable of making it in the outside world. Such shadowing may also represent to the child disapproval on the mother's part of his or her own independent strivings at a time when her approval or disapproval has assumed considerable importance.

If a mother distances from the child precipitously at rapprochement, withdrawing her libidinal availability and her still needed assistance of the child's functioning, the child is confronted with a degree of separation that may overburden the still immature modulating and negotiating functions of the ego. The ensuing sudden and painful awareness of helplessness is likely to result in a too abrupt deflation of the child's previous sense of individual and shared omnipotence. Under the sway of aggressive drive energies stimulated by such deflation, there is a danger that negative representations of mother will be crystallized into a "bad" introject. A subsequent effort to eject this bad introject may then be met with a proclivity on the child's part to identify with or confuse the self-representations with the "bad" introject. Aggression becomes unleased in such a way as to sweep away the "good object" and, with it, the "good" self-representations (Mahler, 1975, p. 117).

Aggression during Rapprochement

Where a mother retaliates in kind in the face of the child's increased aggression at this subphase, a similar situation regarding the formation of an essentially "bad" introject may obtain. Such an introject comes to serve as a source of disapproval, criticism, or aggression, as compared to the needed supportive, encouraging introject that in time can be assimilated, developing into a positive identification that can provide connection and support.

In those situations where the mother fails to adequately restrain and modulate the child's aggression, there is the danger that the child may come to depend on the splitting mechanism to defend against aggression.

Fathering

Where the father is absent or fails to play his valuable role in the parenting of the child, the rapprochement youngster is deprived of important developmental assistance. As we have stated, the father serves as a powerful and necessary support against the pull back to the primary undifferentiated symbiotic phase. The establishment of a libidinally cathected object representation of the father not only promotes separation, but paves the way for the subsequent negotiation of the oedipus. It is the preoedipal love of the father that aids in the relinquishment of the oedipal wishes and contributes to the subsequent establishment of ego and superego identifications.

In many of the cases we have worked with, the problems in separation–individuation have been heightened by failures on the part of the paternal object to form a significant relationship with the child. This has been particularly true of those individuals whose symbiotic experiences have been along parasitic lines. Frequently, clients themselves express the wish that their fathers might have interfered with their mother's intense ties to them.

As previously pointed out the precise contribution of the father in the early years has not yet been fully understood, although much work is currently appearing in the literature on this subject (Prall, 1978). Nor has the effect on child development of one-parent families and the changing roles of men and women in modern society been fully documented and evaluated. However, in view of the importance of early identifications to ego and superego development, there seems to be merit in Burlingham's (1973) view. She suggests that, whatever other development implications there may be in one-parent families, in the absence of two parents, each with a different personality, and therefore offering differing nutrients to the child, there may be a loss, leading later in development, to a "flatter, more uniform, and less rich affective life" (p. 46).

Vicissitudes Related to Sexual Differences

Mahler's observational studies have pointed to certain differences between the vicissitudes of rapprochement as experienced by girls and boys. Though both sexes appear similarly elated during the practicing subphase and respond to the increasing awareness of their vulnerability and their continued dependence with a sobered mood upon entrance into the next subphase, the girls appeared to be more prone to a depressed mood than did the boys. The boys tended to counteract the abrupt deflation of the practicing period mood by their greater motor activity. Whether this, as well as the observation that the boys were more resistant to hugging and kissing, was related to innate or extrinsic factors was difficult to ascertain (Mahler, 1975). Mahler's work suggests that a child's motor capacities may be influenced by maternal attitudes. In describing a little girl, whose motor activities were as developed as those of her two brothers, she noted their mother especially valued all of her children's efforts at independence. This might support the view that where mothers respond similarly to their sons and to their daughters, similar capacities are likely to be fostered in both (Chodorow, 1978).

Although the boys studied by Mahler displayed soberness and heightened sensitivity in the face of their separateness from mother, and concern about her intrusions on their autonomy, they seemed to pursue their motor and perceptual cognitive activities confidently. Under favorable conditions, the active exercise of separation from and the reunion with her by moving away behavior was more prominent in the boys than in the girls (Mahler, 1975). When the boys became aware of the anatomical differences they did not show overt distress, and Mahler concluded that they tended to face their castration anxiety later, during the second or third year of life. Overall, the boys appeared to separate with less stress, seemingly better able to turn to the outside or to their own bodies for pleasure and satisfaction, and to move towards father as someone to identify with (Mahler, 1975). However, where a mother had difficulty in giving up her son's body, passivity seemed to ensue, or the child might struggle to ward off the dangerous "mother after separation." The fear of merger, sometimes seen as central in the resistance to treatment by some adult male patients, may, according to Mahler, have its origin in the situations such as described above (Mahler, 1975).

In the case of the girls studied by Mahler, it appeared that their realization of separateness was more complicated. Mahler has attributed this to their lesser degree of motor-mindedness and to their earlier awareness and response to the anatomical differences. The girls' discovery of the penis confronted them with something that they lacked, thus becoming the "prototype of a wished-for but unattainable "possession" of other children" (Mahler, 1975, p. 91). A range of behavior was observed following the discovery that suggested feelings of anxiety, anger, and defiance. Some little girls sought to undo the sexual differences by attempting to urinate standing up, or other such masculine activities. They also appeared to turn back to their mothers as if they were blaming them or demanding something from them. The girls' disappointment in their mothers and their ambivalent ties to them often led to clinging, dependent, and coercively demanding behavior. By the third year, however, there were indications that the claim for the penis was becoming displaced onto the mother as a person (Mahler, 1975). Identification with mother began to take place and form the basis for feminine gender identity.

Although an observable developmental phenomenon contributing in unique ways to character development, the conflict of penis envy is considered to be normally resolvable (Settlage, 1976). However, in boys, the acquisition of firm gender identity seemed less stormy—which Mahler attributes to the mother's respect for the boy's "phallicity" and his opportunity to identify with father.

While these studies point to sexually determined vicissitudes, it is our impression that serious phallic problems—either prolonged penis envy in women, or excessive castration concerns in men—derive from earlier experiences with loss. In those individuals who have experienced early object loss, the stage appears to be set for excessive fear of the loss of the stool as a body part, and later for misconstruing the absence of the penis as a missing body part. Prior fears of object loss, and of loss of the love of the object, may become transformed into concerns about loss of body parts (Settlage, 1976).

Rapprochement Danger Signs

Among the danger signals at this subphase that may serve to alert the clinician to possible deviations are the child's overconcern with the mother's whereabouts indicated by excessive shadowing or heightened separation anxiety, or extreme coerciveness, clinging, or excessive temper tantrums. Excessive ambivalence and splitting of the object world are additional signs that satisfactory development may be at risk. Finally, we draw attention to those toddlers who are persistently negative in mood and response, and show excessive concern with their own "goodness" or "badness." This suggests what may be a precocity of superego structuralization with the potential for overharsh superego development. Their potential for later pathology in the form of proneness to depression may be overlooked because they pose no active problem for their caretakers.

CONSOLIDATION OF INDIVIDUALITY AND THE BEGINNINGS OF EMOTIONAL OBJECT CONSTANCY

The fourth subphase is a period of rapid expansion of cognitive functions as well as a consolidation of a stable sense of entity and a primitive consolidation of general identity. Where development has proceeded favorably, object and self constancy are on-their-way. The pattern of previous subphases determines the character of this period, influencing the degree to which consolidation takes place. Deviations, developmental lags, and previously unmet needs influence the degree to which previous achievements may "hold" or undergo regression under unusual pressures. If there remains a residue of too much aggression, separation from mother will continue to be uncomfortable and disrupt development. Where object and self-constancy are limited, regression under stress may take place. The firming up of previous accomplishments and those specific to this period may be challenged by the struggles around toilet training, as well as the increased awareness of the anatomical sexual difference and the attached anxieties.

The expansion of cognitive functions and the negotiation of the psychosexual maturational sequence have an impact on the consolidation of individuation. Therefore, cognitive deficiencies or problems in the psychosexual sphere are likely to impose some limitation on the ongoing developmental processes in this open-ended subphase.

The consolidation of individuation is also affected by those accidental occurrences of life such as illness, surgery, accidents, separations, and divorce, occurrences which are endlessly varied and, of course, ubiquitous in human life. Up to a point, the infinite variety of personal experience helps shape the development of human character. However, beyond a certain point that is unique for each individual, developmental stress and accidental trauma may directly impinge on the consolidation of those structures that have already been formed.

DEVELOPMENTAL PREDICTION

Having delineated some, though by no means all, of the potential vicissitudes of the separation–individuation progression, we note Mahler's reminder that, while we may expect that the occurrence of unfavorable experiences and trauma during the first 14 to 15 months of life may lead to a vulnerability to later difficulties, this is not inevitable. Her work suggests that this is only the case if the infant's innate endowment is greatly abnormal, or if the experiential circumstances are stressful and consistently counteract subphase-specific progress far beyond the average expectable or when developmental conditions are, from the beginning so deviant that the effect of the stress is ongoing and cumulative.

SUMMARY AND A CONSIDERATION OF SOME PREVENTATIVE IMPLICATIONS

In summary, it can be said that whether or not separation-individuation leads to a consolidation of individuality and the achievement of a position of on-the-way to object constancy, depends upon the child's innate endowment, the early mother-child and later father-child interaction, and the nature of the child's ongoing life experiences, particularly the presence or absence of acute traumata and unusual stress. The importance of all of these factors in human development is already well known to helping professionals. However, Mahler makes a unique contribution by delineating the impact of these phenomena on a developmental sequence—separation-individuation—thereby adding another vantage point from which both normal development and social and emotional pathology may be examined. Her work, like that of Spitz and other developmental theorists, can now serve as an additional guide for the elaboration of preventative social services and mental health strategies, as well as for the design of ameliorative programs and therapeutic technique.

First and foremost, by deepening our appreciation of the child's own role in development (indeed, according to Mahler "the lion's share" belongs to the child), her work offers added support to efforts at reducing those conditions that have been shown to be deleterious to the healthy unfolding of cognitive and physical capacities. We think immediately of how her work may be drawn upon to further document the necessity for continued efforts to reduce poverty to the lowest possible level. Poor children are clearly children "at risk"—a fact affirmed by innumerable studies. The associated phenomena of poor nutrition of the mother—inadequate prenatal care, higher rates of prematurity, a larger number of very young mothers, less favorable circumstances for deliveries, a higher rate of illnesses such as syphilis that directly effect the fetus adversely—all of these factors constitute serious prenatal assaults. A range of unfavorable post-natal circumstances associated with poverty, such as a greater likelihood of lead ingestion in inadequate housing, as well as poor nutrition and health care, have also been shown to lead over time to physical and/or cognitive impairments (Wilson, 1978).

It is not only the children of the poor, however, whose physical and cognitive development are frequently prenatally compromised. Evidence has grown of the ill effects of alcohol, drugs and nicotine on the developing fetus among offspring of all economic and social groups. It has been established for example, that mothers who smoke during pregnancy are more likely to deliver prematurely, or to give birth to full term babies of low birthweight. Both conditions correlate with a higher risk of impairment (Zinman, 1980). Primary prevention must take these factors into account in order to ensure to the fullest possible extent those capacities in the developing child that are required for healthful negotiation of separation-individuation.

The comprehension of what constitutes adequate maternal care and favorable family relationships after birth, of "the average expectable environment" (Hartmann, 1958) has been sharpened by the work of Mahler. Families, helping professionals, legislators and the citizenry at large could profit from this knowledge. How many parents, even if they are capable of responding favorably, are aware of the need to protect their infants from too early differentiation, particularly when the child's precocious accomplishments are so often an understandable source of pride? How many mothers are prepared for the contradictory behavior of their rapprochement subphase toddlers? How many mothers can appreciate their developing toddlers concern over anatomical differences (particularly when this appears increasingly to be viewed as exclusively culturally determined rather than as a developmental phenomenon)? How many mothers are educated to an awareness that experiences of loss may be cumulative; that intense fears regarding toilet training, or the awareness of anatomical differences may be more than signs of age-appropriate concern, calling for sensitivity on the mother's part, or perhaps some professional help. How many pediatricians, general practioners, public health nurses or other well-baby personnel have such developmental knowledge? In an historical period when speed is so highly valued, greater stress often seems placed upon how quickly the child achieves a developmental milestone, rather than on any other factor. Witness the book "One Day Toilet Training Method." (Azrin, 1974)

Separation-individuation theory also expands our understanding of what may constitute stress and trauma for the young child. Many social, legal and health care practices have already taken into account the findings of other investigators of child development in regard to stress and trauma. The encouragement of early adoption placements, the timing of elective surgery in accord with the child's developmental level so as to avoid such procedures when castration anxiety is at its height, the involvement of parents in any necessary hospitalization of their young children to minimize the negative effects of separation, as well as the establishment of separation and divorce procedures that seek to take into account the "best interests of the child" (Freud et al. 1973) are cases in point. Mahler's studies draw attention to further ramifications of certain of these events, focusing on other aspects that may be potentially stressful, and, in our opinion, affirming the significance of existing preventative efforts. Her findings, for example, are in accord with the medical practices already noted, and also remind us that painful medical proceedures, where they may be safely postponed, might also best be timed so as to avoid a too-abrupt deflation of self or parental omnipotence—that is, to a time when the child reaches a level of on-the-way to object constancy. Another potentially stressful situation that may be added to those already considered is the birth of a sibling before a degree of object constancy is achieved (1975.86,191,192). Given the challenge that confronts a parent in partnering one healthy child through the first three years of life, particularly in modern society, it is not surprising that the close spacing of children's births may prove stressful for both child and parent. Certain studies have shown that regardless of class, sociocultural or ethnic background, the most intelligent children come form the smallest families, or from families in which the longest time interval exists between births (Wilson, 1978). Evidence in a study conducted by Holley and Churchill (Smart, M. Smart, R., 1972) indicates that infants born within one year of a previous gestation, when compared to those born two to five years after the previous gestation—matched for sex, race, hospital of birth, and socioeconomic status—tended to be significantly smaller in birthweight, evidenced lower scores on the Bayley tests at 8 moths, and lower Standford Binet scores at 4 years. When evaluated at one year, the average baby born 12 moths after a sibling had a smaller head and delayed motor development. While this study suggests an effect on neurophysiological development, we may also wish to further examine the psychological effects on mother and child, from the standpont of the separation-individuation progression. Bearing in mind the child's activity and demands during certain subphases, one can see that it takes an unusual mother and favorable circumstances to be able to meet the toddler's requirements in the face of the conditions attendant upon pregnancy. We are, of course, well aware that there are great numbers of intelligent, successful and renowned individuals who have grown up in large, closely-spaced groups of siblings. However, we regard this phenomenon as meriting more consideration than it has heretofore received.

The reaffirmation of the critical role of trauma and exceptional stress upon the outcome of the separation-individuation sequence lends support to the potential value of a wide variety of crisis intervention services that have already been initiated. The development of new programs should be encouraged. David Gil, for example, recommends as part of a nationwide effort to prevent child abuse, the establishment of neighborhood support centers for families undergoing crises such as bereavement, a husband entering military service or accidents of all kinds (Gil, 1970). Such centers would provide a wide range of services including direct care of children and parents when necessary. It is unfortunate that to our knowledge this recommendation has not been implemented to any significant degree. At times such as those mentioned, temporary but prompt assistance can be vital in preventing the entrenchment of problems.

Finally, we should like to point out the pressing need for acknowledgement of the contribution to society of mothers who choose to care full-time for their children during the early years. It is time, in our view, that they are accorded the recognition they merit and are provided with some form of financial security for their future. This would assure them that ultimately care of their children will not turn out to have been a sacrifice that will at a later date, leave them disadvantaged and sometimes impoverished, should their husbands cease their financial support, or the labor market turn them away for their lack of employment experience. Where parents, on the other hand, need or elect to place their children in the care of homemakers, day-care centers, or other substitute personnel, these caretakers should also be accorded the status and remuneration that such an important responsibility warrants.

An understanding of the role of the primary child care provider should help to elevate child care to its proper position in society.

The neglect of our children is not only tragic for those who are directly effected, but in the final analysis we squander our most precious resource and ultimately endanger society itself when we fail to provide optimum care for our children. Speaking of the effect on society of our failure to provide children with the necessary human partnering for their development, Spitz has said,

> "Without a template, the victims of disturbed object relations subsequently will themselves lack the capacity to relate. They are not equipped for the more advanced, more complex forms of personal and social interchange without which we as a species would be unable to survive. They cannot adapt to society. . . . The only path which remains open to them is the destruction of a social order of which they are the victims (Spitz, 1965, 300).

Spitz himself called for the creation of a preventative social psychiatry, in the interest of safeguarding our existing civilization. (301) He was well aware, however, that such a task went beyond the competence of any one profession, but rather constituted a task for society at large. What he affirmed was the helping professional's responsibility to share his or her findings, and to urge their application. It is with this goal in mind that we have sought here, to highlight some of the preventative implications of Mahler's efforts as we have seen them.

CHAPTER 5

Borderline Phenomena in Terms of
Separation-Individuation

While Mahler's observational studies have not led to direct correlations between the vicissitudes of separation-individuation and specific pathological constellations, her work suggests certain developmental occurrences, that may lead to borderline and/or narcissistic organization or that may foster deviant neurotic organization. We have found her contributions to the understanding of borderline development particularly valuable in our clinical efforts. Whether there is actually an increase in the number of borderline clients today is difficult to ascertain. However, we, like many other clinicians, note an increase in our practice of clients whose development appears to be at the borderline level of organization. Broadly speaking, when we refer to borderline individuals, we have in mind those clients whose ego functions are impaired to varying degrees; whose affects, instead of serving as signals, tend to overwhelm them; whose inabilities to tolerate delay or maintain impulse control interfere with adaptation; or whose levels of object relatedness lead frequently to disturbances in interpersonal relations as well as to limitations in their abilities to form a working alliance. They are sometimes the clients whose chronic unemployability and poverty can be understood as more directly related to their severe psychopathology rather than to socioeconomic conditions. Sometimes they are the clients who abuse their children or their spouses, are addicted to alcohol or drugs, or manifest some other form of antisocial behavior. In other instances, they are the clients who do not exhibit obvious adjustment difficulties but seek our clinical services in relation to their profound inner distress. Indeed, in the case of some borderline clients, features that appear neurotic may predominate. This tends to confuse the diagnostic

73

picture, unless we bear in mind Knight's (1954) recognition that neu-roticlike defenses may represent "holding operations" for individuals with borderline structure.

Mahler (1972) has pointed out the similarity between those features commonly associated with borderline pathology and phenomena associated with deviant negotiation of separation–individuation. These include failures in internalization, increased separation anxiety, the failure to bring together "good" and "bad" aspects of both the self- and the object representations, the inundation of ego filtered affects with unneutralized aggression, the alternation of delusions of omnipotence with those of dependency and self-depreciation, and the suffusion of the body image with unneutralized libido and aggression.

In this chapter we shall consider some of these and other well-recognized features of borderline organization, particularly those features identified by Otto Kernberg and Heinz Kohut, from the perspective of separation–individuation. A highly abbreviated summary of Kernberg and Kohut's views will serve as an introduction. Such a summary, does not do justice to the extensive contributions of these major theorists and for a full elaboration, the original texts are recommended.

SUMMARY OF KERNBERG'S CONTRIBUTION

The behavioral indicators that Kernberg considers as suggesting an underlying borderline personality disorder are chronic, diffuse, free-floating anxiety; multiple neurotic symptoms; polymorphous perverse trends; personality structures of either the schizoid, paranoid, or hypomanic type; impulse neuroses and addictions; character pathology such as is seen in infantile personality; and "as if" personalities, antisocial personality structures, and narcissistic personalities. No single indicator is pathognomonic, but the presence of two, especially three, strongly point to borderline organization. These indicators are descriptive, and Kernberg notes that the definitive diagnosis depends on characteristic ego pathology and not on the descriptive symptoms (1975).

In his consideration of the dynamics of the borderline syndrome, Kernberg has focused on the central role of the excessively strong aggressive drive that is defended against by splitting, early forms of projection, projective identification and denial, primitive idealization, devaluation, or omnipotence. These defenses, in turn, distort reality, and the defense of splitting, in particular, is seen as precluding the formation of unified self- and object representations in which good and bad aspects of self or object are brought together. While differentiation of self from object images is thought to have occurred to a sufficient degree to prevent psychosis, ego boundaries of the borderline may give way under the sway of projective identification or fusion with idealized objects. According to Kernberg, this dedifferentiation between self and object, as a result of the defensive efforts employed, may be the reason that such patients at times develop a transference psychosis instead of a transference neurosis. The difficulties in object relatedness associated with borderline pathology derive from an incapacity for realistic evaluation of others and for realistic empathy. According to Kernberg, the borderline personality develops a "protective shallowness" due to the lack of fusion of the libidinal and aggressive drives, and as the result of an incapacity to experience guilt, concern, and a deeper awareness of and interest in others. This shallowness protects against involvement with others that might, in turn, stimulate primitive defenses, especially projective identification or the arousal of fear of attack by another. Emotional shallowness further protects the borderline from a tendency towards primitive idealization of the object that then may induce a fear of submission or merger with the now idealized object. This shallowness guards against the potential rage over the frustration of early, oral demands that might be stimulated in a relationship with an object whom the borderline is likely to idealize. A failure in superego formation, and a lack of ego-integration and maturation of aims, feelings, and interests, prevent the borderline from developing awareness of the more mature and differentiated aspects of other people's personalities. Kernberg points, in addition, to a specific condensation of pregenital and genital aims and a premature development of oedipal conflicts, beginning at age 2 or 3 (1975). As a result, exploitiveness, demandingness, and manipulation of others are prominent. Identity diffusion is a typical characteristic associated with the lack of an integrated self-concept and an integrated stable concept of whole objects in relation to the self. Ego weakness is manifest in a lack of impulse control, lack of anxiety tolerance, and a lack of sublimatory capacity.

Kernberg appears to consider the main etiological factors to be the excessive nature of primary aggression, or aggression secondary to frustration, as well as certain deficiencies in the development of the primary ego apparatuses, and in a lack of anxiety tolerance.

Thus, the role of inborn factors seems primary. Robbins (1976), however, reporting on an unpublished manuscript of Kernberg's, notes that his work on ego formation has been changing, and that his views appear to be more consistent with those of Jacobson (1964) and Mahler (1968), who view drive development as influenced by the proportion, in early life, of "good, pleasurable" experiences and "bad, frustrating" experiences. Robbins quotes Kernberg (1974) as postulating a "primary grouping of pleasurable and unpleasurable constellations of affective experiences and a secondary development of drives as polarizations towards or away from these constellations" (Robbins, 1976, p. 842). Robbins concludes that Kernberg is making a shift in his concept of the origin of the drives towards the developmental point of view, in contrast to his earlier theory of preformation of the drives.

SUMMARY OF HEINZ KOHUT'S CONTRIBUTIONS

In the "Analysis of the Self" Kohut (1971) distinguished the borderline states from the narcissitic disorders by the failure in the borderline to have achieved a cohesive self, or a sense of the cohesiveness of the object. Thus, the borderline personality remains seriously threatened by disintegration, and his or her entire structure is viewed as being at a less developed level. Kohut has considered borderline pathology as related to a primary disturbance of the self that, along with the psychoses, is the result of serious and protracted damage to the self (Kohut and Wolfe, 1978). Closeness is threatening to whatever feeble sense of self exists, and borderline personalities defend sometimes by withdrawal behind schizoid defenses, and in other cases by hostility or suspicion. This, incidentally, may suggest that the frequently noted aggression in borderlines may, at times, serve defensive purposes. Kohut has proposed that sometimes the distinction between the borderline client and the narcissistic client can be made most accurately only on the basis of therapeutic experience. In treatment, as a result of the primitive fear of engulfment related to insufficient self-object differentiation, the borderline individual is unable to devlop either the mirror transference or the idealizing transference characteristic of the narcissistic patient. Kohut ascribes the central defect in the formation of a cohesive sense of self in the case of borderline individuals to parental intrusion during the early stage of self-object relations. He proposes that "at the very point when the nascent self of the child required the accepting, mirroring of its independence, the selfobject, because of its own incompleteness and fragmentation fears, insisted on maintaining an archaic merger" (Kohut and Wolfe, 1978, p. 415).

Meissner (1978, p. 564) has summarized the defects characteristic of borderline organization, as identified by Kernberg, Kohut and others, noting that the areas of deficit are accorded different emphasis by various theoreticians. Meissner includes developmental defects, instinctual defects, defensive impairments, deficits in other areas of ego function and integration, narcissistic defects, impairments in object relations, forms of identity diffusions, and the organization and pathology of the "as if" personality." We now proceed to examine these organizational defects from the vantage point of separation and individuation.

DEVELOPMENTAL DEFECTS

Mahler (1971) considers that the failure to negotiate the rapprochement crisis constitutes a significant pathogenic condition leading to borderline organization. Failures at this subphase may reflect earlier deficits so profound that they cannot be compensated for, even under particularly favorable conditions. Instead of the rapprochement experiences providing an opportunity for the leveling of discrepancies, earlier lesions may be exacerbated and the rapprochement crisis itself intensified. A continued striving at this subphase for missed symbiotic supplies exaggerates the need for closeness, leading to increased coerciveness and to a heightened fear of engulfment. Some children may continue to cling and demand closeness, in which case separation is compromised. Others may defend against the wish for closeness by withdrawl from the object, in which case there is a loss of the vitally needed partnering. In some instances, ambitendency is heightened to the point at which the child appears to be anxiously "coming and going" at the same time. Failures at differentiation may extend into this subphase in the form of greater-than-average separation anxiety and fear of object loss, and failures at practicing may leave their mark in the form of insufficient narcissism and too meagre a degree of individuation to cushion the deflation of omnipotence at rapprochement.

New problems may also arise during this subphase as a result of unusual traumatic experiences in the life of the child or the family, or due to certain stresses inherent in the subphase itself. Particularly ominous is the withdrawl of the mother's libidinal availability at this point, due either to some exigency of life, or as a response to the child's growing separateness and assertiveness. Masterson (1976) has focused extensively on the connection between borderline pathology and the withdrawl of libidinal supplies at rapprochement by symbiotically attached mothers. This withdrawl, according to Masterson, is experienced as an abandonment threat, preventing the child from moving ahead.

Another developmental danger in this subphase is excessive aggression. This may be the result either of the mother's retaliatory aggression towards the child, or of her failure to help modulate the phase-specific spurt of aggression in the child. Where such aggression predominates, it may lead to overreliance on the splitting mechanism that ultimately interferes with the unification of the "good" and "bad" object representations. The child may also take the mother in as a bad introject, leaving the child with unassimilable representations of mother as a criticizing, disapproving, or otherwise negative presence in the mind. This precludes the establishment of those positively based, selective identifications upon which subsequent ego and superego formation depend.

INSTINCTUAL DEFECTS

Aggression and Rage

While the role of aggression has been regarded as primary in borderline pathology, it has not yet been established whether the excessive degree of aggression is due to the inherent strength of the aggressive drive (Kernberg, 1975), to an ego limited in its capacity to deal with the drives (Knight, 1954), or to an impairment in drive development itself, resulting from early deficiences in the mother-child interaction (Loewald, 1972). Mahler, as we have noted before, has proposed that the drives differentiate out early in accord with frustrating or gratifying experiences. Excessive aggression, therefore, may suggest a predominance of bad, frustrating, unpleasurable experiences early in life. Such an excess of aggression early in development threatens vital connections with the object since it leads to expelling maneuvers. Mahler has noted that an excessive need to expel "bad" may lead to exhaustion or apathy in the infant. Under very severe circumstances, regression to the autistic phase may occur, drowning out budding self-awareness as well as the apperception of the "good" part-image of mother, thereby leading to psychosis (Mahler, 1955). Later, in development, such an excess of aggression tends to foster excessive use of the splitting mechanisms, a phenomenon that Mahler has specifically associated with borderline development.

As far as we have been able to ascertain, Mahler's writings have not reflected the current reconsideration of drive theory (Gertrude and Rubin Blanck, 1979; Parens, 1979; and Loewald, 1972). However, in a talk given in the spring of 1979 at The Mahler Symposium in Philadelphia, we understood her to have suggested that the innate force toward individuation might be regarded as an aspect of the early aggressive drive, derived from the innate life force itself. This in some ways accords with the view of G. and R. Blanck (1979) that the aggressive drive is an integral force in separation-individuation. They go on to suggest that, in accord with Freud's (1937) later theories on the drives, the aggressive drive be considered the drive that undoes connections, and libido be regarded as the drive that establishes greater unities, bringing things together. The two drives, working in concert, then foster the progression towards object constancy and serve to maintain separation and individuation. The Blancks (1979) have additionally sought to distinguish between aggression as a drive, and anger, rage, or hostility that, though frequently equated with aggression, are actually affects.

Kohut appears to have something similar in mind when he refers to aggressiveness as "not the raging-destructive baby," but as "the assertive baby, whose aggressions are a constituent of the firmness and security with which he makes his/her demands vis-á-vis self-objects who provide for him a milieu of (average) empathic responsiveness" (Kohut, 1977, p. 118). Destructive aggression, according to Kohut, refers to a "disintegration" product, the result of chronic and traumatic frustration in childhood of the "phase appropriate need for omnipotent control over the self-object" (Kohut, 1977, p. 121).

If one makes the distinction between affect and drive, it would seem that borderline pathology is actually characterized by excessive rage reactions that may employ aggressive drive energies for purposes of discharge. As we have seen in Mahler's investigations, affect development appears to be directly related to object-related experiences as well as to self experiences. The repertoire of affects expands at each subphase with transformations of overwhelming affects into more manageable feelings and the addition of new affects. We have in mind the toning down of "organismic distress" into milder forms of separation anxiety, and the coming into being, at practicing, of the new affect of elation.

In the borderline condition, affect development may be restricted by a failure to integrate good and bad features of self and object. One experiences a range of negative or positive feelings in response to a range of perceptions of experiences with an object or the self. Mrs. Norton, a client, reporting on the improvement of her relationship with her husband, noted that it had made a difference in the feelings she had about him to begin to perceive him as a person with both good and bad features. She recalled that, at one time, her husband's nose picking had enraged her to a point where she either wished he would "drop dead" or she could leave him. She had experienced his habit as a direct affront to herself. When she could weigh this behavior against the now recognized loving things he did, she had come to experience it as annoying rather than enraging. Indeed, she pointed out that sometimes even when she was annoyed she felt some sympathy for him. She had come to recognize the tension and discomfort that underlay his behavior.

Finally, we draw attention to the way in which some borderline individuals utilize their anger defensively. At times, it appears to be used to ward off closeness, or to promote a feeling of strength and power. Mrs. Norton, for example, had indicated, early in her treatment, her awareness that she needed her angry feelings. When she experienced more tender feelings, she felt vulnerable and helpless. When angry she felt in control, on guard, and unlikely to be hurt.

Failure to Achieve Psychosexual Phase Dominance

Another borderline deficit in the instinctual realm is the failure to achieve phase dominance. Kernberg (1975) has referred to the polymorophous perverse characteristics of borderlines. Instead of an orderly progression along the psychosexual sequence, there is frequently a premature development of oedipal strivings. In his view, the excessive development of early, particularly oral aggression, precipitates a defensive advance toward the oedipus in an effort to ward off the rage and fear attendant to the powerful oral dependent strivings. This interferes with a more or less orderly progression along the psychosexual sequence and several sexual trends tend to coexist.

Our experience confirms Kernberg's view that premature advances along the psychosexual maturational sequence may be re-

lated to defensive efforts. Moreover, we have noted that some borderline individuals appear to have employed their sexuality as a
means of compensating for insufficient maternal partnering with the
result that there has been a failure to achieve phase dominance. This
accords with Mahler's finding that in the absence of adequate
symbiotic partnering, certain children thus deprived use the autoerotic resources of their own bodies, or the frankly erotic offerings
of seductive adults, as substitutes for missed symbiotic supplies. A
case in point is Mrs. Smith, a borderline woman who had experienced severe deprivation at the symbiotic phase and at subsequent
subphases of separation–individuation. Whatever closeness she had
obtained from her depressed, overwhelmed, teenaged, unmarried
mother seemed overstimulating, and related to the mother's own
strong needs for physical contact. At the start of treatment this depressed, alcoholic, suicidal woman described how she had, since
childhood, rocked herself to sleep at night. Somewhat later, she
shared the fact that she also comforted herself by masturbating with
a bottle when she could not "quiet her blood" in any other way. She
had begun this when she was 10, at a time when mother had given
her considerable responsibility for the care of her 6-month-old
brother. On one occasion when she had been unable to quiet him,
her frustration and rage mounted to such a point that she experienced an impulse to drown him in his bath. At that point, she took
his bottle and began masturbating. It served to both comfort and
quiet her anger, and had been placed in the service of both self-
soothing and sexual need ever since. This masturbation with the
bottle may be regarded as a condensation of both oral and phallic
aims in a patient who also exhibited profound penis envy. When an
elderly neighbor died, she was shocked to discover herself wishing
that the neighbor had bequeathed her his penis since he no longer
needed it. We came to see, among other things, that the penis was
valued as a breast equivalent and men were envied for their fantasied ability to nourish themselves. While these efforts probably protected Mrs. Smith from psychosis, over time they seriously distorted
the psychosexual organization, and contributed to a deep sense of
shame and lowered self-esteem. The instinctual drives remained at a
primitive level and did not come under the influence of the reality
principle.

The premature development of oedipal strivings can, in some situations, be traced back to sexualized experiences at symbiosis. Mahler (1977) has described the "child-lover-at-the-breast" symbiosis in
which the early mother-child relationships take on seductive tones

(p. 76). A similar frankly erotic relationship may also be established with the father. Such experiences crowd out the phase-specific partnering later associated with the normal practicing and rapprochement subphases and the parent-child relationships may continue to be bizarrely oedipal-like.

Oedipal Negotiation

Mahler (1977) has noted that an important feature in borderline personalities is their failure to proceed in the ordinary way through the developmental experiences that eventuate in a well-defined oedipus complex, and the normal infantile neurosis. Failure to achieve phase dominance along the psychosexual progression, the prolongation of preoedipal object needs, and failures in the achievement of triangulation at rapprochement are among the factors that may interfere with normal oedipal negotiation.

Deprived of this important organizing experience (Rangell, 1972), psychic structure, object relations, and the consolidation of the sense of self are impeded. As we know, the movement towards genital primacy, associated with the oedipus, helps foster a coordination of the general urge towards pleasure that is then directed at a whole, unified object, promoting further consolidation of both the self and object representations. This marks an important shift from part objects to whole objects (Freud, 1905). From the object relations side, the oedipus heralds a new level of loving. The child now moves into a more active position with a greater focus on securing love by way of his or her own efforts. In terms of psychic structure, it is the oedipal negotiation that leads to the formation of that special structure for self-regulation and for the maintenance of self-esteem, the superego. External regulation becomes transformed into internal control. Earlier dependence upon the love of the object gives way to a capacity to provide for oneself some measure of the love and approval once afforded by the object.

PROBLEMS IN DEFENSE DEVELOPMENT

We shall elaborate first on Kernberg's notion of splitting as a primary defense in borderline pathology. Kernberg (1975) uses splitting to describe the active process of keeping apart introjections and identifications of opposing quality in order to defend against anxiety related to instinctual impulses. Splitting itself, in his view, is a fundamental cause of ego weakness and, at the same time since splitting requires less countercathexes than repression, a weak ego falls back on splitting, and a vicious circle is created by which each reinforces the other. Splitting, then, is viewed as a defense utilized by an ego that is actually capable of synthesizing and integrating the good and bad self and object representations. This is in contrast to a developmental view that in some cases would regard the same phenomenon of keeping apart good and bad self and object representations as the outcome of a failure to have achieved the capacity for fusion.

Mahler (1975) notes that early in development the young infant reduces the amount of painful stimuli by expulsion. According to her, the early tension-reducing efforts such as vomiting and spitting in the physical sphere serve as a primitive base for the later splitting mechanism. However, at a time when the infant is incapable of integrating the representations into a whole, this state of affairs actually favors growth. Time is allowed then for building up an uncontaminated good object representation of mother so that when the child is forced by its now developed cognitive capacities to recognize that mother is both "good" and "bad," sufficient libidinal investment should have been acquired to make the bad tolerable. This, of course, requires experiences that tend to be more on the positive side. If, in actuality, the infant experiences a predominance of frustrating bad experiences, then an inordinate amount of aggression may be induced, impairing the capacity for fusion.

Splitting is later employed defensively at rapprochement after some capacity for fusion has been achieved. At a time when the child is drawn back to mother in an attempt to regain the symbiotic merger, the child may defend against that impulse by provoking a quarrel or in some way turning the mother into a "bad" object from whom the child may withdraw. It may also turn the mother defensively into a "good" object, for other purposes.

In cases where the rapprochement crisis is overly intense the child may utilize splitting excessively as a defense. Such a reliance on splitting, as an attempted solution to a severe rapprochement crisis, may then remain as a fixation, leading to borderline orgainzation (Mahler, 1975, p. 229).

Clinically, we encounter clients who have either failed to achieve sufficient capacity for integration of the good and bad object or, having achieved this capability, who continue to rely heavily on splitting as a defense against instinctual demands. Indeed it is possible for the same patient at some times to manifest a failure in integrative capacity and at other times to employ splitting defensively (Stolorow and Lachmann, 1978). Where the failure is in the integrative function, we must address our therapeutic efforts towards the building of unified self and object representations. Where splitting is employed defensively, then interpretation remains the technique of choice. An example of a client who manifested initially a failure in the integrative capacity and later appeared to employ splitting as a defense was Mr. Fine.

Mr. Fine originally seemed to have failed to integrate "good" and "bad" aspects of others, and would act as if he were relating to two different wives or two different daughters. Early efforts in treatment were aimed at reminding him that the person he was enraged at currently, was the same person he had felt tender toward during the preceding session, yet he acted as if she were two distinct persons. At a much later point in treatment, his keeping apart good and bad object representations took on the quality of defensive efforts. In the session following one in which he had praised the therapist for the first time in the three years of their work, thereby acknowledging that something valuable was occurring in the treatment, he came in angry that there were no drinking cups in the bathroom. He regarded the therapist as totally insensitive to the needs of the clients. While other factors were likely to have been involved, this became understood, at that time, as a defense against libidinal wishes that had been stirred up by his acknowledgment of something positive in the therapist. The turning of the therapist into a "bad" object served as a defense against those urges which threatened to lead to feared closeness.

Another defense that is prominent in borderline pathology is projective identification. According to Kernberg, the borderline's efforts to simply project aggressive feelings on to another are unsuccessful. Weak ego boundaries yield under the impact of projected aggression. The borderline person identifies with the individual they have projected the aggression on to, and their continued "empathy" with the now threatening person augments the fear of their own projected aggression. Not only does this defense fail to protect against aggressive urges and thereby reduce anxiety, but the aggressive urges are maintained and increased. This leads to efforts on the part of the borderlines to control the other person in order to prevent him or her from attacking under the influence of a projected aggressive impulse. The borderline feels compelled to attack and control the object before, as they fear, they are attacked and destroyed. According to Kernberg (1975), projective identification is characterized by a lack of differentiation between self and object in a particular area, with the result that the person continues to experience the impulse, as well as the fear of the impulse, while the projection is active, and is therefore led to control the external object.

We would suggest that this phenomenon described by Kernberg may also be viewed as at times representing a developmental arrest and at other times a defensive maneuver. As a failure in development, it represents a manifestation of insufficient self object differentiation. We are reminded that self-object differentiation is not firmed up until object- and self-constancy are well on their way. During the rapprochement subphase, self-object confusion is a likely occurrence, particularly under the impact of strong emotions. It remains a challenging task to determine in any given situation when that which appears to be projective identification represents a blurring of boundaries in a patient who has not yet achieved sufficient self-object differentiation, where regression has taken place at the moment, or when it represents a defense against pressing libidinal or aggressive impulses. The importance of making such a distinction is that where a developmental failure exists an interpretation of defense is unlikely to be effective. On the other hand the presumption that the patient cannot distinguish sufficiently between self and object, when a strong impulse is being defended against, carries patient and clinician off the therapeutic track.

What has been said about splitting and projective identification can also be said of idealization and devaluation. Both of these defenses have their roots in early developmental sequences and are phase-specific until such time as the omnipotent self and object images are transformed into more reality based representations. To the extent that this transformation fails to take place, the object and self-representations retain their primitive qualities.

OTHER EGO DEFECTS

If one considers borderline organization as representative of development that has not proceeded beyond the rapprochement crisis, then it follows that those ego functions that develop in consequence of such achievement will fail to do so. As Blanck and Blanck (1979) have pointed out, internalization and ego organization normally reach relatively stable points with the negotiation of the rapprochement crisis. According to them, this negotiation serves as a "fulcrum" that turns development in a forward direction leading to the achievement of a variety of ego capacities including those that Kernberg has designated as lacking in the borderline, that is, secondary process thinking, anxiety tolerance, and greater impulse control.

Narcissistic Defects

Feelings of emptiness or worthlessness, existing side by side or alternating with feelings of grandiosity and entitlement, are among the narcissistic defects associated with borderline organization (Meissner, 1978). Some borderline individuals regard themselves as persons with special rights, any frustration of which tends to disrupt the sense of self-esteem and the sense of self. Accompanying these often contradictory self and object views is an unusual proclivity to narcissistic injury.

Borderline individuals with narcissistic features are distinguished by Mahler from the so-called narcissistic personalities by the presence of ego defects, particularly in the area of defense development, the relative absence of signal anxiety, inadequate delineation of body-ego boundaries, and insufficient self-object differentiation (Mahler and Kaplan, 1977). These are features not ordinarily present in the more advanced narcisstic organization.

From the standpoint of separation–individuation, narcissistic defects can be understood as consistent with development that has not proceeded beyond rapprochement. While the formation of sound secondary narcissism depends upon adequate experiences at each of the developmental phases, it requires the unification of the good and bad self representations into unified self and object representations and the modulation of omnipotence at rapprochement for further consolidation. In the absence of these achievements, as well as a failure to have achieved a sufficient degree of individuation, the sense of self remains fragile.

In our own clinical work, we have seen particularly struck with the narcissistic problems among those borderline patients who were involved in parasitic mother-child relationships. These patients appear to have been influenced, on one hand, by their mother's seeming overevaluation of them and, on the other, by her actual disregard of their own unique needs. Somehow perceiving themselves as needed extensions of their mothers yet deprived of the normal degree of omnipotence that derives from a satisfying symbiosis, these patients exhibit alternating feelings of grandiosity and worthlessness, or they may experience these feelings almost side by side. One such patient whose mother treated her as if she were indeed a part of herself and waited on her hand and foot, commented that sometimes she felt like a princess, but at other times she wondered if her mother knew of some weakness in her that caused mother to go to such excess in her care. This patient had an extensive reper- toire of grandiose fantasies that she employed to shore up her failing sense of self-esteem, or to gratify herself when she was frustrated. One fantasy that she relied upon heavily was that she was a success- ful opera singer who traveled with a retinue of servants, all of whom immediately carried out her bidding. One could see, at cer- tain points, how various servants performed functions that mother once actually did, well beyond the appropriate time in this patient's life. Her mother, for example, had done all her errands until the pa- tient was married at age 24, drove her back and forth from kinder- garten through college, though public transportation was con- veniently available, and fed her by hand when mother judged her as too fatigued to raise her hand to her mouth.

Defects in Object Relations

The failure to achieve a position of on-the-way to object con- stancy implies that the object remains valued primarily when it grat- ifies. However, this does not seem to accurately reflect the object re- lations capacities of a number of borderline patients who, though borderline in most other respects, seem to exhibit a higher level of object relatedness. We note in many of our patients a capacity for empathy and the ability to relate mutually to certain people. We are reminded that the rapprochement child has begun to value the love of the object, and to recognize that mother has needs of her own, and that her attention must be sought. This achievement, however, is not firmed up until the achievement of object constancy and then, of course, it is only on-its-way. Thus, there is likely to be a range in the capacities for object relatedness and a fluctuating quality, perhaps influenced both by external and internal factors.

The overreliance on splitting, the oscillation between the fear of separateness and the fear of merger, the propensity for a blurring of the self-object distinctions, and, in some cases, the pathological in- ternalized relationships with bad introjected objects are among the factors that impede the development of more mature levels of object relatedness.

Identity Diffusion

With the failure to achieve psychological birth, a firm identity is not established. The individual remains dependent upon others to provide the continuity of identity, satisfaction of this need threatens engulfment at times (Meissner, 1978). The borderline faces a dilemma. Too much separation is overwhelming when there is no adequate sense of self to sustain it. Yet relationship with an object threatens merger. This leads to a search for a position of "optimal distance" from their objects that is rarely achieved. When out of touch with these objects who help stabilize identity, they are lost, yet if they get too close they are also lost.

The False Self or "As If" Personality

We have already pointed to the establishment of a "false self" as a feature of some borderline organizations. This represents an effort to build a sense of self by borrowing personality attributes from others. It has its inception at differentiation, and is frequently associated with a parasitic symbiosis. Mrs. Carter, whose problems will be elaborted upon in Case Study 1, affords an example of this arrangement. When she entered treatment, she described herself as an actress who carefully copied desired behavior and characteristics of others. She was the actress, the audience, and the critic, and her life was a series of studied, planned, and evaluated situations. She was filled with terror that there might not be anyone real behind the guises she assumed.

SUMMARY

In summary, borderline organization can be viewed in terms of separation-individuation theory as one of the possible outcomes of failure to resolve the rapprochement crisis adequately. Some of the symptoms reflect fixations at earlier phases, and others are more clearly derived from failures at the rapprochement subphase itself. However, borderline organization is not simply a repetition of earlier struggles as they originally took place. Development continues despite earlier affronts but these early lesions have a significant ongoing effect on the organizing processes (Blanck and Blanck, 1979).

Under the impact of the innate force towards individuation, each individual makes certain unique adaptive attempts at compensating for that which has been missed. Such efforts may not only distort development, but also block future developments. This accords with Spitz's (1959) view that when a normal integration between development and maturation is disturbed, there is, nevertheless, a tendency towards compensation that leads to some form of integration, deviant as it may be. In other words, when the developmental partner fails to provide requisite nutrients at the critical time, or when innate factors prevent the child from taking full advantage of what may be available, the child will make use of other means to meet prominent phase-specific needs. An integration will take place that differs from the norm, and even if the requisite partnership is forthcoming later on, it will not be possible for the child to take advantage of it because the compensating though deviant structures will remain operative. Thus, the patient who continued to masturbate with the bottle to comfort herself, utilizing the autoerotic resources of her own body as a compensation, may well have been saved from more severe pathology by her own efforts, but she paid a developmental price. Therapeutic intervention must, in such cases, be addressed to the reduction of these compensatory adaptations as well as to the promotion of those development processes that have been blocked.

Part

Two

CLINICAL
APPLICATIONS

CHAPTER 6

Transitional Life Tasks and Clinical Intervention

The achievement of self and object constancy while on-its-way following the first round of separation–individuation is probably a life-long endeavor. As in the case of the resolution of the oedipus complex (Ticho, 1978), the consolidation of object constancy remains an open-ended task. New phases of the life cycle see new derivatives of earlier processes at work and new levels of achievement may take place at different ages and biological stages, as well as in relation to new life tasks or in response to the inevitable crises of human existence. Adolescence, young adulthood, the middle years, and other stages offer both new opportunities for consolidation and advance, as well as imposing new demands that may overtax existing capacities and structures. The way in which the first round of separation–individuation was experienced and the level of those achievements set the stage for future development. Up to a point, old conflicts may be reworked and previous gains consolidated, but certain failures or vulnerabilities derived from earlier experiences may render past achievements tenuous and subject to depletion or regression. Where earlier accomplishments were minimal, the sense of self and object constancy may be easily compromised. The average expectable stresses attendant to new life phases that when favorably negotiated lead to further developmental advances may, in such situations, be experienced as traumatic and overwhelm the individual's limited resources.

Even under favorable circumstances, transition points, whether related to biological changes or new external requirements, involve stress. This confronts the individual with complex challenges and revives aspects of earlier conflicts. Separation–individuation anxiety and anxieties attendant to the oedipal negotiation are inevitably stirred up at those nodal points that recapitulate earlier struggles. Marriage and parenthood, for example, require a new degree of separateness from one's original family and, at the same time, revive unconscious conflicts from all phases of psychosexual maturation.

Transitions along the life-cycle, require changes in status, in role, in ego functioning, and, sometimes, even in bodily appearance, all having potential consequence for the sense of self and the nature of one's object relations. The nursery child moves ordinarily from being one of a few in a family to one of many, requiring a shift both in self-perception and in object relatedness. The school-going child who until this time has eaten and gone to the bathroom more or less on an attuned time schedule must extend his or her capacity for delay to meet the routines and requirements of an institution. From the family whose demands can, to a degree, take cognizance of the inevitable shifts in mood, energies, or health of the adolescent, the working teenager or young adult must begin to accomodate to the impersonal scrutiny of a more exacting and demanding employer who ordinarily expects attendance, punctuality, and job performance regardless of minor aches or pains. From being the child of her parents, the new mother must very quickly become the nurturer and protector, postponing her own needs for gratification in favor of the more compelling needs of her infant.

Frequently, changes in physical environment, separation from familiar persons, places, and things, even new styles of dress and grooming impinging on the bodily self, attend transitions. New challenges may occur propitiously when developmental achievements have paved the way for handling the task at hand and at times of relative intrapsychic quiescence during which energies may be more easily mobilized. However, they may also converge with unusual maturational and developmental pressures. We think of the adolescent who must move to a new community and school, far removed from old friends and familiar activities. In most cases, traumatic crises may further burden transitional experiences, as in the case when leaving home to attend college coincides with parental divorce, or where the young parent is confronted with the loss of his or her own parents during the first months of parenthood.

Where self and object constancy have been as firmly established as possible during the first three years, an individual will have greater independence from the environment and wider latitude so that they may more easily undertake the normal transitional tasks of life and possess greater strength to deal with those unusual stresses that are universal. Indeed, mastery of the "average expectable" transitional tasks ordinarily affords an expanded feeling of self, and deepens and strengthens existing capacities, as well as promoting new ones. However, it is likely that a degree of vulnerability and a need for reaffirmation from the new love objects will continue through life (Settlage, 1977).

Whether or not physiological changes and the new life tasks that come in their wake will strengthen or deplete the individual's resources depends upon the level of their development and maturation at the time, the nature of the tasks confronted, and the synchronicity among maturation, development, and the challenge in question. To the degree that various tasks revive former conflicts, the nature of the reworking of these conflicts and their mastery will depend upon the ego strength and self-integration already achieved, as well as the environmental circumstances that exist at the time. For example, the child who has failed to fully achieve the degree of self and object constancy ordinarily necessary for school attendance may have a favorable chance for further development in a school that takes such matters into account. On the other hand, if the kindergarten teacher values self-sufficiency and containment, and is troubled and unduly annoyed by the child who has difficulty at this transitional point, the school situation may serve to aggravate existing difficulties.

As therapists, we are frequently called upon to serve clients who are facing difficulties of varying degrees in dealing with stress in negotiating one or another transitional life task. We may be required to give a developmental assist at such a point to individuals who, having achieved a fair degree of structuralization, can rather easily regain their equilibrium. With help, they may utilize the experience ultimately in the service of further consolidation of self and object constancy. In some instances, intervention may be aimed at improving the environment so that, with a better match between environmental expectations and the individuals' adaptive capacities, movement forward is promoted. There are, however, situations of greater gravity that call for longer, more sustained therapeutic efforts to enable the individual to achieve a higher degree of self and object constancy so that he or she may confront phase-specific tasks more adequately, and be equipped to handle those challenges that inevitably lie ahead.

Where difficulties in negotiating life tasks can be traced to failures in the achievement of self and object constancy, therapeutic interventions are addressed to issues related to separation and individuation. This may aid not only in the restoration of equilibrium and an advance in the individual's capacities to cope with the tasks at hand, but in some cases may help promote a higher level of general development. In this chapter, case illustrations from the treatment of clients who have had difficulty negotiating four common life tasks—schooling, marriage, parenthood, and bereavement—are considered.

SCHOOL

Nursery Program

The first test of the child's self and object constancy is frequently provided by entrance into nursery school. We begin with a consideration, therefore, of the relationship between subphase inadequacies and attendance at nursery school. Because of its complexity, we leave aside the important matter of separation from mother, and substitute care before the age of 3, which is an increasingly common phenomenon today. However, it is at about age 3 that the young child acquires the capacity to sustain a whole mental representation of mother for a few hours of her absence. When nursery school placement can be arranged primarily to accord with and to meet the child's needs, this placement at about 3 conforms with our understanding of the child's developmental timetable. Self and object constancy are sufficiently stable then so that the child can comfortably move into the wider world, capable of enjoying the adventures and stimulation of the new environment. The child, at this point, can begin to transfer to the teacher the expectation of being cared for that had been previously established in the relationship with mother. He or she can carry to school the self-valuation and confidence that had been established as a result of the favorable negotiation of the first round of separation-individuation.

However, children who have attained object constancy still experience a temporary normal regression when actually confronted with physical separation from mother. In a study of nursery school children, Speers, et al. (1971), concluded that a normal recapitulation of the separation–individuation process takes place initially. Children were observed to seek closeness with their mothers (symbiosis), then to move away (practicing), and finally to move further away, wooing mother with their accomplishments (rapprochement). Ultimately, they reached a point at which they appeared to experience mother's leave-taking without anxiety. The degree of regression, the behavioral expressions, and the speed with which the separation–individuation sequences were retraced to regain a relatively anxiety-free level of object constancy were unique to each child. Actually, Speers and his associates came to consider that a failure to regress in the new and unfamiliar environment of nursery school and to repeat the separation individuation process might, in itself, suggest failures that threaten future development. Further noted in this study was the way in which certain children defended against object loss, either by playing mother excessively, or by becoming intensely involved in activities in a rather driven way. This, incidentally, may appear to the observer as a form of hyperactivity, often mistaken for organicity rather than evaluated in terms of possible separation problems.

The qualified nursery school takes into account the child's and parents' needs. It is to be expected that some degree of excitement and tension will be mingled with feelings of pleasure on the part of child and parents. It should be noted that entrance into nursery school poses developmental tasks for the mothers as well as their children. Thus, nursery schools generally provide an opportunity for both parent and child to become accustomed to staff and to the physical plant. Time is allowed for slow and sensitively handled disengagement. The normality of regression is understood and staff and parents are prepared for forward and backward movements (Freud A., 1965). At certain times, the child will require additional support from the teacher even under favorable circumstances. The teacher's soothing and attunement, at times of regression, and encouragement of the child's forward ventures at the appropriate moment are in the service of promoting continued consolidation.

A failure to become acclimated to the new environment, excessive anxiety or signs of depression, as well as overactivity or pseudo-self-sufficiency may serve as signals of potential danger. Assessment of the severity of the problem will, of course, be based on pre-nursery school levels of development as well as on the adjustment to nursery school. Where serious pathology is suggested, early referral for evaluation, treatment, and possibly a therapeutic nursery program may be in order. Less serious subphase inadequacies may be identified and call for modifications in the normal nursery school arrangements and supportive assistance for child and/or mother by a skilled staff person. Intervention at this early point in the life of the child can be of vital importance.

Let us look at a brief intervention made by a social worker on the staff of a nursery school on behalf of a 3-year-old girl, Carol, who seemed to profit from what we might term a developmental assist.

Carol was about to be withdrawn from nursery school in the face of what seemed to be a protracted period of separation difficulty. In contrast to her pre-nursery school behavior and mood, which had been favorable, Carol was unusually fretful and seemed less able to tolerate mother's leaving than would have been anticipated. Mother had been sitting in a corner of the room and while Carol would make brief and seemingly enjoyable forays into the activities and the group, she all too frequently returned to mother's side. Mother was, herself, becoming increasingly discouraged and humiliated, questioning her role as a mother. In the social worker's talk with Carol the following exchange took place:

Social Worker: Nursery school teachers help children feel good at school and help them have fun and learn new things.

Carol: But if you cut your finger at school there are no bandaids.

Social Worker: Oh, sure there are. Let's both look in Miss Mary's cabinet where we keep our bandaids. If you ever needed one that is where we would get it. If that did not help, we would call your mummy and see what else she does to make you feel better.

Carol: My mommy always gives me two bandaids.

These and other similar simple interventions were relieving to Carol and apparently served to convey the notion that there could be a transfer from the idea of mother-bandaid-help to teacher-bandaid-help. We note that Carol was wise enough to be self-protective and hesitant to rush into a new experience where bandaids might be unavailable and help not forthcoming. We are aware that her concern about cuts might well be suggestive of an unusual degree of castration anxiety, which, coupled with her somewhat excessive separation anxiety, should alert us to keep a careful watch on Carol's continued development. However, in the process of these interchanges, in which teacher and sometimes mother participated, Carol was helped, rather quickly, to use her excellent cognitive capacities and previously acquired sense of trust in mother, along with the degree of object constancy previously achieved to move forward. She continued to make a successful adjustment in the program.

In the case of Rosemary, another 3-year-old child in the nursery, a somewhat lengthier intervention was required.

After several weeks of nursery school, Rosemary continued to cry for her mother, experiencing pain that could be relieved only by mother's presence. The teacher could occasionally provide relief by holding the child on her lap, but this would not last if the teacher had to move away. Only rarely could Rosemary become interested in the toys or play of the other children.

Exploration with the mother showed her to be a young woman with low self-esteem, multiple phobias, and a poor self-image. She had been forced to work as a result of the father's recent abandonment. Mother had mustered up courage to seek the nursery school placement for

Rosemary as a partial solution to her work schedule. However, she experienced the child's nursery attendance as a deeply felt additional loss.

Mother's feeling of loss and her fears and panic about her own and Rosemary's safety and well-being were transmitted to Rosemary. A referral for treatment for mother's long-standing problems was made. The nursery school staff undertook to provide special time for Rosemary, reading books to her such as Mommy's at Work, (Merriam, 1971). These helped in conveying ideas about mother's whereabouts, existence, and safety. The staff provided special closeness for Rosemary at snack times. Talking with Rosemary during the school day about her mother's actual whereabouts, and her mother's well-being, was initiated. For example, comments such as "Your mother is having her coffee break at her job now, just as we are having our snack," provided further reinforcement for the development of greater conviction that mother existed when not seen, and would return. Over time, Rosemary began to talk about her mother herself, which suggested that she could now more easily use the internal object representation on her own.

A knowledge of separation–individuation theory can be a helpful tool to the nursery school teacher. The small child's need for mother and the behavior and moods it leads to are frequently misunderstood. The teacher may experience this as her failure rather than an aspect of development, often normal, though sometimes pathological. Increased understanding of the developmental progression enhances the teacher's capacity to promote the nursery school child's ongoing development, and facilitates the identification of "children at risk." Appropriate steps may then be taken for prevention, or remediation, at a favorable developmental juncture.

Later Schooling

Children may experience separation anxiety and problems derived from subphase inadequacies at later points in their educational careers. Certain shifts may be particularly taxing, as when the child moves into a departmentalized program at junior high and is faced with an increased number of teachers and changing groups. For some children who have been sustained by the presence of one teacher and a familiar group of classmates, this alteration in school program may, in itself, upset the developmental balance.

Clara was one of those pre-adolescents who became increasingly anxious during the first weeks of junior high. She had trouble finding the classrooms at period changes, felt distracted, and, in contrast to her former high level of academic work, began to have difficulty in learning. When seen by the school counselor, whom she sought out, Clara noted that she felt confused and preoccupied during the day. At first, her increased difficulty appeared to be related to her mother's illness, which coincided with entrance into junior high. However, it was subsequently learned that her older sister, with whom she had been very close, had left home to attend a boarding school. Clara and Kim had shared a bedroom since Clara's birth; had had the same friends; sometimes dressed alike; and, though two years apart, behaved, at times, as if they were twins. Clara pointed out how reassuring it was at night when she felt apprehensive to look across the room and see Kim sleeping. Often, she recalled focusing on Kim's breathing if she awoke from a bad dream. It appeared to the worker that the convergence of junior high, with its increased demands; mother's illness; and her sister's departure from the home had overburdened Clara's capacity for tolerating separateness. Interpretations, such as the following, were offered in response to appropriate material, to help Clara understand the origin of her increased anxiety:

> We can see that you have been unusually close to your sister, and have taken strength from her. At times, it was almost as if the two of you were one. You have not really discovered your own strength as separate from her, and have not had much of a chance to learn what you could do on your own. Now Kim has left, mother has been ill, and you don't even have the same teacher all day to keep a sense of continuity. You know, though, in view of your accomplishments at school before, you may really be able to do more on your own than you have realized. Having always been with Kim you haven't had much experience coping with scarey feelings on your own. Perhaps, through our talks, we can strengthen that part of you.

Brief support from the counselor as well as clarification and some working through of separation issues enabled Clara to move ahead, and begin to take advantage of the new challenges and opportunities afforded by the school. She touched base with the counselor infrequently during the term, but then, from all reports, was able to become involved with her peers both at school and during after-school hours.

School Adjustment Problems and Learning Difficulties

Clinical experience in a mental health clinic with learning disabled children, and in a school-based mental health program, has increased our appreciation of the way in which failures in the achievement of self and object constancy may lead to learning and behavioral difficulties at all levels of schooling. In the absence of a reliable inner representation of mother to sustain the separateness from her, and without self constancy and the degree of individuation that implies, the child lacks many of the important capacities necessary for learning and the ability for self-regulation of behavior. Pressed to deal with excessive anxiety or depression, and lacking the capacity to cope with such affects, behavior and learning abilities may prove problematical. Indeed, as we have noted, failure to negotiate the rapprochement crisis leaves the child fixated at immature levels in the very areas that are necessary for successful school performance. It is the capacity for frustration tolerance, anticipation, reality testing, signal anxiety, secondary process thinking, impulse control, and the acquisition of a reality-based sense of self that assures the recognition of the need to study in order to learn. The belief that one can learn as if by magic is superceded by the reality.

In our experience, some of the younger children described by their teachers as withdrawn or uninterested in class work seemed to be preoccupied with trying to maintain some inner connection with their mothers. When we, or their teachers, spoke with them about "mommy," they became more alert and involved. We came to view their classroom behavior as a manifestation of the "low-key" behavior described by Mahler in relation to the practicing phase child. We inferred that their apparent withdrawl might reflect efforts at "imaging" mother, in an attempt to hold on to the sensation of well-being associated with her. While promoting some degree of equilibrium, and serving to stave off anxiety, such efforts absorbed the child's energies, and diverted his or her attention from the task of learning. In certain such instances, the teacher's lack of understanding and frustration with the child exacerbated the youngster's problems and led to secondary difficulties.

Some common school problems may be better understood when viewed from the vantage point of separation–indivudation theory. The "hyperactivity" of certain students may represent frantic efforts to defend themselves against feelings of loss and fear, much like the overactivity of the nursery school child described earlier in the chapter. Certain school phobias may be related to severe separation problems. Failures to adequately negotiate the rapprochement subphase may account for considerable difficulty, both in learning and in adjusting to the demands of the school setting from the standpoint of behavior. Among the problems related to the rapprochement subphase are those that derive from failure to come to terms with the lack of self-omnipotence. The acquisition of knowledge requires postponement, an acknowledgment of outer reality, mastery through effort, and the acceptance of "not knowing." Where the illusion of omnipotence has been retained, the child is incapable of the sustained effort that learning requires. Failure and frustration are likely to be experienced as narcissistic injuries. Feelings of shame and anxiety are frequently aroused, which, in turn, may be defended against by denial, or projection of blame, aggression or flight from the academic experience (Herman and Lane, 1979). Some adolescents who manifest school discipline problems can be understood as guarding against the loss of their feeble sense of self through their negativistic behavior. This is reminiscent of the 2-year-old's efforts at asserting autonomy.

We have been deeply impressed with the efforts of certain teachers to apply their understanding of separation–individuation theory in the classroom. In a first grade class, a teacher became adept at recognizing certain pupils' manifestations of separation anxiety through excessive noisiness and movement when she was far across the room from them. In the past she had interpreted and responded to this behavior as "naughtiness." She began a practice of calling to these children at specific intervals, commenting on what they were doing, and reminding them she was aware of them. With one of the youngsters who had unusual difficulty, she would leave an object on his desk when she moved away, asking him to keep it until she stopped by in a little while. A pencil, a small pad—it mattered little what the object was—the effect seemed to increase significantly the child's capacity to tolerate the teacher's distance.

College

College life today imposes unusual demands upon students, requiring a higher degree of individuation than in the past when colleges served *in loco parentis*. Our experience suggests that some adolescents who have failed to achieve self and object constancy have great difficulty in coping with the pressures and freedom that prevail in many college situations and are well advised to remain close to home and work through, in treatment, those tasks of separation and individuation that remain incomplete. In the case of young people with lesser degrees of difficulty, clinical assistance at school or in the college community may enable them to remain at school and to develop further.

We have seen a few students who, having experienced a crisis around separation while away at college, have sought counseling while at home on vacation. Brief intervention has enabled several such students to return to school, sometimes continuing in treatment at college and sometimes not. We offer the following illustration of such a short-term intervention given to Mary, an 18-year-old college student. Mary was seen for eight sessions during her Christmas holiday, and follow-up, some six months later, revealed that she had adjusted satisfactorily upon her return to college and did not pursue a recommendation for ongoing treatment.

Mary had begun to experience severe depression shortly before the Christmas recess of her second year at an out-of-state college. She was referred for brief counseling during the vacation to help her determine whether she should transfer to a local school.

When seen, Mary indicated that she had expected to feel more comfortable when she returned home but was actually not feeling any better. She was reluctant to transfer for a variety of reasons and thought that if she could understand what was happening to her, she might be able to continue in her present school, which she would prefer.

An attractive, articulate young woman who had done well academically at college and who had enjoyed the campus activities, Mary indicated that she had been content at school until about a month before the vacation when she had become confused and felt at "a loose end." Only upon questioning was it learned that at about that time she had terminated a relationship with a boy friend whom she had begun going with the first week of college. She could not see, however, how her depression could have anything to do with the ending of that relationship since she had long wished to part from her boy friend. He was a demanding person who required all of her free time and whom she had begun to experience as "suffocating" her. Their interests were very different and she felt limited in her freedom. She could not pursue certain activities that had begun to interest her without enraging him. She had experienced relief when they ended their affair.

College represented for Mary her first separation from what was described as a close-knit family who had done "everything together." Her brother, six years her senior, had attended a local college and left home to get married the preceding year. She recalled that as a sad time for the family. She was particularly proud of her good relationship with her mother, whom she had considered to be her "best friend" until she went to college. She had confided in her practically every significant detail of her life until she had left home. Then she found it necessary to withhold certain information such as her sexual experiences and her limited drug experimentation. Mother and she had never been parted until she went to college. Even when at age 11 she had been operated on for appendicitis, mother had stayed with her in the hospital.

Mary explained that she had anticipated being homesick at college in view of the closeness of her family experience. However, she really had not had the time to be, for she had quickly formed such a close relationship with her boy friend. Initially, they were inseparable at school.

Out of the material that Mary shared it became clear that the termination of her relationship with her boy friend had confronted her with what seemed to have been her first experience without an almost constantly available partner. The boy friend had afforded her the closeness that she had formerly experienced with her mother, and had served to postpone the experience of object loss she might have faced earlier. It was important to clarify that it was not the loss of the boy friend himself that was so significant, but rather the loss of what he had come to represent intrapsychically. On one hand he had replaced mother and, on the other, he had drawn her away from mother. According to her, their sexual involvement was the first "real secret" she had kept from her mother. She was uncomfortable with withholding this knowledge for it made her feel "far away" from the mother in whom she had always confided. She rationalized that she was simply protecting mother from worry. Later, she pointed out that knowing her mother she felt she would have also conformed to the prevailing patterns today as related to sexuality and drugs. Thus, she seemed to find a way to keep a bond with her.

We came to consider that her depression involved a certain amount of guilt about separation as well as being a response to the loss that she was experiencing. It was pointed out that her profound reaction was understandable in light of the prolonged, intense, and out-of-phase closeness that she had had with mother, and the absence of slow, gradually paced dosages of separation that ordinarily pave the way for smoother separation. As long as she had her boy friend she had not had to experience what it was like to be alone and to encounter the sadness that ordinarily accompanies the realization of loss.

Acknowledgement was made of Mary's obvious capacities to function independently. That she had the age-appropriate wish to do so was also indicated by her desire for greater freedom from her "suffocating" boy friend. The acknowledgment of her developmental strivings was in keeping with an effort to support the highest level of development. There was a suggestion, implicit in these interventions, that one needs practice in dealing with small amounts of unpleasant affect in order to develop a better tolerance for those experiences of loss that are inevitable.

Mary's feelings in relation to not telling mother all the details of her life were explored further. She expressed concern that her mother would feel badly if she knew that Mary was less open with her. Slowly it became evident that she felt mother depended upon their closeness for her well-being and that Mary's strivings for independence might be hurtful to mother. The guilt, insofar as could be ascertained, was related more to somehow failing mother than to what she was actually doing. We have come to see that in certain circumstances the separating children experience guilt in regard to the wish to move away, and feel that their mothers will be harmed. This may represent a form of reversal.

These sessions proved helpful. Mary was relieved to discover some comprehensible basis for her discomfort. She had feared that she was going "crazy." The thought that there was strength and value in her wish to do something differently from mother and even to keep secrets from her seemed to relieve some of the guilt. It was proposed that since from what she could assess when she returned home her mother appeared to be faring well, it might be that she had turned things around. She had felt as if her mother would be as upset about their moving away from one another as she was. For the purposes of this brief treatment we focused on her sexual activities and her limited drug use as serving the purpose of creating intrapsychic distance from mother, which was the painful aspect for her. To what degree these phenomena had additional meaning remained unexplored.

From the beginning, there was an understanding that our focus would be on seeking to identify and clarify as much of the problem as we could. The possibility that longer term treatment might be indicated was raised at the beginning of the contract. By the fourth session, Mary had decided to return to school though she was still mildly depressed. The fact that she would lose money and time were advanced as the reasons for this. However, she noted that, after being home for ten days, she missed the freedom and activities available at school. She felt that while she anticipated a struggle she was in a better position to contend with it. Treatment facilities in the area of her college were suggested and she thought that she would feel comfortable seeking help, if she felt the need. While she had initially come for these sessions in order to comply with her parents' request, she now felt that out of the brief experience she had derived something for herself that would facilitate her going on if it was indicated. She thought the sessions had been interesting. The therapist sought, at this point, to encourage her to seek further help by suggesting the prophylactic value of treatment even if she were not overtly uncomfortable. In view of the life tasks ahead, it might be valuable to attempt to further strengthen some aspects of herself. It was noted that her intellectual interest was a positive attribute for future therapeutic work.

Six months after return to school, her father phoned, at her request, to say that she was doing well. He noted that she had expanded her interests, particularly in extracurricular activities, and had a feature role in a forthcoming dramatic presentation. We cannot know whether this developmental assist will lead to further consolidation of object and self constancy. This was a case in which individuation had, it seemed, preceded separation, so that Mary had greater capacities than she was utilizing. These were supported in the treatment. While considerable effort was directed at helping Mary reflect upon her material and discover connections, it should be noted that in this time-limited exchange, the therapist did utilize a more educationally oriented approach than would ordinarily be indicated in an open-ended treatment situation.

That Mary made what appeared to be good use of this approach may testify to a great deal of strength in her. She had, after all, been able to go off to school, to perform relatively well even when upset, and to utilize this brief therapeutic experience. Our impression was that Mary had the advantages of good inborn capacities, a positive symbiotic experience, and favorable conditions during differentiation and practicing. She appeared to have foundered at rapprochement and we suspected that this might have had something to do with the mother's failure to gently encourage her forward thrust. Indeed, her mother appeared involved instead in keeping her close. Unfortunately, one of the problems with short-term treatment is that one has only a brief time to gain an understanding of the client, and we sensed that there were many important issues that we failed to touch upon in this limited work.

MARRIAGE

The capacity to establish an enduring, reciprocal love relationship with a marital partner is rooted in the phases of symbiosis and separation–individuation, as well as being dependent upon the outcome of the oedipal negotiation. The experience of early union between mother and infant leaves a "residue of longing" that ultimately prompts the search for a lover in later life (Bergmann, 1971, p. 39). This was recognized by Freud (1905) when he proposed that the finding of a love object represented the refinding of an earlier love, the prototype of which was the infant at the breast. Symbiosis leads not only to the search for a love object but fosters those capacities that make love possible. Empathy and compassion as well as the ability to invest significant meaning in one special person, experienced as different from all others, orginate in the early dyadic experience.

The capacity for loving and being loved develops and is transformed during the subphases. From a valuing of the love object based on need-gratification, the child's awareness of the love object as a person in his or her own right with individual needs grows, and feelings towards the loved one begin to transcend need-gratification. Over time, the love of the object acquires profound importance and its loss comes to represent a powerful threat. Sensitivity to approval and disapproval by the love object begins, and the child comes to appreciate that he or she must become more active in the pursuit of love. Although it is not until the resolution of the oedipus that the capacities for loving reach fuller measure, with affection and sexuality becoming integrated and capable of being directed towards a nonincestuous love object, the early preoedipal experiences are essential building blocks in this development.

Self and object constancy, developed in the first three years, insure that the reawakening of feelings derived from the symbiotic phase do not bring with them a loss of the sense of self (Bergmann, 1971). The capacity to be alone in the presence of the mother (Winnicott, 1958), acquired during the subphases, paves the way for the ability to remain separate within the context of a deeply felt love. With object constancy the marital partner can be valued despite his or her imperfections, physical separation, differing interests and views, disappointments, and the countless stresses of marital life. With self constancy, self-worth is maintained despite the partner's intermittent disapproval, emotional unavailability, or geographic distance. Firm boundaries permit emotional intimacy and physical union without fear of merger, and enable the partners to temporarily put aside their own needs in favor of their partner's without fear of the loss of self.

Problems during symbiosis or in the subphases may impede marital adjustment to a greater or lesser extent and in numbers of ways.

Deviations at symbiosis may lead a partner to overvalue nonverbal attunement, or to be incapable of that measure of empathy required for sustained love. The search for understanding "without asking" is manifest in a variety of marital problems.

We refer to those partners who cannot express their wishes directly because their mates "should know" and if they have to "ask" then they do not feel loved. On the other hand, there are marriage partners who are unable to "tune in" to their spouse at all, and require constant verbal explanation in order for them to be sensitive to the other's needs. We think of a young woman whose husband had severe headaches, and though he was in obvious pain, she could not express sympathy, or diminish her demands upon him. She insisted that his silence when ill, was intolerable to her and that if he could only ask her to help him she could do so. There was, indeed, evidence that when she understood another's needs, she did have the capacity to respond but her own attunement to the nonverbal was minimal. While there were other factors accounting for this, we learned, over time, that this young woman herself had had a very meagre symbiotic experience. The patient's mother appeared to have had some difficulty relating to her until the patient began to talk, which was at an early age, around 1½ years. At this point, mother, who seemed to value her little daughter's verbal proficiency highly, seemed then able to respond better to the child's directly expressed needs. We came to regard this experience, in part, as connected with the patient's own great difficulty in "tuning in" to her husband, and her overreliance on semantic communication.

Insufficient self-object differentiation may account for some marital difficulties. Where the sense of self is fragile, the intimacy of marriage may be experienced as profoundly threatening. Certain sexual problems, for example, are clearly related to fear of merger. Instead of orgasm representing a temporary regression "in the service of the ego" (Kris, 1952), it becomes experienced as dangerously engulfing. In some marital situations, the couple's interaction represents the constant attempt to maintain distance and prevent merger. The incessant and trivial bickering characteristic of certain couples frequently reflects this defensive effort.

We observe among some couples attempts to use their marriages to repair early deficits, to compensate for previously missed object-related experiences, or to maintain a sense of personal equilibrium through their partners. There are those who clearly seek to obtain supplies missed at symbiosis. Their need for gratification, attunement, or union with a more omnipotent object prevails. Sexual experiences are frequently valued in terms of the wish for the cuddling, holding, stroking that was missed earlier, with genital sex having little significance. Some marital partners try to replicate experiences associated with the practicing phase. Among these are some who use their partners predominantly for "refueling" purposes. An example was Mr. Y., who noted that he could not tolerate a business trip of more than three days' duration, and was actually held back from advancement in his work by this. He found that after two days away, he was preoccupied with getting home to see and talk with his wife. He noted that it was as if his spirits needed a "lift."

Evidence of a recapitulation of the rapprochement struggle has already been referred to in the case of those partners whose argumentativeness seems aimed at guarding their autonomy. Mr. and Mrs. Stone was such a couple. They argued over the most inconsequential matters. One major argument took place about whether ice cream thrown down the kitchen sink would block the drain. Purchasing a new piece of furniture sparked a three-day fight. Indeed, their difficulties intensified with their improving financial condition for there was greater opportunity to purchase things and, therefore, more room for disagreement. In each situation they sought to highlight their differences and to play out the struggle for self-assertion.

The way in which individuals locate partners with whom they may achieve an unusual degree of "fitting together" is often impressive (Hartmann, 1939). Such arrangements are, however, tenuous. A significant change in one partner may threaten the precarious balance. When, for example, Mrs. Allen was forced for financial reasons to go to work in a company that prohibited personal telephone calls in the office, Mr. Allen became increasingly upset. Accustomed to calling home several times during the working day, he could not tolerate the increased separation. He had been able to feel safe at work as long as he thought he could reach his wife by dialing the telephone. In our work with him, he noted that he had now begun to understand better why he had previously been so angry when his wife went out shopping in the evening. He had thought that he was simply annoyed or hurt because she did not choose to be with him. He had viewed her insistence on going as an effort to assert herself, which it actually was, and a lack of sensitivity to his needs. Frequent arguments took place at such times. Mrs. Allen became resentful at what she experienced as her husband's efforts to control her. When both Mr. and Mrs. Allen came to appreciate that he had actually been unable to tolerate the anxiety attendant to her going out and being beyond his "telephone reach," and that his anger was defensive, they were able to begin to approach each other differently. As so often proves to be the case, anger had served as a protection against feelings of anxiety and depression.

To some degree, marriage normally affords opportunities for gratification of earlier needs that still remain and exist in all of us. It is when such needs predominate that they contribute to an unusual degree of strife. Whether marital difficulties can be dealt with by a developmental assist of short duration or require more sustained, longer-term treatment either conjoint and/or individual, depends upon the nature and severity of each partner's intrapsychic problems, and the particular way in which these reverberate with those of the partner. We have, sometimes, been suprised at the progress that certain couples make with what we would consider to have been a minimal amount of help. Mr. and Mrs. Armstrong were seen for a consultation at a time when Mr. Armstrong was considering leaving his wife. They quarreled continuously and, as time went on, their arguments had become increasingly acrimonious. They were seen for three joint sessions, and each was seen alone twice. A recommendation, based on an assessment of their individual problems, was for individual treatment. It appeared to the worker that the efforts of each to repair their respective problems through the marriage had heavily burdened the relationship, and had clearly exacerbated deep-seated difficulties that antedated the marriage and impeded their adaptation in other areas of life. Both, however, were reluctant to move into treatment, and decided that they would first like to see what they might do with what limited understanding they had gained during the consultation.

It had quickly become apparent that Mrs. Armstrong sought to have her husband "tune in to her" and was deeply disappointed and angry at his failure to do so. She appeared to be an unusually competent woman who ran her household with great efficiency and who tended to be withdrawn and uncommunicative. She was frequently annoyed at her husband's failure to assist her with household chores, to take the initiative in planning their entertainment schedule, and to assume greater responsibility for the children's care. When asked how she made her wishes known to her husband, she acknowledged that she did not. If she had to ask him, then there was no value in his help. If he could anticipate and relate to her unexpressed wishes it was for her a test of whether he cared for her or not. If she had to ask, then he would only be doing it because she insisted, not, as she wished, out of love and understanding. She was able to see that her long-standing need to prove she could do everything herself might make it difficult for those around her to realize that a part of her wanted to be cared for and assisted. It was possible for her to relate these needs to the fact that as a child she had had to become independent very early in order to cope with life. Her mother had died when she was 5, following a long and incapacitating illness, and she had been raised by a succession of housekeepers.

Mr. Armstrong was surprised to learn of his wife's wishes, feeling that she seemed anxious to take care of everything herself. He had always felt that he could not live up to her expectations, and had gradually withdrawn, involving himself in hobbies and other activities that afforded him that measure of success he did not experience in his role as husband.

The consultation terminated with the therapist's leaving the door open for their return but they were not heard from again, and the therapist considered this to have been an unsuccessful contact. Nearly five years later, the therapist met the couple in the lobby of a theatre. They approached her, reminded her of their earlier meeting, and commented that their brief therapeutic experience had been a turning point in a marriage that had improved significantly over the years. Unfortunately, we have no way of knowing what distinguished this couple from other couples who appear, initially, to manifest very similar problems but who require far more intensive and longer treatment before any change is achieved.

PARENTHOOD

The notion that parenthood is a developmental phase in the life-cycle has been explicated by Benedek (1959), Erikson (1950), and others. Issues from all developmental sequences are revived and new opportunities are present for developmental advance. Earlier conflicts may be reworked, and in the process of parenting, mother and father may grow along with their offspring. Once again, though, earlier fixations and vulnerabilities may overburden the psyche, precluding continued development and interfering with the capacity to parent. Among the problems that may be revived are those that originate in deficiencies in symbiosis or in the subphases of the parents' own separation–individuation.

The "good enough" (Winnicott, 1953, p. 94.) parents draw from their own favorable symbiotic exchange in their fitting together

(Hartmann, 1958) with their infant, and, at the same time, their achievement of self and object constancy enables them to maintain a clear distinction between their developing infant's needs and their own needs. The capacity to gradually shift their responses, attitudes, and the nutriments they provide in accord with the phase-specific needs of the child depends upon their own earlier developmental accomplishments. The capacity for intimacy as well as a firm sense of self enables the parents to nurture, and assures their reliability and the steadfastness of their attachment. Their capacity for separation, on the other hand, permits them to foster and value their child's development towards ever-increasing degrees of separateness—in other words, towards psychological birth.

From pregnancy on, parental self and object constancy is challenged. Biological changes attendant to pregnancy introduce varying degrees of physiological and psychological stress. Ordinarily encompassed, the bodily changes may threaten the sense of self of those women whose identities are fragile, and in some cases, may interfere with the husband's perception of his wife as a constant object. We have in mind those women who experience estrangement from themselves when pregnant as a result of their altered appearance and the changing feel of their bodies, as well as those men who manifest anxiety in response to their wives as becoming "unfamiliar" to them. The impact of pregnancy on mother and father is, of course, influenced by whether the pregnancy was wanted or not, the readiness of the couple to assume the financial responsibilities of parenthood, and other factors in addition to those that touch upon matters of self and object constancy.

For some women the developing fetus is experienced as so much a part of the self that they fail to take cognizance that despite their oneness they are, in fact, two. For these women, pregnancy often represents an ideal state in which deep symbiotic needs are richly gratified. The birth, in such instances, may represent, unconsciously, a loss rather than a gain, the disruption of a highly valued experience of merger. It is in such cases that postpartum depression may follow delivery.

Until recently, obstetrical practices have generally failed to take into account the emotional needs of parents and the family-to-be. They have been particularly stressful for men and women whose capacities for separation are limited. Women have given birth in isolated hospital conditions, left alone for long periods of time during the labor, and attended by strangers. Fathers have frequently been treated as "outsiders" and have felt shut off from the experience and from their wives. For both mothers and fathers-to-be who possess limited "basic trust," or fear of strangers and have not achieved object constancy, such arrangements have been particularly hard. We are now witnessing a major revision in obstetrical care with the advent of home deliveries, birthing centers, rooming in, Lamaze and other methods of delivery that stress advance preparation by the parents and active participation in the birth experience. A variety of procedures are being developed to reduce the mechanization of the birth experience and to promote the appreciation of birth as a normal life process rather than an illness. Although developed to improve the delivery experience for the average family-to-be, and to promote bonding among the family members, these procedures may prove particularly significant for parents with special needs, therefore also serving a preventative function. This would be particularly true if, along with the other improvements, attending personnel could be sensitized to indications of unusual need on the part of some parents for postpartum supportive services, in much the same way as they are now alert to the physical needs of those infants-at-risk who require special postnatal care.

Under the most favorable circumstances, parenting is a long and demanding task. While recognizing in the postpartum "blues" a more or less common reaction to the birth experience and the early period of child care, our culture has done little to provide significant supports to the new family. The recent establishment of Mothers' Centers—programs in which parents are developing mutual support systems—is an effort in that direction. Reports on the discussions that are an integral feature of the Center's overall program indicate that these women experienced the birth and assumption of their role as mothers as traumatic to varying degrees. They used the group discussion to reconsider and rework experiences associated with pregnancy, delivery, and their earily responsibilities toward their infants, even though a considerable period of time had often elapsed since they had given birth (Turrini, 1977).

In caring for their babies, mothers draw upon their own early symbiotic experiences and their subsequent identification with their mothers in the child-care role. The mother begins to relate to her infant's needs, aided by the signals that a healthy baby provides, out of unremembered but preserved experiences of being cared for herself. Both the ability of the infant to summon the mother and the ability of the mother to receive and respond to the infant's signals play an integral role in the development of an optimum mother-infant dyad. Where either the infant's sending power or the mother's capacity to receive and respond are limited, development may be at risk. For mothers whose own early symbiotic experiences were less than optimum, their capacity to tune in to their infants may be minimal. It is difficult to provide that which we have not had ourselves. Some mothers may require considerable nurturing themselves in order to be able to nurture. Such is thought to be the case with certain abusing mothers, for whom nurturing environments are being structured in the hope that they, in turn, may be more able to provide for their infants when they have themselves been better provided for.

Early parental care draws not only upon the symbiotic past of the mother and father but, at the same time depends very much on the level of self and object constancy that they have previously achieved. The infant depends upon the mother's capacity to form and maintain a deep attachment, whether the baby is smiling in her arms or crying and awakening her from a distance in the middle of the night. The mother, too, is dependent, during the early period of parenthood, upon her husband's capacity to remain attached to her at a time when she may be less available to him both physically and emotionally. At each level of the child's development from birth on, the parents' capacity to value the child, whether present or absent, whether gratifying or frustrating, is tested. The practicing toddler must rely on the mother's keeping him or her in mind when out of sight. The rapprochement child seriously taxes a parent's capacities to remain steadfast at times when the toddler's behavior imposes great frustration upon the parents.

Self constancy is similarly challenged. Unhappy, fretful infants who, despite their parents' most devoted effors to comfort them, continue to express dissatisfaction, can induce deep feelings of failure, ineffectiveness, or frustration in the most experienced and confident of parents. A firm foundation, however, of self-regard makes it more possible for parents to support one another, reach out for help, and continue to empathize with their infant's distress without suffering a serious depletion in their own self-esteem. The self-worth and self-confidence of parents is taxed all along the life cycle, as anyone whose child has brought home a failing report card or who has received a complaint about his or her adolescent's behavior can testify to.

The parents' capacity to partner the child's negotiation of the separation–individuation tasks further depends upon the parents' self and object constancy. Both mother's and father's own experience of loss in relation to their child's increased separateness must be encompassed. Parents must be capable of varying their offerings and finding new levels of relatedness that are responsive to the child's changing personality and needs.

Identification of problems and intervention achieve the most favorable outcome if provided before birth and during early infancy. We think of Mrs. Robbins, a young mother who shared with the nurse at the prenatal clinic her blissful fantasies of the time when she would hold her baby, rock it, and finally have a real-life "doll" of her very own. Aware of the deprivation in Mrs. Robbins's own early life, this sensitive and concerned nurse gently commented that it seemed as if Mrs. Robbins was imagining her baby as a tiny infant for the rest of his or her life. What did she think the baby might be like when he or she walked or talked? How did she imagine she and her husband as parents then? Mrs. Robbins expressed, initially, her surprise that she frankly had not even pictured her infant-to-be as existing out of her arms. Whether the few talks they then had about Mrs. Robbins's anticipations of her future infant and herself as a mother proved helpful, we do not know. We can only hypothesize that they were probably an improvement over simply leaving Mrs. Robbins to continue to focus totally on her infant-to-be as a part of herself, and as primarily a source of gratification of her symbiotic needs. Pharis (1979) in a study of expectant parents has proposed that the family is born in the minds of the parents-to-be long before the delivery. Thus, prenatal attention to the parents' psychological as well as biological needs may ultimately facilitate the parents' capacity to foster their offspring's psychological as well as biological birth.

We think of another brief and early intervention made by a pediatrician familiar with separation–individuation theory. Mrs. Tines, dressing her infant after a routine examination, became incensed when the baby wiggled and impeded efforts to dress her. Mother was obviously frustrated and appeared embarrassed by the baby's behavior. She admonished her little girl for being "bad" and apologized to the pediatrician for taking so long to dress her youngster. Dr. M. tried to reassure the mother that actually her little daughter was responding to mother's fine care and "doing her proud." He suggested that the infant's ability to move about and exercise her growing body was a demonstration of her healthy developing physical self, and was her way of starting to move about a bit on her own. He acknowledged that the moving was not easy for mother, but essential for the baby, and was a sign of how well both mother and infant were doing.

While infancy is a particularly critical developmental period for parents as well as child, subsequent developmental stages such as the oedipal negotiation, latency and adolescence also have a critical

impact upon parents. The child's negotiation of each phase rever-
berates to varying degrees with the parents' own early experiences
and touches upon important unconscious issues. Parenthood, as Benedek (1970) has noted, continues throughout life to play a central
role in the self-regard of both mother and father. Even in old age
parents cling to the status that parenthood affords them.

We have selected a brief vignette of work done with a mother
who responded to her son's marriage with a great sense of loss. At
the marriage of a child, a parent is inevitably faced with a discontin-
uation of direct parental responsibilities, and with a new kind of
separation. In some sense, it is like a retirement and confronts a
mother, particularly one who has devoted her full-time efforts to
child rearing, with a marked change in status, activity, and purpose.
Even in those situations where the mother has been otherwise occupied, she is faced with an important task. This task is heavily burdened in the case of parents who have depended too much on their
children for closeness and for narcissistic gratification. Separation
anxiety, depression, or a depletion of the sense of self are frequently
precipitated at this critical juncture in the lives of mothers who have
not achieved self and object constancy.

Mrs. B. became depressed when her son married. She hated her
daughter-in-law and nothing the young people did satisfied her. Even
the ribbon used to tie her Mother's Day gift was considered "no
good." A young social work student began to work with Mrs. B. at the
clinic. Slowly, her failure in self-object differentiation and her lack of
self and object constancy became apparent. In a moving session, this
mother recalled her anger when her son, then 14 months of age, had
so much enjoyed fondling his blanket. She recalled trying to pull the
blanket from him. The student, who was familiar with the positive
significance of the transitional object (Tolpin, 1972), proposed that
Mrs. B. must have provided favorable early mothering since the child's
capacity to value a transitional object was testimony to earlier good
feelings with mother. The independence that her son began to
achieve in this way also reflected the good start he must have had.
When Mrs. B. began to be able, with the student's support, to see her
early mothering in a positive light, as opposed to feeling that her
son's individuating efforts reflected negatively upon her, there was a
gradual development of more positive self and object representations.
As she worked through some of the anger toward her son for leaving
her, she came to recognize that, in some way, her earlier anger toward her own unavailable mother had become displaced upon her

son. In time, Mrs. B. began to consider what else she might do with her interest and time and became involved in a career outside of the home. When the student left her field placement, Mrs. B. had a difficult time, and the losses of her earlier life, including the loss of her son, were reworked again in the termination phase.

BEREAVEMENT

Freud (1917) has proposed that the death of a loved one is normally encompassed over time, through a psychically demanding, painful, and time consuming process of mourning. The normal mourner is ultimately compelled by reality testing to acknowledge the death of the loved one and, in the interest of preserving the narcissistic satisfactions associated with living, slowly decathects the representations of the object. While mourning does not and should not succeed in withdrawing all of the investment in the object (Furman, 1974) sufficient libido is freed so that the mourner becomes once again capable of loving. An intrapsychic, enduring connection is maintained through the process of selective identifications with the deceased, which ultimately enrich the personality of the mourner and promote further adaptation.

Viewed from the standpoint of separation and individuation, the capacity for normal mouring depends upon the achievement of self and object constancy. A sufficient degree of self-object differentiation is required to insure that the loss of the object is not experienced as a loss of the self. Sufficient capacity for reality testing must exist for the individual to acknowledge and face the death of the loved one and sufficient secondary narcissism and confident expectation is requisite in order that pleasure in living may serve to help initiate the painful work of mourning. The achievement of object constancy also assures that a unified, whole representation of the object uniting both good and bad features will make it possible to tolerate ambivalence and to form selective identifications with an object that has been perceived as separate and whole.

Pathological depression may follow the loss of a loved one in persons who have, in fact, achieved self and object constancy. Since Freud's "Mourning and Melancholia" (1917), an extensive and illuminating literature which elaborates on a wide range of complex psychic phenomena that lead to pathological mourning, has been developed. However, in keeping with our focus, we offer a case

illustration in which failure to have achieved object and self constancy constituted a major factor in a prolonged mourning.

Mrs. Marcus, a middle-aged woman, began her twice-a-week treatment, which spanned a six-month period, some two-and-a-half years
following the death of her 30-year-old son, John. He had died in an
automobile accident while intoxicated. From the beginning of contact
she sought to focus on securing relief from the unrelenting, intolerable depression she had suffered since the loss, noting that she experienced herself as an unhappy person whose troubled childhood, un-
satisfactory marriage, and seriously disturbed son had made her feel
"jinxed" by life. She insisted that she was seeking help only for those
difficulties that she saw as related to her son's death and did not wish
to become involved in a longer-term treatment program addressed to
her more basic difficulties. She wanted only to reduce the amount of
extra discomfort and to be free to resume the level of functioning she
once had on her job, in her home management, and with a small
group of friends whom she had formerly enjoyed.

Incapable of making even minor decisions, on the verge of tears if
not crying a good part of the time, unable to enjoy activities, and
generally continuing to experience the intense feelings she had had
immediately following the tragedy, Mrs. Marcus had first sought help
about a year after her son's death. She had seen two therapists at different times for about five or six visits, terminating each arrangement
with the feeling that the therapists had not understood her. Both
therapists had interpreted her depression in part as a manifestation of
her rage turned back upon herself, and in part as a form of self-punishment and punishment of her husband with whom she felt she
shared the guilt for her son's many emotional problems, Mrs. Marcus
agreed with their interpretations, but felt they had not been helpful.
She could see that her insistence, for example, on having John's photographs throughout the house, including one on the refrigerator
door, was a form of self-torture, but this understanding had not enabled her to remove them. She could also see that her inability to
take advantage of the opportunity to move from her crowded, inadequate housing, or to make her life more comfortable in any way, per-
petuated her state of misery. However, an understanding of the way
in which her indecisiveness led to her discomfort, and thereby served
the purpose of self-punishment, did not enable her to cease her rumi-
nating, obsessive activity.

When seen by this therapist, Mrs. Marcus appeared to be an intelligent, overwhelmed, profoundly sad woman who wept throughout

the first few sessions. She was desperate for relief and immediately expressed her hope that the therapist would find a way to rid her of her discomfort. She indicated that her wish was that the therapist would say something that would put her situation in a different perspective, and likened her expectations to those one ordinarily associated with a minister's offerings. She had, indeed, sought comfort from her clergyman, but he did not seem to have "the right words." At some level this longing expressed her wish for a magical solution and at another level she appeared to be seeking the comfort or soothing that a young child derives from a mother's reassuring words.

Mrs. Marcus was the only child of a psychotic, blind mother who had been hospitalized for varying periods of time since Mrs. Marcus was 3 years old, and a father who had abandoned the family when she was 8 years old. Since the time that she was 10, her mother had been permanently institutionalized and Mrs. Marcus had been placed first in an institution and then, at her request, in a foster home. She had lived in three foster homes between the ages of 11 and 16, the moves being determined by the needs of the foster families. At 16, when still another foster family with whom she had been particularly happy planned to relocate, she left school, took a room in a boarding house, and went to work as a file clerk. She met her husband in a program for servicemen and married him when she was 18. He went overseas shortly thereafter and she moved in with his family, which she found satisfying. His mother treated her kindly. She recalled how they had shared together in keeping the image of her husband clear through their conversations about him. Although upon his return she quickly found their relationship incompatible, she was delighted to become pregnant, feeling that that was one of her most satisfying life experiences.

Mr. Marcus was described as withdrawn, depressed, and uninterested in anything other than his work as a watchmaker and television viewing. However, she felt fortunate to have married at all, appreciated the fact that her husband was sharing of his income so that they could have a home, and was glad not to be alone. Her son had been diagnosed as emotionally disturbed in kindergarten. A tantrumous, impulse-ridden youngster, he had been placed in special classes throughout his school career. She had, in opposition to her husband, expended time, effort, and money of her own to secure treatment and special programs for John, which proved of little help in the long run. John was hospitalized in his twenties after a suicide attempt, was involved in illegal activities for which he was arrested several times and was in and out of her life, seeking help frequently when he was in trouble. She deeply regretted that at about the time of the accident she had refused his request for money, feeling that he would only spend it on drugs or alcohol. She felt that she had failed to take cognizance of the severity of his emotional limitations and regarded her refusal of his wishes as a precipitant of his tragic end.

It was evident in this treatment, as in the past treatments, that rage, guilt, and self-punishment were significant features of the clinical picture. However, additional material emerged that suggested alternative explanations of some of the already described behavioral manifestation.

For example, in one of the early sessions Mrs. Marcus described how in her early twenties she had passed a man in the street who resembled a picture she carried in her wallet of her father. Following him into a store, she inquiried as to who he was and introduced herself to him. He denied knowing her, but she thrust a paper into his hand with her name and address on it. Later, she received a letter from him indicating that he was her father but had been too ashamed to acknowledge it. As a matter of fact, he said he had traced her whereabouts through relatives and had for a long time visited the neighborhood, hoping he would find her. However, he really had no way of recognizing her. A reunion was effected, though there was less association than she would have desired. He was then living with a woman who had several children with whom he got along well. His visits were infrequent and uncomfortable. He died two years later. She lamented that he had no longer seemed the merry, music-loving father that she had recalled. She stressed, however, how she had clung to his picture, feeling that it represented the only means by which she could maintain the memory of him.

This led to her recollection of her deep fear as a child that her mother would forget who she was when she went to visit her in the hospital, for she really could not develop a picture of her as she was blind. She further recalled how strange her mother used to look to her when she was brought to see her by relatives. Ultimately these memories led to an expression of her deep fear that she might forget how her son looked and what he was like, and then it would be as if he had never existed.

With this association, she wondered if perhaps that was the reason she felt compelled to have his photographs all over the house. The therapist confirmed this understanding, adding that Mrs. Marcus seemed unaware of how clearly she actually did have her son in mind, and how clearly she had conveyed the picture of him to the therapist. We had not required photographs in our sessions to call him to mind. Perhaps a time would come when she would feel more confident of her ability to recall him, so that she would no longer require photographs on display in her house. The pictures semed to force her to think of him, in contrast to her remembering him in a more natural, relaxed way. About three months following this work, Mrs. Marcus removed those photographs that were placed in such inappropriate spots as on the refrigerator and on the inside of her closet.

It later turned out that she also worried about not feeling sad lest without the feeling she might forget her son. Forgetting and being forgotten were themes that continued to emerge. Sometimes they derived from experiences of earlier losses, such as from father's abandonment, and the repeated losses of mother.

As time went on, the nature of her relationship with John became clearer. He seemed to serve certain functions for her in some ways that she felt were missing in herself and in other ways that could be seen as need gratifying. It became possible to identify more precisely what she had lost when she lost him (Freud, 1917). We came to see that his impulsive, acting-out behavior had brought excitement and adventure into her otherwise drab life. Moreover, his violent behavior represented valued strength, power, and omnipotence. She felt stronger in his presence. She felt that if she were in need, he would protect her. If he were alive, she would not have to worry about her old age. She, herself, was much preoccupied with whether her own mother was well tended. She visited regularly, though mother had not recognized her for many years, and tipped the hospital personnel well. However, no one would dare to mistreat John's mother. He would forcibly insist on good care for her and service personnel would fear him. She was reminded of how, when they went to an eating place, any dissatisfaction with the food or service would enrage him. He would make the kind of scene that would bring immediate attention. While she had been embarrassed, she had at the same time felt a kind of respect for him and a confidence that he could take care of things. She cried when the therapist pointed out that now we could both appreciate that, in losing her son, Mrs. Marcus had lost someone whom she regarded as a protector and how frightening that must have been. She responded by saying that it was only in her imagination that he could protect her. It was what she had chosen to see, for actually he was too troubled to be able even to manage himself. This then reminded her of her father. He had tried to protect her from her mother's anger, but in the end he was not strong enough to take it himself. It was at that point that she disclosed for the first time that her father had had two hospitalizations for depression.

It turned out that John was like her father in other ways. He had, according to her, made her laugh. He had a good sense of humor and when she was sad he would tell her a joke. He also shared with her an appreciation of dance music and she brought several record albums to show the therapist what they had shared. She saw him, despite his problems, as frequently having brought a quality of liveliness into the home. These qualities, too, reminded her of her memory of a father who, when he came home, would tell her a story or sometimes play a harmonica to which she would dance. An elaboration of this and other material revealed oedipal derivatives that were not dealt with, however. Instead, the emphasis was placed on how meaningful it had been to have had such an opportunity to enjoy these familiar pleasures with her son and how much she must have missed them.

While concentration was on her current loss, she came to see the way in which her son's death had revived feelings associated with the earlier loss of her father, including abandonment, loss, and rage. Emphasis was also placed on the way in which, in losing father, she had lost those functions that she had not been able to provide for herself. Father's loss was, as in the case of her son—as if she had lost a part of herself.

An interesting feature of this work was the way in which Mrs. Marcus's own sense of humor began to emerge—for only a few moments and only intermittently. The therapist joined in the humor, pointing out that, clearly, Mrs. Marcus had followed in her father's footsteps as far as a sense of humor was concerned and it seemed from what she said that her son had learned it from her. An attempt was made to convey a sense that not only was there something of value in the father but that she had acquired a capacity for humor herself, which in turn could enable her to be entertaining to others. However, following a session, in which Mrs. Marcus had commented that she simply had had a good time, she returned to her former depressed, helpless self and the therapist hypothesized that relinquishing the depressed affect had its dangers.

Slowly Mrs. Marcus began to regain her previous level of functioning. She was able to concentrate better on her secretarial work, resumed some social contacts, purchased a new home, and seemed more involved in living. By the sixth month she began to express an interest in terminating. Her new home was at some distance and she had considerable work to do to get settled. She felt satisfied that she had regained her former level of competence. She reminded the therapist that throughout her life she had been more or less depressed and she did not believe that if she came to treatment for life that she would ever get over the pain of her son's death. The therapist was reminded of Mrs. Marcus's insistence when she began the treatment that she did not want help for basic problems.

At about this time Mrs. Marcus related an experience that suggested why she might need to maintain a depressed affect. She told of one time when she had momentarily felt very happy. She had been promoted on her job with a significant raise in pay and a genuine statement of appreciation and recognition from her employer. Following this, she began to have nightmares involving her mother, who had been moved to a different hospital. Mrs. Marcus had become intensely worried about the quality of care in the new hospital. She began to awaken at six in the morning, a time when she thought her mother would be taken for breakfast. She would imagine her mother feeling her way down the corridors, having difficulty locating the dining room, and would begin to cry as she thought her mother might in such a situation. She noted that this had gone on until she, herself, had a gall bladder attack and was hospitalized. Somehow that seemed to get her mind off her mother. It is possible that her success on the job at one level represented an oedipal-like victory leading to a need for punishment or at another level represented a new level of separation from her mother, which she met by joining her in suffering. However, at that time in the treatment, it seemed to the therapist that Mrs. Marcus felt closest to her mother when she was sad and that the affect associated with happiness represented separation. The therapist interpreted to Mrs. Marcus along these lines. Her response was that in light of the misfortunes that had befallen her since birth, she could not imagine being free of sadness. Her firm insistence of this tended to confirm the hypothesis, made initially, that in some way she needed to maintain an overall depressed affect. It was postulated that the affect served as a tie to the both the lost mother and to some degree the father, as well as constituting an integral aspect of the sense of herself. It seemed possible that a certain level of depression might have served as a defense against a more profound object loss associated with psychosis. Incidentally, we have left aside, but were aware of, the possible involvement of hereditary factors in view of Mrs. Marcus's family history.

Mrs. Marcus's wish to terminate was respected and she was encouraged to return if she so wished. The value of her efforts and her accomplishments were acknowledged. Six months following the conclusion of treatment she wrote to say that she was enjoying her house and several activites, but she continued to cry for her son and was certain that that would never change.

In summary, we might regard Mrs. Marcus as a depressed woman whose affect had become crystallized around the loss of her son but, at the core, this affect was itself an important component in pre-serving a connection with lost objects and in maintaining a precarious sense of self. Failure to have achieved both self and object constancy left her vulnerable to additional depression when faced with the loss of objects that served need-fulfilling and narcissistic purposes and that were not sufficiently differentiated from the self. This short-term treatment helped her to understand, in part, what she had lost in her son and what she experienced as missing in herself that in a sense he had provided when he was alive. An effort was made to relate this to her past life, which failed to provide those factors which would have led to a more solid sense of herself. Focus was placed, at the same time, on what she had received from past objects despite the severe limitations of her early life, and how she had extracted so much from so little. The many adaptive efforts she had made both on her own and her son's behalf were affirmed. Finally, her wishes to hold on to her basic mood, so to speak, were respected. The work appeared to have provided what Mrs. Marcus had sought: a restoration to her for-mer level of adaptation. Whether it contributed to some advancement in her level of self and object constancy is questionable.

SUMMARY

In the normal course of life we encounter a series of tasks the ne-gotiation of which challenges our adaptive capacities. Whether tran-sitions result in personal growth, or lead to some degree of dis-integration, depends on the level of psychic structuralization, and particularly the strength of the ego and the state of self and object constancy that has been achieved. Where an age-appropriate level of development has been reached and the tasks occur at phase-specific times, transitional life tasks may be faced as challenges that mobi-lize the individual's resources and stimulate further growth.

However, when a transitional life task becomes linked with ear-lier unresolved or partially resolved conflicts, or requires capacities not yet achieved, a given task may serve as the precipitant of dis-tress, leading to decompensation as opposed to consolidation.

Transitional tasks may threaten an existing balance between id, ego, and superego, or jeopardize a vulnerable sense of autonomy. More broadly speaking, transitional tasks may, for one reason or another, interfere with the feeling of safety (Sandler, 1960). In such an event feelings of anxiety will be stirred up. Where the transitional task is experienced in some way as bringing about a loss, then depression may ensue.

When the individual has failed to reach the position of on-the-way to object constancy, the negotiation of life tasks will be severely compromised, and the likelihood is that, at new points in the life cycle, the challenges will be experienced as severe crises. There are those other individuals who have probably achieved a significant degree of separation and individuation but who, in the face of certain tasks, regress, or must struggle unusually hard to deal with the current task. They often get through without help, but, in our experience, remain vulnerable. In the absence of progressive development or resolution of a phase specific conflict, consolidation fails to take place. This is somewhat similar to those counterphobic efforts that force us to perform a feared activity, but of course do not ameliorate the underlying concerns. We think of those clients who report severe anxiety at school entrance that they "got over." However, subsequently they manifest separation anxiety at other points and, in retrospect, it would seem they would have been better served by being helped to "work through" their earlier problems as opposed to "getting through."

We think that where helping professionals are sensitive to the significance of self and object constancy in coping with transitional tasks, they can be alert to individuals-at-risk, and provide intervention that may serve prevention. In some instances, only long-term, sustained treatment will help advance development to the point at which an individual may face and deal with the many transitions and tasks of the life cycle. In other cases where development has gone further but vulnerabilities exist, limited support may help an individual to deal not only with the task itself, but to move forward developmentally. As Erikson (1964) has pointed out, each new stage in life is a turning point, and as such, may not only be a period of increased vulnerability but may also constitute a time of heightened potential.

The Promotion of Object Constancy and Self Constancy

The treatment of Mrs. Carter has been selected to illustrate the therapeutic challenge posed by certain borderline patients whose ego modifications reflect both developmental failures and the adaptations they have made in their endeavor to compensate for deficits in the maternal partnering. Treatment efforts are required in such cases that address not only the need for repair of deficits but also for reduction of the compensatory integrations that have come to block further development.

Mrs. Carter, a 32-year-old intelligent, attractive, competent-appearing young woman who functioned well in a responsible job, manifested those features associated with borderline organization. These included an "as if personality"; the use of others for primarily narcissistic purposes; a failure to integrate the "bad" and the "good" self- and object representations into whole self- and object representations; a tendency towards self-object confusion; a profound fear of engulfment as well as fear of separation; instinctual defects; an overreliance on grandiose fantasies; severe narcissistic defects; and the continued employment of the defenses of splitting, denial, idealization, and projective identification. Under the pressure of longings for closeness that threatened merger, she withdrew from intimacy and seemed, at times, to manifest schizoidlike defenses.

Having experienced a parasitic symbiosis, Mrs. Carter had differentiated prematurely and experienced major problems throughout the subphases. From early on, she had turned back to herself for mothering, attempting to serve as her own developmental partner, and increasingly resorted to grandiose fantasies to compensate for the lack of real mothering. This turning away from her mother and back to herself further deprived her of those nutrients that the mother or the father could provide. She had, over time, fashioned for herself a superficial outer personality that was modeled in accord with idealized features of actual persons as well as derived from impressions she had formed of movie and television stars. Her unique efforts were made possible by her excellent inborn endowment, her precociously developed ego capacities, and the fact that, while the maternal partnering was significantly limited, there were some positive aspects that she took advantage of. These and other features will be considered along with a condensed summary of those efforts made to foster reorganization and promote development during Mrs. Carter's twice-a-week treatment, which extended over a period of six years.

Presenting Problems

At the time she sought treatment, Mrs. Carter was experiencing concern about her forthcoming marriage to an older, somewhat demanding man who unlike herself had never been married before. She felt that while she liked him and had much to gain from the marriage economically and socially, she really did not love him and that from her side the relationship involved considerable pretense. Divorced for the past two years, following a previous six year marriage, Mrs. Carter was doubtful of her capacity to achieve a successful marriage. However, she felt her son needed a father, since his biological father had moved to a foreign country and was unlikely to play a role in the child's life. She had engaged in a number of affairs during and following her marriage and now felt it was time to settle down. However, she felt anxious as to whether she could manage the relationship and did not once again want to appear to have failed with a man. She noted that she was primarily interested in attracting men, and once they were won, she tired of them or became disappointed in them. She usually sought out successful married men whose attentions toward her, rather than toward their wives, made her feel valued. She had a sense of "sharing in their glory." She recognized that these actual or fantasied liaisons served as an important source for raising her self-esteem. She added that when she was depressed, which was frequent, she fantasied a new affair to "lift her spirits."

Mrs. Carter was nonorgasmic, finding sex burdensome but necessary in order to achieve the other satisfactions she derived from a man. She did gain a feeling of self-worth from her capacity to impress her lovers with her sensuality. Over time, however, she became tired of pretending. Indeed, she frequently preferred fantasied affairs that she could choreograph to suit her needs more precisely. She had no particular wish, she pointed out, to become orgasmic though she did regard her sexual capacity as indicative of an unwelcome flaw in herself. Mrs. Carter stressed that her previous affairs had all ended amicably and that she continued to feel a deep sense of gratitude to her lovers, as she did to her divorced husband, for their kindness and attentiveness to her.

Gradually, it appeared that Mrs. Carter's deepest concern had to do with a growing feeling of unreality about herself. While formerly proud of her "acting ability," she was beginning to feel as if she was becoming incapable of distinguishing between the "real" her and the "actress." Indeed, she wondered whether there was a "real" her. She was constantly planning how to act in a certain situation with certain people. Then she observed and evaluated herself. She kept losing track of herself and required photographs to afford her a sense of continuity. She could not, at the beginning of treatment, clearly recall many events before she got married, and searched old photograph albums for evidence that she really existed during earlier years.

She experienced herself as a different person depending upon whom she was with. At work, she was competent and efficient; with men she was seeking to attract, she was seductive, witty, and helpless in a "feminine" way. With her mother, she was childlike, unassertive, and "childishly" dependent, asking for mother's help and advice even when she did not require it. Possessed of many social skills, she had frequent, though superficial, social contacts and relatedness. She viewed people as an audience, deriving much from their praise and admiration, but fearful of too much closeness with anyone.

Mrs. Carter had considered treatment several times when she was depressed but felt she would be unable to be open with a therapist. She believed that she would be driven to impress the therapist as she did others. She also thought of it as frightening to consider being alone with a person for the time a treatment session took place. However, she was becoming more desperate and felt she had to do something.

Mrs. Carter was, at the time, residing with her mother. Her father had died of cancer several years before. She had returned home following her divorce, and while she resented mother's intrusiveness, she appreciated her care of her son, Dick.

During the beginning of treatment, Mrs. Carter complained continuously of frustrations and difficulties that she had experienced, both in the past and in the present, in her relationships with the important persons in her life. However, she denied that she was actually angry with these people, insisting that she was simply hurt. To be angry appeared to be at variance with her preferred view of herself as a warm, positive woman who was forced to endure unkindness from others. When she began slowly to acknowledge a certain amount of anger, she became fearful of some vague retribution. In about the second year of treatment, she confided that actually she was aware of a continuous state of anger. As she expressed it, she could feel herself angry as she awoke and would wonder who she would find during the day to direct it toward. She did not understand why, but she felt she needed to feel angry. It served purposes that we began to discover as the treatment progressed.

FAMILY HISTORY

Mrs. Carter was the only child of middle-class, parents. Her now deceased father had been a traveling salesman, frequently absent from home. She deeply resented his having played so minor a role in her life and spoke of him with disdain for a long time in the treatment—on those rare occasions when she mentioned him at all. She saw her mother, on the other hand, as making her the center of her life. Mother waited on her "hand and foot," feeding her until she went to kindergarten, driving her back and forth to classes until Mrs. Carter went to college and also sleeping with her, during father's trips, until she was in college.

Mother

She viewed her mother as a strong, giving, caring, stoical, reliable person. To the rest of the world, mother also appeared a mild-mannered, self-effacing, patient, and religious woman. However, Mrs. Carter saw another side of her mother, that is, a woman who was capable of wild rages, impatient, screaming, and constantly critical. Mother had, when she was about 3 or 4, hit her with a fireplace poker, which had left a scar on her arm. Mother was also recalled as forcing food on her, administering painful enemas, and as withdrawing into a cold, hostile silence, or closing herself in her bedroom when she was incensed with Mrs. Carter. At first, she could not recall what she did that would have provoked her mother, except to eat slowly.

Mrs. Carter felt that as long as she complied with her mother's wishes and stayed close to her, they had gotten along well. Mother was giving and attentive. They shared secrets together and "we won't tell Daddy" was a well-recalled phrase. The secrets consisted of purchases that they had made while the father was away, or their regular watching of soap operas on television, which father considered a waste of time.

Mrs. Carter viewed her mother at times as having prevented any relationship between herself and her father, wanting Mrs. Carter "all to herself." On the other hand, she felt that if her father had loved her, he would have assumed a role in her life.

Mrs. Carter expressed great perplexity regarding her parents' relationship with one another. Even though it appeared to her that mother preferred her to her father, when he was home she was sent to bed early and the parents dined together, even through her high school years. She had been shocked, too, to see how her mother had mourned her father's death. She noted that she herself had experienced little pain at the time. What had she lost?

Childhood

She recalled herself as a withdrawn, outwardly compliant child who, for the most part, rebelled and expressed anger toward her mother in secret ways. She used to wait to go to the bathroom until the last moment in the belief that this annoyed her mother, who was so preoccupied with her toileting. She also bit her nails and twirled her hair. Another expression of her anger and wish to thwart her mother was her sullen behavior in front of mother's friends. She was well aware that her mother was proud of her and wanted to show her off, but Mrs. Carter refused to be pleasant. Mother's friends were always urging her to smile, and she was silently hopeful that they would get an impression of how unhappy she was. She also felt that, in a way, her somber expression was similar to the "gloomy" faces she associated with her parents during her early years. As she grew older, she actively sought to smile in order to be different from mother.

Her clearest memories centered around eating. Mother had fed her until she was 6. This seemed to have something to do with mother's concern about her nutrition but, most importantly, Mrs.

Carter viewed it as evidence of mother's intolerance for her own rhythm of eating. Mother sought to hasten the feeding by playing games in which she would distract her and then "pop" the food into her mouth.

Provided with an abundance of clothes and toys, it was her feeling nonetheless that mother did not take her preferences into account. She hated her clothing, and recalled throwing her school lunches away.

Fantasy Life

As the treatment progressed, Mrs. Carter related many fantasies that occupied her thoughts as she was growing up. She had family romance fantasies that were distinguished by the sumptuous feasts her lost, rich, giving, famous, smiling, indulgent parents would provide for her, as well as clothes that would suit her well. She also had long, involved fantasies of becoming famous and being admired and adored by other famous personages. When she was angry, her fantasies turned toward revenge and she would imagine the offending parent dead and she, the bereaved child, showered with pity by all those she knew. An alternative to this was the fantasy of her own death, which would evoke guilt and repentance on the part of her parents, as well as revealing, to the church congregants, how "sinful" her parents actually were in their ill-treatment of her. Only one joyful family memory was recalled at the start of treatment, of herself as a little girl donning her mother's hats and making her ordinarily sober parents laugh. She repeated this activity frequently and it was a source of family pleasure.

Schooling

A good student, she was apparently acknowledged by her teachers, and as she grew older, she became involved in certain school activities in which she achieved success and recognition. At school, she felt free and recalled enjoying herself. She was described by those who knew her as talkative and outgoing. She could imagine herself being like that but could not recall the feeling of herself as that kind of person.

Marriage

Mrs. Carter and her first husband went together for about three years prior to their marriage. In retrospect, she felt she had valued the sexual aspects of their relationship above anything else. It seemed to her that for the first time she was doing something that her mother did not know about and would not approve of. They married when she graduated from a local college. She felt that her major reason for marrying was that it afforded her the chance to go off on her own and "escape" mother's control.

Mrs. Carter considered that she and her husband were more like friends than intimate marital partners. They lived very separate lives except for sharing in certain social activites. She appreciated, however, his willingness to engage in long periods of sexual foreplay, and while she did not achieve orgasm, she had been "grateful" for the time and effort he expended to give her pleasure. She also appreciated his fathering "her" child. Furthermore, she had never felt compelled to impress him. She had already felt superior to him by virtue of her education and intelligence. Thus, she could be more herself. On the other hand, his limited sophistication and his menial occupation prevented her from gaining any measure of importance through their relationship.

Motherhood

She had fantasied having a baby since she was a little girl. She would have something of "her own" and furthermore demonstrate that she could be a better mother than her mother had been. She appeared to have formed her maternal ideal on the basis of a total disidentification with her mother. She would allow her children a full measure of freedom and would love and accept them for what they were. She translated this into reality and her extreme permissiveness with her son had led to his having serious difficulties in impulse control. The nursery school teacher had expressed concern about Dick, which troubled Mrs. Carter, who regarded the school as trying to "crush his spirit." She was proud of his strong will and assertive capacities, seeing them as an evidence of his "manliness." Mrs. Carter was pleased that he "could still" suck his thumb when he was 4. It proved that she was not rigid, like her mother.

The False Biography

The history was developed over the course of this lengthy treatment. Initially, Mrs. Carter had great difficulty recalling her early life but, in time, many gaps were filled in. Also, in time, we came to appreciate the extent to which the past had become distorted, primarily as a result of her overreliance on those defenses that conflict with reality testing, namely denial, splitting, projective identification, and primitive idealization and devaluation. We also considered that, during the early period of development, the integrative function of the ego might well have been impaired by the difficulty of fusing such unusually contradictory images as her mother presented, because the balance seemed on the side of frustration and aggression. It was, as has been pointed out, the prevalence of libidinal feelings toward the mother that favored fusion of the object and of the drives (Spitz, 1965). Moreover, her premature, defensive disengagement from mother and her turn toward herself limited her object related experiences. Preoccupied with herself, she appeared to have frequently missed what was occurring about her. In addition, her excessive employment of denial, splitting, and projective identification resulted in distortion of the actual objects. Immersed in fantasy, she had come to prefer the objects in her mind. Real persons were used for need gratification or for purposes of imitation.

An example of how the object representations were subject to distortion may be illustrative here. While the picture of Mrs. Carter's mother as a controlling and intrusive person seemed confirmed over time, there were moments when the facts presented about the mother tended to suggest the exaggerated quality of Mrs. Carter's representations. Also, there were positive aspects of mother that either were denied or disavowed by Mrs. Carter when they emerged in her productions. At one point in the treatment, Mrs. Carter, when referring to her mother's domination, raised a question about her own acquiescence in this matter. Slowly, a picture unfolded in which she revealed that she had felt it "beneath" her to have to appeal to mother for anything she wanted. She felt it was her due, and to ask or fight for anything negated its worth.

In this connection, she remembered herself as a little girl, hidden behind the bannisters in the upstairs hall, watching her parents as they ate their dinner together. She would tiptoe back to bed and run the water in the bathroom so they would not realize she had been watching them. When she spoke of this, early in the treatment, it had been within the context of how frightened she had been of being scolded. The same incident was later examined from the perspective of her feelings at having been "cast away" by mother when father was home. She had then expressed rage, which led to some appreciation of the way in which the oedipal arrangement had been experienced by her as a deep blow to her self-esteem. However, when this came up much later, Mrs. Carter indicated that another reason for hiding from her parents when she was watching was that she had not wanted them to know she was interested in them. If they did not invite her to the table, she would not give them the satisfaction of thinking that she wanted to join them. She would "abandon" them and "demean" them as a form of revenge; this was, incidentally, reflected in contemporary social relationships. She did not want people to feel they really mattered to her for it would give them an advantage and would also make her more vulnerable to their disinterest. She stressed too, that even if her parents had noted her presence and asked her to join them, she would have been troubled. It would have been demeaning because it would have meant they felt sorry for her, rather than they recognized that she deserved to be there.

Finally, we draw brief attention to the distorted picture of Mrs. Carter's father. He certainly did not play the requisite role as catalyst of separation–individuation and failed his daughter, developmentally, in many ways. However, he was, in actuality, not the disinterested, totally uninvolved parent that was recalled by Mrs. Carter. He was, we learned, the father who sat up all night with her when she was ill, the man who built her a much treasured doll house, and the man who had written her humorous poems to keep her abreast of his travel experiences. Sometime during the treatment, she said that her mother reminded her that it was her father who had come home from work to take her to the hospital following a serious accident, and had remained at her bedside until she was out of danger. She could not recall this and had difficulty, at first, believing it. She was convinced that it was her mother who had taken care of her. However, in time, she did begin to recall the warm feelings associated with her father taking her shopping or bringing her gifts from his many trips. Since we shall not have the opportunity to detail the therapeutic work around the father, we would like, at least, to note that the retrieval of these and several other more positive memories, much later in treatment, did facilitate a revision of the paternal object representations, some enhancement of them, and the consolidation of a more positive representation of father. This fostered a more affirmative view of herself as a beloved daughter, contributed, in some measure, to a more positive feeling toward men in general, and led to a belated, though muted, mourning of his death.

METAPSYCHOLOGICAL ASSESSMENT

Before elaborating on Mrs. Carter's development through the separation individuation sequence we offer a highly abbreviated assessment, along some of the lines, proposed by A. Freud (A. Freud, Nagera, & W. E. Freud, 1965).

Assessment of Drive and Ego-Superego Positions

Mrs. Carter appeared to have moved along the psychosexual maturational sequence towards the oedipus without, however, moving firmly from phase to phase. Oral, anal, and phallic trends appeared condensed. The impact of early oral experiences shadowed each phase. Genital sexual behavior, for example, was viewed primarily in oral terms. Whatever enjoyment she achieved in sexual experiences derived from sucking and being sucked. When angry at her partner, as she often was, she had a strong urge to bite him. At times, intercourse appeared to assume an anal significance, and yet was described in oral terminology. During sex she felt as if food was being forced upon her by an intrusive partner who determined the timing and amount of the activity. Sexual arousal was feared to the degree that it reminded her of how she could be lulled by her mother's story telling while being fed. The penis represented food being "shoved" into her mouth at such times. Her wish to be competent and impress others, a possible derivative of phallic narcissism, took the form of striving to impress her partner with the speed and fervor of her orgasm, reminiscent of efforts to gain praise for eating quickly as a child. Oedipal-like material that emerged in the course of the treatment suggested a search for the satisfaction of predominantly preoedipal wishes through the oedipal arrangement, a familiar feature of borderline development as explicated in Chapter 5.

Narcissistic cathexis of the self was maintained primarily through fantasy, through sharing temporarily in the importance of others, and through the acquisition of their acknowledgement and approval.

Object relationships were of a need-gratifying or narcissistic type. Others were valued to the degree that they could help maintain her self-esteem by providing her with supplies that she felt she either required or was entitled to.

Mrs. Carter's aggressive drive was directed towards the object world in the service of maintaining distance or powering her angry affects. Aggression was also directed towards her body physically by nail biting, and onto her self through her strong reaction formations.

Her innate capacities were intact and in some areas she appeared to have superior endowment. However, certain ego functions such as memory, synthesis, and reality testing could either be temporarily impaired under the impact of strong libidinal or aggressive strivings or temporarily relinquished in the service of defense or adaptation. For example, she knew that she could not become a successful performer without training, but frequently thought and behaved as if she could. Reality testing could be reinstated by a question such as "Do you really feel you could be an excellent ballet dancer without training, practice, and experience?" Her ego functioning was further limited by certain inhibitions. Though she had learned to play the piano as a child, she had at about the age of 13 refused to touch the keyboard. In part this was explained by her as her way of depriving her mother of pleasure. Subsequently, however, we came to appreciate that this represented an inhibition to avoid anxiety related to sexual implications attached to piano playing.

Danger was primarily experienced as coming from the outside world. She feared people being angry at her, intruding upon her, controlling her, using her, abandoning her, or withdrawing their offerings from her. Predominant were fears of separation, loss of love, and engulfment.

Mrs. Carter employed a range of defenses including denial, projection, projective identification, splitting, reaction formation, rationalization, and, to some degree, repression. Her withdrawl into herself, her employment of fantasy, and her use of her anger were additional means of defense. Her defensive activity frequently failed to provide her with a feeling of safety (Sandler, 1960) and one felt her strained effort to keep anxiety under control.

If we regard the superego as the heir to the oedipus and the final structure to be formed, it would not be accurate to talk of superego in a woman with a less than structured personality. She seemed to have achieved what Jacobson (1964) has delineated as the first stage in superego development: the incorporation of values around cleanliness with the formation of pregenital reaction formations. Fastidious in appearance, meticulous in her housekeeping, and preoccupied with hiding any evidence of her bowel and bladder functioning, she was constantly defending against instinctual impulses. She ran the shower each time she urinated, lest someone hear the sounds. A wet toothbrush left on the sink, her husband's burping, or the sound of someone urinating filled her with disgust. She took elablorate pains to avoid exposing herself to the sounds of others and to prevent anyone from being aware of her bodily activities. It should be noted that this behavior was clearly overdetermined. Her concern about sounds was ultimately traced back to primal scene phenomena. Furthermore, this had all somehow become incorporated into her feelings of entitlement.

Disgust rather than guilt was her predominant affect and someone burping in her company was more offensive than someone cheating on their income tax. Her value system centered around control, strength, and cleanliness (Blanck & Blanck, 1974, p. 69).

Mrs. Carter did have an ideal regarding how she and others should behave, but this in no way guided or restrained her behavior. She was uncomfortable about her lying, her extramarital affairs, and certain illegal transactions she had been involved in. However, she rationalized that people had to "cheat a little or tell small lies" in "today's world."

Assessment of Conflicts

At the start of treatment Mrs. Carter's conflicts appeared primarily in the interpersonal realm. Struggles were viewed as between herself and others. This was in keeping with a level of development in which she lived more in the immediacy of the moment, at the social exchange level, and in her body, as opposed to living in the mind (Lichtenberg, 1975). Eventually, internal conflicts became clearer. Intrasystemic conflicts in the id were manifest between activity and passivity, feminity and masculinity, and between the two drives. Conflicts within the nascent superego evolved around conflicting identifications. On one hand she sought to identify with her representations of powerful parents who boasted of "getting away with things," and on the other hand she sought to emulate a kindly, much admired childhood neighbor who seemed to her to stand for "honesty, love, and respect." The ego was weakened immeasurably by conflict between the function of reality testing and those dedfenses, such as denial, which distort reality.

Intersystemic conflict has been more difficult to identify. The inhibition of the piano playing suggests a conflict between id and ego or the superego forerunners. Clearly there was conflict between her aggressive id wishes and the demands of reality. On the whole, however, intrasystemic conflict, that is, conflict within the structures, predominated. This accords with the findings of Blanck and Blanck (1974, p. 143) that in nonneurotic or borderline clients conflict is more likely to be intrasystemic.

Symbiosis

We shall now examine, in line with our purposes, our understanding of Mrs. Carter's progression through symbiosis and the subphases of separation–individuation.

The parasitic symbiosis between Mrs. Carter and her mother has already been described. While seeking intense closeness, her mother appeared unable to respond to Mrs. Carter's own unique needs. This was manifest very early in life by the mother's lack of attunement around feeding. While the mother in later life described how she had followed her pediatrician's advice with regard to timing and quantity of intake, evidence suggests that this lack of attunement extended to other child care areas and was characteristic of the mothering experience.

Out of this parasitic symbiosis in which, incidentally, there was closeness in terms of the mother's needs but an insufficient attunement to the baby's needs, Mrs. Carter failed to experience the sense of well-being that is ordinarily associated when a better fit between mother and infant prevails. This incompatability between mother and infant appeared to have led to premature awareness of the distinction between self and object. Furthermore, the intrusive, smothering quality of the symbiosis fostered a defensive effort to escape. A deficiency in confident expectation and an impairment in narcissism were the outcome of this unfortunate set of circumstances.

The less than optimal symbiosis also left Mrs. Carter deficient in several aspects of ego development. She remained under the pressure of missed symbiotic needs though she ultimately developed strong defenses against them. Nonetheless, to some degree the wishes persisted as evidenced by her need to be understood without words. The mother's failure to soothe and calm and to respond more appropriately to her signals of distress, led to an inability, on her part, to achieve both the capacity for self-soothing and the capacity to utilize anxiety as a signal. For a long time, she presented a panic-like quality in the sessions that she dealt with by speaking rapidly.

Rejection, slight, disappointment, or failure overwhelmed her and she would respond with nausea. It should be noted that Mrs. Carter had not employed anything that resembled a transitional object. Since the transitional object depends upon the transfer of soothing originally derived from a satisfying early merger, this failure to create a transitional object was understandable (Tolpin, 1972). The fantasies that did provide a means of narcissistic enhancement and a discharge of narcissistic rage are not regarded as transitional phenomena. These, and prolonged thumbsucking, represent, in some sense, autoerotic experiences that did foster a degree of independence from her mother. However, as Tolpin has indicated, it is the addition of the maternal functions to autoerotism that furthers the infant's capacity for sustained self-soothing (1972).

We also considered that the excessive frustration of the first year led to a predominance of aggressive drive energies over libidinal drive energies. This arrangement impeded the fusion of the good, gratifying mother and the bad, frustrating mother, with concomitant impairment of the fusion of the drives (Spitz, 1937). These, and other failures, cast a shadow on subsequent subphase development, and led to Mrs. Carter's prolonged tie to the "mother in the flesh" for need-gratification and to an accompanying fear of separation, lest either she or mother be destroyed.

Differentiation

Mrs. Carter's premature differentiation led, as we have noted, to precocious ego development, efforts to provide mothering for herself, and to the development of a "false self." It was clear that her efforts were propelled by considerable aggression. From early on, she sought to disidentify with mother, which impeded the separation process to the degree that she failed to achieve those internalizations that maintain connections. Furthermore, the insufficiency of attunement at symbiosis prevented the development of sufficient confident expectation, which ordinarily cushions the turns away from mother. We would hypothesize that these phenomena might account for the realtive lack of curiosity and pleasure that Mrs. Carter manifested in regard to the wider world as well as her limited interest in other people as persons in their own right. The turn to the other-than-mother world, instead of leading to genuine social relationships, had led to a use of others primarily as objects from whom she could learn how to function and to gain what she felt she needed.

We finally would like to draw attention to the relationship between Mrs. Carter's defensive premature differentiation and her propensity towards depression. Despite the difficulties inherent in a parasitic symbiosis, there must be the provision of certain satisfactions by the mother. Mother's and infant's needs must, at times, coincide. While attunement is less than optimum, there must be a certain degree of it. Thus, Mrs. Carter in freeing herself from the "bad" experiences inevitably lost whatever was "good."

Practicing Phase

Mrs. Carter achieved the ordinary developmental milestones early and began walking at eleven months, much to her mother's pride. Mrs. Carter considered that her mother "claimed" her achievements and, thus, she experienced them as belonging to mother. She felt that mother encouraged the activities she wanted her to pursue and was troubled if Mrs. Carter wished to do certain things mother would prefer doing for her. For example, if Mrs. Carter wanted to do her own sewing, mother would be hurt.

We considered that some of her current behavior might suggest the quality of the practicing experiences. There was a conspicuous absence of joy in her activities. Her achievements were significant only to the degree that they proved she was capable and could secure admiration from others, or could demonstrate greater competency than mother. If she failed at an activity she became physically nauseated and emotionally despondent. Practicing activities failed to contribute to that sound sense of secondary narcissism that is associated with the feelings of joy and efficacy in the functioning of that phase.

Rapprochement

Mrs. Carter entered the rapprochement phase heavily burdened by earlier deficits, particularly an excessive degree of aggressive drive energy or rage. Severe temper tantrums during this period suggested a rapprochement crisis beyond the norm, and mother's response, which took the form of retaliation or withdrawal, failed to help modulate Mrs. Carter's aggression or to contribute to the gradual deflation of omnipotence. Furthermore, the object world remained split due to the failure in the integration of good and bad self-representations and good and bad object representations.

There were indications that Mrs. Carter had experienced heightened longings for mother during this subphase. She recalled herself sitting outside the bathroom door while mother bathed, and crying when it seemed that mother was there too long. Interstingly enough, she recalled, in a subsequent session, how disgusted she had been, as a child, to discover that mother had frequently forgotten to flush the toilet. She felt that it was thoughtless of mother to confront her with her toilet products and was angry in the session. The worker considered that this devaluation might represent a defense against the libidnal wishes that had been stirred up with the memory of wanting to get closer to mother—the mother "behind the door."

Thus, Mrs. Carter remained fixated at a borderline level of organization, having failed to move beyond the rapprochement subphase.

INITIAL PHASE OF TREATMENT

For at least the first year of treatment, each session consisted of precise accounts of the myriad problems she had with the important figures in her life—husband, mother, child, employer. She had married Mr. Carter after the first eight months of treatment. There were many concerns with him. She began to discover faults, particularly habits that bothered her. He burped after meals and she saw this as an insult to her. Along with anger came renewed fantasies of affairs and thoughts and wishes regarding the death of others or her own death. She was insistent that she would not have another affair, and though she came close, she did not actually act out in this way during the six years of treatment.

The major focus of her complaints remained her mother. She was fearful of not responding to mother's suggestions, criticism, or desire to give her things for fear mother would retailiate by withdrawing. An understanding of her powerful need for mother and her fear of the loss of her need-gratification was developed. Mother phoned daily, advising on the weather, the current choice of cheapest foods, and so on. Sometimes it seemed she was in the sessions. Mrs. Carter complained about the intrusion but recognized her need for her mother. Finally, she pointed out that she felt she would never be free until her mother died. Immediately upon saying this, she became anxious lest talking of such things would kill mother. She sought reassurance from the worker that mother would be all right. At other times, she would worry about the impression she was making on the therapist with her "nasty" wishes.

Mrs. Carter's usual stance was stiff and rigid. It was as if she was trying to hold back, or hold herself together. It was apparent, later on, that she was frightened, and the attempt was to keep her fear down by controlling her whole body. There were, however, other times when she became the consummate actress. She could become very lively as she repeated what she had said or done, or a frightened little girl who was intimidated by mother or husband. Then, there was the role of the defiant child who stuck out her tongue behind her mother's back, or the remorseful wife and mother who wept when talking about the hardship her actions had imposed upon her husband and son.

Therapist-Client Relationship

During this initial phase, the therapist appeared to be someone Mrs. Carter found "useful." She received her complaints, enabled her to consider alternative ways of viewing experiences, provided a limited amount of information such as where she might secure counseling for her son, and was "there" without judgment or demands.

Interventions

The interventions that were offered in response to her material focused on her fears, her disappointments in herself and others and their profound effect upon her, as well as her need for mother and her fearful efforts to disengage from her. When she expressed apprehension that mother would be angry at what she was saying about her in a session, the therapist inquiried as to how mother would know. This led, over time, to an understanding of how she experienced mother as capable of reading her mind. This was traced back to their close and prolonged tie. Her inability to say "no" was examined and was understood, partly, in terms of the threat that her aggression and anger posed for her. She was unable to use her aggression in the service of separation, for it was so closely connected to her destructive wishes and fantasies. Later, it became evident that her inability to say "no" was also related to her feeling of "entitlement," to the conviction that she ought not to have to assert herself.

When she complained that her husband's carelessness about his personal habits, particularly his burping, was an insult to her, question was raised as to whether or not there might be another explanation. She finally considered that, perhaps, he was having abdominal discomfort. At that time her anger was understood as reflecting her overall feeling that people were either acting for her or against her; they were not people in their own right. In time, she began to make a conscious effort to consider alternative explanations for people's behavior, and found herself less angry or less hurt. She was surprised to consider that, perhaps when her mother was quiet, it might be because she was fatigued, ill, or depressed.

Interpretation of Defense

Mrs. Carter frequently anticipated what she expected the therapist to say in relation to certain events. It became clear that this represented in part her symbiotic mode of relating and in part an effort to shut the therapist out. She often acted as if she were playing both the therapist's role and her own role in a session, just as she did in reality. In other words, the exchanges went on within herself and sometimes failed to take into account the interpersonal reality.

Defenses were also interpreted. It was difficult to ascertain whether her propensity for seeing a person as wonderful one day, and the next day wanting to run away from the individual because of her disappointment, was a sign of developmental failure to fuse the object, or whether it represented an active defense to ward off an instinctual impulse. Initially, an attempt was made to promote fusion of the good and bad object representations by reminding her that the husband whom she had admired on Thursday was the same one whom she was wishing dead, on Friday, for burping. Later, when similar behavior appeared to be more clearly defensive, it was interpreted accordingly.

Increased reality testing was promoted when Mrs. Carter became better able to see that her profound fears of abandonment were partly the result of her tendency toward projective identification. When she was angry she frequently projected the anger onto her husband. Then, knowing that when angry her own first thought was to run away from him, she presumed he would be wishing to run away from her. The final result was, of course, to increase her anxiety. We were also able to trace the forerunners of this process back to mother's withdrawing from her when she was angry, as well as

Mrs. Carter's own early efforts to shut mother out. Here she introduced memories of how, when mother would speak to her, she would "shut her ears" at times and try to think her "own" thoughts.

MIDDLE PHASE OF TREATMENT

Therapist-Client Relationship

Gradually, it appeared that Mrs. Carter began to regard the therapist as someone who was on "her side." When confronted with an unreasonable demand made upon her by her husband, she would think of the therapist and gain the strength to say "no." With the discovery that no great harm befell her or her husband or their relationship, she became more courageous. When she finally refused an unwanted gift from her mother, a matter upon which she had ruminated for weeks, she was surprised that her mother "took it so well." For the first time, she wondered whether mother was really as needy of Mrs. Carter's needing her as she had thought.

Thus, the therapist seemed to become the "good" object and mother usually the "bad" object, with husband, more often than not in the early years, being "bad." To her, the therapist was a need-gratifier who did not intrude, offered questions, and encouraged her to think and do what she wanted when it did not hurt others.

A shift occurred when Mrs. Carter saw the therapist with a recently purchased secondhand car. She was thoroughly disappointed. She could not believe the therapist could not afford a new car. When the therapist inquired as to what bothered her about the car, Mrs. Carter became enraged. Was she going to have to teach the therapist what the consumer problems were with a secondhand car? While it became apparent that she felt demeaned by associating with a therapist who drove a second-class car, the degree to which she resented the feeling that, perhaps, the therapist was going to want advice from her was significant. Actually, it was the first time she seemed to notice the therapist as anyone but the person sitting across from her. One could speculate that the car also represented a devalued woman without a phallus, or that she had the need to devalue the therapist as a defense. However, the therapist picked up where the affect seemed strongest, and that seemed to be in relation to her anger that the therapist might want something from her.

This led, in time, to her informing the therapist that she did not want to know anything about her. She thought of the therapist as someone whom she could always count on. In fact, sometimes she comforted herself that if all went badly she could ask the therapist to intervene, on her behalf, with her husband or mother. She recognized this as a wish she had had as a little girl with regard to her father. She would pretend that he would protect her from mother. She did not expect to actually ask or to get this from the therapist, but it was a comforting thought. However, she did not want the therapist to come alive as a person. When she phoned, she preferred getting the answering machine to speaking with the therapist personally. Indeed, she sometimes thought of the therapist as a recording machine who simply registered what she had said. This was understood, at first, as representing an effort to keep the therapist from assuming any further significance for her, which would threaten her with control by the worker. In addition, she did not want to get close because she felt the therapist would use her for her personal needs. Distance also preserved the therapist as "good." She did not need to risk findng out anything she disliked.

Therapeutic Gains

As time went on, Mrs. Carter made a number of developmental gains. Most important to her was a growing sense of reality about herself, with some diminution of her need for photographs. As she recalled more from the past, there were fewer gaps in memory, and she developed an increased sense of continuity. As she increased her direct verbal communications, relying less upon being understood without words, her interpersonal relationships improved. Greater distinction between thought and deed tended to quiet her fears of the magical power of thought. She was able to experience her son as a more separate individual and, consequently, to perceive that he needed limitation and guidance. She was particularly gratified with his improvement, and, over time, gained a greater sense of competence as a mother.

In about the third year of treatment, she began to express some discomfort about her sexual difficulties. As her relationship with her husband improved, she was becoming uncomfortable about her "acting" during the sexual experience. She began to feel that she was deceiving him and that this prevented them from having a more gratifying relationship.

Mrs. Carter was, always fearful of acknowledging gains lest the therapist regard them as a sign that the treatment should be brought to an end. She anticipated that the therapist would wish to get the treatment over as soon as possible.

LATER PHASE OF TREATMENT

In about the fourth year, the treatment took another turn. Mrs. Carter began to express dissatisfaction that she had to make such an effort to improve things. It was true that if she told her husband that she preferred the movies to staying home and watching television, he was glad to take her and they had a good time. However, she felt that he ought to know by now what she liked and that she should not have to make such an effort to achieve what she wished. No longer compelled to achieve a measure of need-gratification through the symbiotic mode, her feelings of entitlement began to predominate. Once she informed her husband of her preferences, it was his obligation to bear them in mind. This seemed to be in the service of maintaining her sense of omnipotence. The therapist responded by acknowledging that it would have been good had she had her needs met more responsively when she was a little girl. However, even children have to make an effort to inform people of what they desire and have to strive actively to have their needs fulfilled. We could begin to see now how hard it had been for her to make the necessary efforts, for to become active on her own behalf conflicted with the feeling that she should achieve what she desired simply because she deserved to.

At this time, she expressed, in far greater detail, her fantasies about being a movie star, famous politician and so on. She imagined what it would feel like to be glamorous, how she would behave, and how others would see her. She noted that she wanted to achieve the success through fantasy and without effort. While this accorded with her wish for omnipotence, it also came to be understood as indicative of the fear that if she were to try to realize these wishes by effort, she would discover her lack of competence and ability.

This awareness brought Mrs. Carter and the therapist to a realization of the profound feelings of inadequacy that lay at the core of her being. While on one hand she had employed the notion of mother's preoccupation with her to sustain a sense of importance, on the other hand there also lay behind this a feeling that mother had been so protective and involved because of the recognition that there was something wrong with Mrs. Carter—some profound deficits in her. Maybe she was a disappointment from the beginning and somehow she had felt mother's displeasure from early on. She had often wondered if her mother might have preferred a son. As one might imagine, this led into her phallic concerns, her feelings of inadequacy, and her envy of men who have what they want simply by being men. The recognition of the anatomical differences had been, as we came to appreciate, experienced as another traumatic blow to a woman already deficient in the narcissistic realm. Indeed, she had protected herself against this recognition by denying the differences. Now, it became possible to understand why she failed to see anything inappropriate in bathing with her then 5-year-old son. She had asked, when this came up in the past, "What is the difference?" While attempts had been made earlier to deal with the denial implicit in this, it had no meaning until we began to gain a fuller appreciation of the depth of her feelings of inadequacy.

ENDING PHASE OF TREATMENT

Worker-Client Relationship

Except for the anger attendant to the car incident, Mrs. Carter had managed to maintain a positive therapist-client relationship by distancing at first. Later, when she began to have more feeling about the therapist, she used such defenses as denial and overidealization. Thus, there was little opportunity within the therapeutic encounter to deal with her anger, and particularly with her inability to integrate the good and bad aspects of the object, for it was clear that she made every effort to maintain the therapist as a "good object." However, this finally changed when the therapist wanted to raise the fee in the latter part of the fourth year of treatment. Mrs. Carter's financial circumstances had clearly improved and it no longer was appropriate to continue her on the reduced fee at which she began treatment. She was incensed, considering the therapist selfish and uncaring. She had fantasies of getting worse and requiring hospitalization. Not only would the therapist experience regret over having treated her so badly, but everyone would then be aware of the therapist's lack of sincere concern for her. This was recognized as not only real anger in the current situation, but a revival of her lifetime rage at mother, which she was dealing with in a familiar way. While the therapist could appreciate her anger, she remained firm about the fee. In time, Mrs. Carter became calmer and the material could be dealt with more interpretively. She recognized that she was responding to the raise in fee as a direct assault on her feelings of entitlement and as a replication of a failure to meet her need to be taken care of. Her efforts to coerce the therapist into relating to her as a needy, dependent child were in the interest of securing a sense of closeness by way of need-gratification. However, she further noted that if the therapist had acquiesced, she would have had her feelings confirmed that she was, indeed, helpless and inadequate. Moreover, the therapist's acquiescence would have been reminiscent of her mother's response to her childhood temper tantrums. It would have made her feel that the therapist was also weak and ineffectual, which would have been frightening. The therapist's capacity to tolerate her anger, which persisted over several weeks, without retaliating or withdrawing, appeared to be reassuring and, in some way, diminished the unreal feelings of power and destruction that she had experienced as related to her rage.

When the fee increase went into effect, some two months later, there was a decided shift. Mrs. Carter noted that somehow she felt more "grown up." There was a feeling of achievement. She felt reassured that she could not rob people of their strength as she thought she had done in the past when mother, who seemed so strong, became overwhelmed by her temper outbursts. Attendant to this was a recognition that she had distorted the picture of mother, creating of her a powerful person so as to defend against the fear that mother was really weak. She was unable to integrate a picture of a crying mother with one who could still protect and take care of her. She was then reminded of her earlier unvoiced rage at the therapist when the worker had a cold. She had wondered how someone who could get sick could help anyone as vulnerable as she. She had not mentioned these feelings, both out of a concern that she was bad for being so uncaring, and because she had made every effort to deny that the worker was really ill. She recalled how frightened she had been at anything that would anger her about the worker, which generally had to do with the worker seeming to be deficient in some way.

This led to further consideration of both her fears and her rage. We came to appreciate that she used her anger for a variety of purposes. She felt stronger and more capable of coping when angry. Her anger also preserved her distance from others. When sometime later she noted that anger made her feel more like a man, we came to appreciate that, in some ways, it had come to represent a phallus.

A dream presented in the fifth year of treatment, following the above, helped us to get in touch with the profound fear of merger against which Mrs. Carter had for so long defended. The dream occurred following her acknowledgment of certain gains she had made in the treatment, and her expression of appreciation for the therapist's efforts. One of the gains she described was the fact that she occasionally achieved orgasm. It should be noted that she had had an orgasm, which she had been initially pleased about, during the third year of work. However, very shortly afterwards, she had indicated concern lest the therapist feel that it was the result of the treatment, and claim credit for her gain. She had, at that time, indicated that she was not sure she would want to have another one. This was the last time that her sexual experiences had been discussed in any detail in the treatment.

Fear of Engulfment. In the dream, Mrs. Carter had been having her portrait painted. She had been aware of concern as to how it would come out and pointed out that she had been deliberately ingratiating toward the artist in the hope that he would paint a favorable picture of her. He painted a serious, unsmiling woman who looked older than the way Mrs. Carter viewed herself, or wanted to view herself. She was unhappy with the completed portrait, but felt better when her friends reassured her that it was not an accurate resemblance.

Her first association was that she knew why she preferred photographs to looking at herself in the mirror—she always looked better in pictures. She then noted that there was something about appearing old that bothered her and she was much reassured when people told her that she looked young and had youthful interests. She then paused and asked herself whether perhaps her fear of looking older had something to do with her mother. In actuality, she is taller and thinner. However, she has had a fear of looking like her—looking like her would mean being like her. She thinks she could easily become like her mother, that is, "bossy and irritable." She sees a smiling person as being different from mother. She has worked hard on developing a smile. Smiling represents youth and lightheartedness, as opposed to being nonsmiling, old, and weighted down by responsibility—that means being mother.

Actually, she thought if you blindfolded someone who knew both herself and her mother, he or she might not be able to tell the difference. Despite all her efforts, she really is selfish and would, if she allowed herself, have temper tantrums and seek to dominate, just like mother. She has come to realize why she married a domineering man—he keeps those qualities in check in her.

As she worked on this dream in the session, she became apprehensive and went on to say that her greatest fear has been that she would be like her mother. If she did, she would "disappear" and become mother, or mother would become her. She added that somtimes her handwriting reminds her of her mother's. It looks scribbled, particularly if she is fatigued. She gets a shock and has the feeling that her mother has been in the room and written on the page. It is almost as if mother is inside her doing the writing. She expressed the idea that if she resembled her mother, she would feel as if she were her. She added that she gains reassurance from photographs because, in those, she looks very different from her mother. However, she does function like her mother in a good way, that is, when she is efficient—but she gets frightened then, as if she is a "clone" of her mother. "How horrible," she added, "if there were two of us. Think of all the damage the two of us could do!" This dream captured not only the fear of engulfment but clearly gave expression to the fear that the bad self and the bad object would merge and destroy all that was good.

TERMINATION

Much working through followed all of these efforts and the consolidation of her gains was a slow and arduous task with alternating forward and backward movement. However, over time, the self and object representations became more integrated and more clearly differentiated. The real relationship between Mrs. Carter and her mother improved. While mother still tried to direct her, she was able to help mother reduce her current twice daily telephone calls to once or twice a week. She was able to respond to her intrusions with humor and noted that mother seemed to be changing in response. Her persistent need to act differently from mother subsided and she was able to value the positive capacities that they shared, such as mother's excellence at dressmaking and her interest in poetry. She became free to take what suited her and leave the rest without fearing she would merge with her mother.

By the sixth year of treatment, Mrs. Carter, following a summer vacation, raised question about whether the time might be approach-

ing when she could consider ending the treatment. Though she had
not handled all the exigencies of her complicated family life as well
as she wished to do, she did feel pleased with the way in which she
had dealt with most of the challenges. She really knew what it was
to experience people as having their own needs, sometimes responding to her and sometimes responding to whatever was happening in
their own life. She had come to recognize that there are good days
and bad days for everyone and one does not "wash out" the other.
She could get angry without having the concomitant need to fanta-
size about "affairs" or anyone's death. She felt as if a "veil" had
been lifted from her eyes. Instead of life being a drama in her mind,
she could regard people as real and herself as real. More and more,
she asked questions instead of trying to read minds. She had always
wondered how she would exist without her familiar feeling of anger
but noticed that she has done better without it, and did not have the
"empty" feeling she anticipated. What is most important is that criticism, losing a golf game or some other failure, no longer sickened
or overwhelmed her. The feeling was so different from when she
used to feel better and not want the therapist to know in case the
therapist encouraged her to end treatment, or claimed the achievements as her own. She thought they should both feel proud of what
she had gained. She wondered how the ending would take place.
She wanted to continue to experience the therapist as a person, not
as a machine. She worried that she would end treatment by pushing
the therapist away, "rubbing her out, so to speak." She would see
this as an effort to avoid the pain that she anticipated at the termination of such a long and significant relationship.

Termination took place eight months later. Mrs. Carter's observations of what she, herself, felt had been growth-promoting in the
therapeutic effort are summarized.

According to her, the therapist served as a model for how a person could look at things as sometimes good, sometimes bad, and
sometimes in between, and still maintain a feeling of connection
even during the times of anger. She also had learned that she could
not destroy a person through her rage, and that no matter how unpleasant she had been, the treatment had continued and she had not
been abandoned nor encouraged to leave. She had found herself beginning to use some of the means by which the therapist had helped
to comfort her and no longer found herself so agitated and frightened. Most important of all, she noted that something happened that
had enabled her to "allow the therapist" to come close. She thought
it had taken her almost three years to realize that the therapist was
not going to use or manipulate her. She felt that what led to this rec-

ognition was the therapist's responsiveness to meeting her need in regard to appointment schedules and, initially, to the need for a reduced fee.

Mrs. Carter noted that even after she began to experience the therapist as trustworthy, it took much longer to appreciate that such positive feelings would not lead to her being "swallowed up." She commented that, in time, she realized this fear was in "her own head." She added that there really had been other people in her life from whom she could have received more comfort, understanding and closeness, but she could see, in retrospect, that she trusted neither them nor herself sufficiently to allow for such assistance. Perhaps, she reflected, the most valuable result of the therapeutic work was that slowly she was seeing that she and her husband could help one another. He could now advise her on something to do with Dick, and instead of feeling criticized, she actually felt his interest in her and Dick, and frequently his ideas made all the difference in easing a situation. She felt a new level of closeness with the friends she was making.

DISCUSSION

We have sought to illustrate a treatment effort on behalf of a woman with borderline organization who had, early in development, attempted to provide herself with missed nurturing, as well as to form a false self. Her narcissistic defenses as well as a profound fear of engulfment led to a withdrawal from significant object relations. Thus, she was deprived of those experiences with important others that are requisite for the development of self and object constancy.

The therapist was challenged to become more than a "machine" for Mrs. Carter. This involved acquiring a meaning for her and attracting her outside the narcissistic orbit she had created. This was not an easy task. Efforts to become engaged with her in some way were easily experienced as intrusions to which she responded angrily. For example, when she sometimes would become involved in what appeared to be a lengthy soliloquy, the therapist might inject a question to which she would, at times, respond as if she had been interrupted. She would remind the therapist that it was "her hour." Agreeing that it was, the therapist might then question what part she wanted the therapist to play in it. In time this led to an appreciation of the fact that, while she did want something from the therapist, she feared a repetition of the early mother-parasitic relationship.

In general, however, the ordinary therapeutic tasks that a therapist performs were sufficient in this treatment situation. Interpretations were offered, when the material was appropriate, of the fears, needs, or wishes that her withdrawal from others guarded against. The opportunity to be listened to nonjudgmentally, the acknowledgment of her real efforts at adaptation in the face of developmental exigencies, and the provision of both preverbal reconstructions and interpretations of current anxieties, conflict and defense, and affect and transference manifestations were part of the technical repertoire.

Certain parameters were employed, including a flexibility about appointment time and a reduced fee for several years of treatment. The changing of appointments to meet Mrs. Carter's working schedule was intended to provide an atmosphere in which her needs might be met in a more attuned way. It was pointed out from the start that this accommodation would be made, if possible, within the limits of the therapist's schedule. Mrs. Carter requested such changes infrequently. Her responses to the changes were analyzed. Early in the treatment she indicated that somehow it felt good to have someone meet her time needs. Later in the treatment, she pointed out that when the therapist changed the appointment because of a conference Mrs. Carter was to speak at, she felt that the therapist was respecting her as someone who also performed important work. As has been previously noted, Mrs. Carter ultimately came to regard this flexibility around time as indicative that the therapist valued her as a unique person. The reduced fee, another parameter, was initially necessary in light of Mrs. Carter's real financial circumstances. It was pointed out, when the arrangements were first made, that when her financial situation altered, the fee would be reconsidered. However, when her situation did change, following her marriage, the therapist decided to postpone the consideration of a higher fee until Mrs. Carter's fear of the therapist's wish to control or intrude upon her might be lessened. It was hoped that, when she achieved a somewhat more positive, real view of the therapist, a base might be developed for clarifying the transference manifestations that could be anticipated at the consideration of a fee raise. Several months following the fee raise, Mrs. Carter did inquire as to why the fee had not been raised earlier. The therapist then pointed out that she had waited until she felt that Mrs. Carter was more familiar with her and had achieved a greater measure of trust so that the fee raise might be utilized therapeutically. The therapist after all, had chosen to accommodate to Mrs. Carter's financial need and could also accommodate to what she regarded as her psychological need by waiting until the fee raise could be placed in the service of her treatment.

An important contribution to the therapeutic outcome was the therapist's capacity to tolerate Mrs. Carter's rage without retaliating, and without submitting to her efforts to coerce. The repeated interpretations of the conflicts she was acting out, or of the way she was utilizing her anger as a protection against frightening libidinal feelings, were integral aspects of the treatment process.

Out of these and many other efforts, it became possible for Mrs. Carter to slowly give up those defenses and compensatory adaptations that tended to block further development, and to then retrace those developmental steps that had been missed, utilizing the therapist as a partner. Ultimately, Mrs. Carter acquired a higher capacity for internal regulation of self-esteem and for mutuality in her relationships with others, indicative of a significant move towards self and object constancy.

The Therapist as Developmental Partner

Mrs. Brooke grew up under conditions that, in retrospect, seemed to have been overwhelmingly adverse. She was both physically and emotionally badly neglected, though not abused. As an infant, she received only minimal care; as a child, she lived literally from hand-to-mouth much of the time, without adult guidance or nurture. In early adolescence, she became a near-delinquent. It was not until well into adolescence that her life assumed some measure of structure and predictability. As an adult, she struggled between total failure to achieve a happy life, and marginal adjustment. It was not until a physical disability became severe that she received the emotional help she needed—and then only because her medical advisor was alert to her most basic requirement.

Mahler's thesis is that infants with adequate inborn ego apparatus, who achieve a fairly good symbiotic experience, are not likely to become psychotic however unfavorable succeeding subphase experiences are. Memory traces of need-satisfaction are retained, and the infant develops the capacity to use the mother as a "beacon of orientation" (Mahler, 1968, p. 64). This client could, later in life, connect with those who offered help. Evidence is persuasive that, in this case, the client, as an infant and child, could extract every ounce of care from whoever offered it in the environment. This accords with Mahler's observations relative to the innate capacity of some individuals to do this, substituting for actual loss of the mother. She paid a price in developing serious pathology involving a psychosomatic condition and inordinately low self-esteem, which, in turn, led her into acceptance of an intolerable life situation. She was unable to avoid repeating her own childhood with her second family.

The deleterious effects of alcoholism on a family unit are illustrated. Although many community agencies were involved in this situation, it was not until Mrs. Brooke received sustained individual treatment that the intergenerational cycle of neglect was interrupted.

BACKGROUND HISTORY

Mrs. Brooke, a 35-year-old married woman and mother of six children, was referred by her medical practitioner. He recognized that her severe skin condition was, in some measure, related to her emotional state. The involved history was collated over the first year of the six-year-long, twice-weekly treatment.

The client, the youngest of three children, grew up in the heart of a big city under the most deprived emotional circumstances. By the time she was six years old, her parents were together only sporadically, the oldest sibling was living with a grandmother, and she and her brother were with the father who was at home only irregularly. Her mother had started to drink heavily when she was an infant, and was, by this time, a confirmed alcoholic who sometimes lived at home, or with any man who would take her in.

When the parents were together, there were frequent violent fights often interrupted only when Mrs. Brooke, then a child of 6–8 years, called the police, who dragged her mother off since her father was usually less intoxicated and could act as if his wife had caused all the trouble. During the course of treatment, Mrs. Brooke recalled the chaotic unpredictability of her life at this time—there was seldom an adult in the house with the two small children, then both under 10 years of age. Both mother and father came and went irregularly. There was often no food in the house—she and her brother would be fed by parents of friends, or would ask the neighbors for scraps "for the dog" that the children would eat themselves. She learned, as an adult, that her father left his wife money for food but she used it for alcohol, and when inebriated would forget that she had the children to care for. Few clothes were provided; housekeeping was primitive. There was no one to ask for advice or help with schoolwork, to learn from, to talk to, or to share problems with. She tried to console herself with the fact that she was "free" to come and go as she pleased; there were no external restrictions such as the curfew her many friends had. However, the loneliness and longing for predictable adult care was overwhelming. Mrs. Brooke recalled, for example, running home at night, heart pounding with fear, and looking up at lighted apartments with their shades drawn and wishing that she was in one of those rooms being cared for and nurtured.

By the time she was 12, she had been involved in many minor delinquencies, was truant from school, and had become so much trouble to her father that she was sent to a correctional home where she remained until she was 16 years old. It was there that she learned personal hygiene and domestic skills and completed several years of schooling. Although the discipline and work were extraordinarily hard, she was provided with the structure and predictable environment that probably saved her from a totally disordered life. The religious training provided a holding environment and a background of "unequivocal" morality against which to measure her behavior. She identified with one teacher, in particular, who was kind, warm, and constant—a figure who emerged in the treatment as composite wished-for mother-therapist.

On her release she found a job, lived with a relative and refound her former neighborhood friends. By this time, she was a pert, lively, attractive young lady with much street wisdom. At 19, she married an attractive but delinquent man, bore two children, and within three years was deserted and ended the marriage. By this time, she was being supported on state funds and struggling to maintain herself and the children. Feeling alone and exhausted, she agreed to live with a man whom she disliked and feared, having known him since childhood—for that was preferable to her fear of living by herself. When she became pregnant, she agreed to marry him, despite her experience with his tempestuous mood swings, which often erupted into violence and verbal abuse. He had been an abused child himself.

There are four children of this marriage ranging in age between 14 and 22 years. The marriage has been one that, in some ways, was a repetition of that of her own parents. She feared her husband as her mother had feared her father. She had no expectation of respectful treatment, and her low self-esteem precluded effective protest. She failed to protect her children, as she herself had never been protected, and they were seriously abused by the father, and always exposed to parental conflict with its physical and verbal excesses.

At the time treatment began, Mrs. Brooke was employed as a machine operator, a job she had held for several years. Tension between herself and her coworkers had mounted since her appointment as a supervisor. This was the result of her difficulty in handling the interpersonal problems that arose. Her skin problem had become so severe that she finally had to resign and apply for disability benefits.

Mrs. Brooke had been working a night shift while her husband worked a 5:00 A.M. to 4:00 P.M. shift. The result was that they were home together for only a few hours at a time, and she had only the sketchiest notion of what went on while she was at work and her husband was with the children. In addition, she obviously closed her eyes to some of the clear evidence of her husband's abusive behavior.

Mrs. Brooke's skin condition is one in which she experiences itching and when she scratches, giant wheals are raised. The wheals might last a few hours or a few days, and the episodes of itching might occur daily for some days, or at longer intervals. Before treatment began, their occurrence seemed to be entirely unpredictable and purely happenstance. The existence of allergic factors was, however, clear, and Mrs. Brooke knew that she could not wear certain fabrics next to her skin. She obtained relief from medication but the dosage now required was high enough to be producing very unpleasant side-effects. It was at this point that she accepted the referral for psychotherapy.

INITIAL PHASE

Mrs. Brooke, sulky and skeptical about therapy, nevertheless had confidence in the doctor who had made the referral and was pleased at his obvious concern for her. Never having felt cared for or valued, she expressed surprise at the interest shown, especially as the fee agreed upon was low enough for her to afford. The provision of a consistently benign atmosphere in the treatment provided a new experience for Mrs. Brooke. She was soon aware that something different was happening to her and said, "No one has ever listened to me before the way you do." This experience and observation was the beginning of a different vision of her past life, and was used to help her empathize with the lonely little girl she must have been, rather than the "tough" one her family had always told her she was. She had grown up not questioning this.

The therapist asked that Mrs. Brooke pay attention to the events, thoughts, and feelings that had preceded a skin reaction, and to whatever emotional reactions might be going on during an attack. The reason for this was explained in simple terms: "Sometimes what we feel and think can have an effect upon our bodies." Examples were sought out of her own experiences—rapid heart rate when she was frightened, trembling when angry, or fast breathing with tension; in this way, an ego function of self-observation was engaged and exercised.

Over a period of time, it became clear to Mrs. Brooke that there were, indeed, connections between her emotions and her physical reactions. Her skin would react almost before she was aware of being angry or frightened, for example.

Among the many theoretical considerations that were borne in mind during the treatment was Mahler's conceptualization of the early differentiation of the aggressive and libidinal drives as well as her stress on the fact that aggression must be neutralized if it is to be available for development. It was postulated that the traumatic experiences of Mrs. Brooke's early life favored the development of aggression over libido and that there was insufficient opportunity for drive modulation. Discharge to the interior continued long beyond the phase-specific time.

Although the highly complex matter of somatization will not be discussed, Schur's (1955) conclusion that verbalization discourages somatic discharge and aids the neutralization of drive energy was affirmed. There was a firm and consistent effort to help the client put her feelings into words. Later she was encouraged to try to distinguish shades of feeling and to name them.

There was a gradual improvement in the frequency and severity of the skin outbreaks, and although Mrs. Brooke has never been completely free of this condition, the improvement has been so marked that she now requires a minimal amount of medication for maintenance. When she is under unusual stress, she continues to react with a temporary flare-up of the skin condition. However, because she understands the probable connections and is usually able to reconstruct, put her feelings into words, and work on solutions, an increase in medication is not needed and she can tolerate the discomfort with more equanimity. She has also become more able to respond to signal anxiety rather than becoming overwhelmed by panic reactions. The growth of this capacity has mitigated the chronic tension of her life.

ONGOING TREATMENT

As client and therapist spoke together about the content of her fears and angers, memories of the past were revived and connected

with the present. The adaptive or nonadaptive nature of her responses, the function they had served in the past as well as their ap-
propriateness in the present, and how well or badly they served her
in her current life were thought through together.

She had been left alone and unprotected so much of the time as
a child that she had needed to pretend to herself, and everyone else,
that she was "tough" and to act it. (Her past delinquencies as a child
and young adult were considered in this context). Now she could
admit to the worker that she was very often frightened, both physically and emotionally, and frequently puzzled and confused about
how to behave in current life situations.

She put up with her husband's brutal behavior rather than risk
being without him, for without him there was no one, and she felt
helpless and afraid. There were times, too, when he was very kind
and helpful and then she would identify with his terrible childhood
and feel close to him. She spoke of her conviction that men were
"breakers of women" and that she felt impotent in the face of that.
When this view was related to her childhood experience with her
own parents, she became fully aware of its inappropriateness in the
present. She could not, however, act upon this understanding until
she had better learned to protect herself and until she felt less vulnerable to possible desertion by her husband.

In terms of the needs of a developing individual, it seemed that
Mrs. Brooke had suffered some subphase inadequacy at every level
of development except, perhaps, at the autistic phase. She had experienced unpredictability in nurture, had witnessed great rage between her caretakers, and had thus not been helped to modify her
own anger. There had been no reliable models for identification until she was an adolescent. She had not learned to protect herself by
having been protected. Her intellectual assets were clear, although
they had never been tapped, and her physical charm and appeal
were obvious assets. She connected with the worker and her object
hunger was apparent so that she could use the worker as a partner
in development. Her current functioning was such that the therapist
assumed that she must have experienced at least adequate symbiosis
and some degree of nurture in subsequent phases of development.
Indeed, Mrs. Brooke later recalled her mother saying, "You were my
favorite, you looked like my family." Later in treatment, there were
fond memories of mother's warmth—buying clothes together, having
her lovely black hair braided.

Treatment took on the dimension of the therapist becoming a
constant, stable force in the client's life, a real object who lent her

ego as a sustaining adult does to a growing individual. Scrupulous attention was paid to the fact that Mrs. Brooke was no longer a child, and her autonomy was always respected and encouraged. The experiential quality of the exchange provided opportunities for growth.

The therapist was aware of the client's inability to protect herself and, therefore, to protect the children who had been and were still often seriously at risk. This was an urgent matter. Mrs. Brooke cited incidents in which she would become involved with her husband in arguments that led to a physical encounter, during which she suffered physical injury. She was encouraged and helped to find alternative self-protective ways of dealing with her husband. In conjunction with this, she began to recognize that by not being able to stop him, she, too, bore a share of responsibility for the abuse of the children.

When the therapeutic alliance was firm enough, the therapist asked directly about Mrs. Brooke's reaction to her husband's abuse of the children. One of her first responses was a statement which puzzled the therapist: "He knows that I won't call the police." As this was explored further, a number of vivid childhood memories reemerged, this time with expression of deep feeling. She reiterated what she had told the therapist months before about her mother screaming to her to call the police when she and her husband fought. When the police came, it was the mother whom they took away as Mrs. Brooke had stated before. In the present discussions, Mrs. Brooke recalled that she had sometimes been relieved that it was mother not father who was taken. As an adult this realization filled her with shame because she knew that it was father who was really to blame. She felt that she had betrayed her mother and hated herself for that. She deserved to be punished! Putting this insight into perspective, she could better understand her current difficulty in "calling the police"—that is her difficulty in trying to stop her husband's violence. She had been unconsciously fearful that the police might mistakenly take her away for the childhood "sin" of wanting mother out of the way. Expansion of this idea, together with the growth of good feelings about herself and less fear of her husband, helped her to diminish and, finally, end the abuse. When she told her husband that she would "call the police" he knew that she meant it. In addition, the example Mrs. Brooke set for the children in not allowing herself to become physically entangled with her husband was important. In the beginning she would stop herself from provocative verbal sparring with him, as this usually led to violence.

If this still did not end the threatening incident, she would force herself to get away from him physically until they both calmed down. Her instructions to the children were to get out of his way, physically whenever possible, and to avoid verbal provocation. If the targeted child could not do this for himself or herself, another child learned to act as protector by pulling or pushing the sibling out of reach, often shouting reinforcing instructions designed to encourage self-protection. Of course, the fact that the children were by now old enough to behave in this fashion was facilitating. For a long time, Mrs. Brooke tried to make sure that no one child was ever left alone in the house with father.

The verbal abuse has continued but the family has learned to endure it for the most part. Prominent in this phase was Mrs. Brooke's deepened understanding of and sympathy for the events in Mr. Brooke's life that had been influential in shaping his violent reactions. As she understood this, she helped her children to modify the picture they had of their father so that the younger ones, at least, could consider the idea that it was not their "badness" or "unlovableness" that was a prominent factor in their father's rage towards them. It was anticipated that this understanding, although conscious, would allow them a more realistic view of themselves and their past lives, and have a beneficial effect upon their self-esteem in the future. There is hope that they will not become abusing parents.

Mrs. Brooke had worked outside of her home for most of her life and she soon became restless and bored without a job. With encouragement and support, she obtained a high school equivalency diploma and was then referred to the Office of Vocational Rehabilitation. Her counselor there worked with the therapist, and Mrs. Brooke was given the opportunity to enroll in a para-professional course at a local college. After three years of study, she obtained an associate degree, which has equipped her for the satisfying position she now holds.

During this time there were many problems to negotiate. Mrs. Brooke needed steadfast encouragement from the therapist who, at that point, was the only person available to give it to her. As time went on and she had some success, Mrs. Brooke became more able to rely on herself and was less easily discouraged by failure. She could connect with some of her teachers and by reaching out to them with more confidence, received help and encouragement from them as well. A process similar to what Mahler describes as "mirroring" occurred.

As her circle of friends broadened, she was, in reality, less and less dependent upon the therapist. As she examined with the therapist her performance in class, she learned to evaluate her strengths and weaknesses with some precision. Her self-esteem grew upon the reality of mastery. When she failed to do well, instead of becoming so discouraged that she was tempted to give up, she was able, with support, to stretch her frustration tolerance and "try again." When she seemed to be on the verge of overestimating her abilities, the therapist would gently help her modify her "omnipotence" without too severe deflation. In this context, there were times when Mrs. Brooke also overvalued the therapist and her achievements. This was dealt with, but not as covert hostility, although the possibility of that being there was, of course, considered and probably true. For a time, Mrs. Brooke was allowed to share in the therapist's "glory." When expedient and timely, the therapist was able to help the client reduce the idealization to life-size and appropriate admiration and gratitude for a task shared and well done.

A serendipitous outcome of Mrs. Brooke's experience in studying was her enhanced awareness of the problems her youngest daughter was having with her school work. In identification with the therapist's role, Mrs. Brooke became involved with this youngster and her school work, and tenaciously persevered until the school authorities provided appropriate remedial resources while she offered help at home.

Mrs. Brooke's changing reactions to the therapist's absence through illness and vacation has reflected her growth. As might have been expected, the first period of separation, after about a year of treatment, was traumatic. The patient knew where the therapist would be, she received letters, and provision had been made for her with another therapist if she wished to be seen. Her skin condition became very troublesome, she cried a great deal, and finally got some comfort through telephone contacts with the alternative therapist. She reacted, in fact, as if separation meant abandonment. Over the years, she has coped with increasing ease, using those resources and comforts she has acquired in the other-than-mother world to sustain herself. She no longer needs the therapist in the flesh.

The Development of a Symbiotic Orbit in the Treatment of a Schizophrenic Man

The Bryson case was chosen because it illustrates the use of Mahler's work in the care of a schizophrenic man. Therapists need a way to understand the needs of the psychotic patient and strategies for management. The Bryson case is of special interest because, despite the use of major tranquilizers prescribed by a medical adviser, it was and remains the organizing work of the therapist that was necessary for growth and stabilization.

Although Mahler has not written about treatment of adult psychosis, we have been able to draw on her research and insights as a guide in treating people suffering from schizophrenic processes.

The Bryson case presents the use of some of her findings about the symbiotic phase. Guided by her findings that schizophrenia results, in part, from failure to achieve "oneness" in the symbiotic phase, exploration and reconstructions are sought with the patient about the first year of life. This case illustrates how facets of the preverbal experience can be explained by the therapist and become useful as organizing principles in treatment.

BACKGROUND HISTORY

Mr. Bryson, a 28-year-old man of a deeply religious family raised in a large city, came to the mental health facility seeking help in obtaining a job. Mr. Bryson was the youngest of three and the only one living at home. His parents were both professionals and about to retire. When Mr. Bryson graduated from a local college at the age of

21, he suffered his first break with reality and was hospitalized. He had never held a job and was receiving social security disability payments.

As Mr. Bryson spoke of his goals in the initial interview, he told of the elaborate delusions that he experienced daily, and had been experiencing over the past ten years. He believed the television spoke to him; that he was a state governor; that the food outside of his home was poisoned; that his girl friend from childhood appeared in many places, wearing disguises; and although he reported that sometimes these were crazy thoughts, sometimes they were real. In short, Mr. Bryson had been undergoing a paranoid schizophrenic process for the past ten years. These symptoms had persisted despite the use of various major tranquilizers.

Mr. Bryson's sense of humor revealed an ego capacity for self-observation. His fund of knowledge about political, historical, and social issues was broad. His approach was liberal and humanitarian. Under stress, Mr. Bryson's delusions would increase, as would the fragmentation and disintegration of his thinking. Stress for Mr. Bryson might occur when he became ill with a mild infection, upon hearing a heart-rending sermon, or when his mother threw him out of the house. His parents had suffered excessive panic all of their lives.

In the course of the three years of treatment, Mr. Bryson was provided with rehabilitation training for clerical work, individual and group therapy, group and individual work with his parents, family daycare, and hospitalization. It was Mr. Bryson's capacity to form a relationship, and his hunger for a relationship in which he could feel safe, that was the basis for the changes that occurred. Often the stimulating activities that he undertook as a result of the rehabilitation programs required efforts, in the treatment, to cut through the panic these stimulants catalyzed in him.

INITIAL TREATMENT

From the beginning, Mr. Bryson asked to be given coffee at his sessions. His ability to seek food within the relationship was treated as the highest level of his object-related capacity and a seeking out of the longed-for positive symbiotic state that he had never experienced. He was asking for good food in good company. The request for coffee was respected also as an attempt to master his fear that food was poisoned in places outside of his home, and as an attempt to engage in the world outside of mother. All sessions began with a trip to the coffee machine in the mental health center. In over three years of weekly sessions, Mr. Bryson never failed to reveal a new aspect of inspection of the spoon, sugar, coffee, table, and room where the machine was placed. He was knowledgeable about the studies of carcinogens in the world around him and saw them demonstrated in the Center's coffee room. Each issue was divested of its horror as it came up at the beginning of the session. Since the coffee machine was located in the middle of the clinic, Mr. Bryson had a good opportunity to meet other staff members there. He had a nice flare for the theatrical and a stage presence, and engaged in humorous remarks with all the staff. In the course of beginning the interviews in this coffee-social encounter, he formed a relationship with the entire staff. Through the therapist to the larger unit, the Center became a home away from home, representing, for him, a steady constant place that he could come to when in need—a place where he would not be poisoned.

As Mr. Bryson engaged in the solution to his anxiety states, he reported experiences and memories that provided important bases for the work. Mr. Bryson was born three years after the death of a sibling. That deceased child's death remained an active event in the life of his family. This child had never been mourned. The therapist reconstructed that his mother's fears had been intensified by that loss, and that when he was born she had lovingly, but with terror, hovered over his every move and breath as a neonate and later as a small infant so that he had come to experience terror about his every move in life. Mr. Bryson confirmed this idea, recalling that he had not walked until the age of 2½ and then not until the pediatrician one day stood him up in the office and told him to walk, which he did. The explanation of his infancy that focused on the aspect of the "taking in of fear" in the preverbal period (the first months of life) during the symbiosis is, in this case, a global reconstruction illuminating one facet of the chaotic affect in the early dyad, and its effect upon him. The "explanation reconstruction" represented an organizing principle both for Mr. Bryson and the therapist.

Mahler's theory helps us review the experience of the first year of life. We examine the nature of the attitudes and capacities within both parties of the dyad, the infant and the caretaker. One might note that even in the above reconstruction, the emphasis was on both the mother's terror that she could not control, and the active position of the infant "taking in" that terror. With the emphasis on the "taking in" experience of the child, we temper the view for the client of the self as a passive victim. By presenting the mother as "lovingly hovering with fear," we are reporting accurately on the positive nature in the mother, for the purpose of bringing to the client's attention the goodness in the mother, in order that he may retain connections with her, rejecting only those parts of her that were not good for him. In this way, we are promoting the ejection of the Bad Mother image that was not possible for him during his symbiotic phase.

Drawing on Mahler's theory, one can see that, as an infant, Mr. Bryson was able to form a symbiotic unit, a self-object experience with his mother, but that the affect of panic dominated the symbiotic experience. He never experienced the whole fused omnipotent "oneness." As can so clearly be seen, in this case, "confident expectation" was never achieved. Differentiation was impeded by the fear that "to move" was to become sick and die. To turn away to the outside world in the differentiation period, to crawl or to walk in the practicing period, was to die. All autonomous aggressive drive thrusts were contaminated with panic and annihilation anxiety. Safety was thought to lie only in physical closeness to the mother. But even that was no relief from the panic and danger. The beginning sense of self was depleted, experienced as dangerously fragile, and the developing motor functions and interests were inhibited by both his own and his mother's fears. Again, note the emphasis on his fears, as separate from his mother's fears. He could not acquire positive regard for the strengths of his body or musculature nor develop a sound body image. A minor viral infection, such as a cold, could set off ideas of disintegration. He had no internal concept that his body could withstand an illness. When he became sick, he literally expected to die. On such occasions, he had grandiose fantasies that one could explain as his attempt to deny his vulnerability and to protect himself from the annihilation anxiety he experienced. When he experienced disintegration panic, therapeutic intervention was addressed to his perception of internal fragility. It was interpreted that he experienced mildly unpleasant bodily discomfort as a totally destructive force that he was incapable of conquering. It was suggested that this was the view that his mother had of him—it was not factual. Indeed, it was a view that altogether disregarded the capacity of the body to heal itself. On one occasion, Mr. Bryson presented the view that his racial group was genetically weak as further support for his body vulnerability belief. When his "scientific evidence" was challenged, he began to check this out, to discover that he had fallen for propaganda. He was absolutely ecstatic about this insight and chagrined at having accepted propaganda, and experienced considerable relief. Therapeutic interventions that embodied new ideas and perceptions about him as an individual came, over time, to change his inner perception of fragility and served to increase his sense of body integrity.

Mr. Bryson's beginning optimism was dependent upon regular visual contacts with the therapist. Therefore, discussions in advance of vacations focused on anticipating what kinds of problems the worker's absence would raise for him. He was asked to participate in organizing conditions that would minimize his distress. He was told of the therapist's vacation itinerary and postcards were sent to him from each place the therapist visited. In addition, substitute sessions were arranged for him with other staff members at the clinic. These efforts were explained to him as helping him feel, and know, that the therapist would still exist even though physically absent. Giving him an explanation of the tools (e.g., the postcards) engaged his cognitive and intellectual capacities, stimulating participation of his ego functioning and increasing his level of self-awareness.

ONGOING TREATMENT

In the first year of therapy, Mr. Bryson could maintain a more positive than negative view of the therapist except under certain stress. On one occasion, the therapist became a member of the Ku Klux Klan, and the doctor providing medication became J. Edgar Hoover. But, as the constancy of the relationship continued, some self images became stronger, and more positive object images of the worker developed. In the second year, after one vacation break, Mr. Bryson bounded in, euphoric, yelling that he was a Viking, pounding his chest, saying Vikings did not need their mothers. Interpreting that he must have suffered great anxiety and loneliness while the worker was away ended the Viking ideation in one session. By the third year of work, the therapist-client relationship never became contaminated with paranoid ideation. Also, by this third year, Mr. Bryson would, with humor, ask for his "mother" at the clinic appointment desk. This was an expression of one incorporated love experience that had been needed and missed in the symbiotic period.

The real admiration the therapist held for him was also a central factor in his arrival, with positive affect, into this symbiotic like experience. The therapist's capacity to appreciate his assets, his fine intellect, his basically healthy body; the therapist's attunement to the level of his suffering; the admiration for his ability to have survived the terrible psychic deprivations; the therapist's capacity to work with, understand, interpret, and even admire his delusions that were often adaptively disguised wishes for success, power, love, and connectedness—all provided him with a view of himself different from that which he had ever experienced before. The gleam in the therapist's eye, a new mirror, is likened to the mirroring experience of the early dyad and can be thought of as narcissistic supplies in the new environment that, over time and accompanied by interpretation, could be taken into himself. In the third year, those delusions and panic that did arise could be disassembled in the treatment sessions within the atmosphere of the positive libidinal-affective experience with the therapist.

Mr. Bryson's life at home with his parents was often fraught with episodes of panic. The eruption of unneutralized hostility was ignited by any family member. Panic and rage were contagious and acted out in sometimes violent ways. None of the family members could contain the flow of aggression once it got under way. Each member threatened abandonment of the next, which served to increase the panic. Throwing household items at one another was common. Putting Mr. Bryson out of the house with a "never-darken-the-door-again" stance was common.

Two examples of specific episodes are given. In one, Mr. Bryson had opened the refrigerator door and held the door open while he looked for something pleasing to eat. His mother became panicky that all the electrical supplies would be used up by the open refrigerator door. Her tension erupted into yelling at him that he was wasting all the electricity, and besides, was wasting his life away eating and getting fat. (Mr. Bryson was not fat.) Mr. Bryson threw some eggs at his mother. His mother called her therapist screaming that Mr. Bryson had tried to kill her. When the therapist challenged the egg-throwing as an attempt at murder, the mother replied, "But he knows I must have a low cholesterol diet." The therapist retorted with humor, "You mean he tried to 'undiet' you to death?" With this, the mother and the therapist laughed together and the unneutralized panic and fear came under control. On another occasion the police were called by the parents and the police called Mr. Bryson's therapist at his request. They had separated Mr. Bryson in one room, the parents in another. The parents wanted Mr. Bryson jailed or hospitalized. The police became confused. Lengthy discussion between the parents, Mr. Bryson, and the police resulted in the plan that Mr. Bryson would take some money and go to a motel overnight. When this plan was all worked out, the parents capitulated and Mr. Bryson was allowed to stay home. We note the need here of a team approach—in the first instance with Mrs. Bryson's therapist, in the second with the police and Mr. Bryson's therapist. On two occasions, Mr. Bryson was hospitalized as a result of this kind of family action episode. However, on at least twenty occasions in three years, hospitalization was avoided by timely therapeutic intervention.

One is naturally drawn to the idea that Mr. Bryson would have been better off living separately from the parents. The hospital team made many attempts to help Mr. Bryson live in separate quarters, family daycare, and an apartment of his own, among other places. These efforts were doomed to failure because Mr. Bryson could not live without seeing his mother. It is interesting to note that, on one occasion, he lived in an apartment outside of his mother's area telephone exchange, and each call to her house increased his panic. The extra set of numbers symbolized a geographical separation, and caused greater panic as Mr. Bryson experienced himself as outside a fantasied safe orbit with his mother.

After three years of work, Mr. Bryson would occasionally hold a job, could get control of the panic and delusions with the worker's help, and had some greater access to pleasures in life. Yet, Mr. Bryson remains basically unemployed and dependent upon social security disability and continuous clinical services.

DISCUSSION

This case illustrates the major significance of the early dyad in the development of mental health. We are assuming, in this case, adequate innate endowment though probably a high anxiety level within the neonate. The combination of neonatal anxiety vulnerability and chronic panic of the mother set the course for incomplete symbiosis in the sense that the omnipotence and grandiose wholesome symbiotic affective experience was inhibited. Early intervention might have saved this man. His mother had needed help to mourn the loss of the previous child; she needed help for herself for her panic; she needed help to approach Mr. Bryson—the infant—with hope and optimism. Her problems were apparent to many along the way: the obstetrician, the pediatrician, and later, the school personnel. Too many professionals are afraid to step forward and refer people for help; too many are themselves afraid of the concept of help, or the connotation of therapy; and too many needs go by noticed, brushed aside.

Mental health policy issues highlighted include the value of the use of telephone contacts, extra treatment sessions as needed for stabilization, and the importance of the location of family day care for the mentally ill.

The fallacy of the view that physical separation of the patient from the family will solve problems is demonstrated. A great deal of money and effort is often wasted upon the attempt to effect such separation when, in fact, such effort would be better directed towards the improvement of clinical services. In this case, the provision of outpatient care was still less expensive than hospitalization would have been, despite the many professionals involved.

Mr. Bryson's greater independence from his environment was contingent upon the relationship with the therapist, and the arrival at a positive, uncontaminated idea of a person and place to go to get help. We cannot say that object constancy was attained, for it was not. But an "idea" of help could sustain itself long enough for Mr. Bryson to reach the therapist. This suggests that the small amount of delay of gratification that Mahler cites as possible for the infant in symbiosis was achieved. We think that the arrival at a positive nonparanoid affective relationship with the therapist is a success, both in human terms and in cost to society. The achievement of a higher level of positive perception by Mr. Bryson of the therapist and the world outside himself, despite the necessity for continued treatment, is a valid accomplishment. Mr. Bryson has not been made dependent upon the therapist, as some might say; rather, he has been enabled to use the environment (the therapist and the clinic) for greater independence from that environment. This aspect is very important for, to date, no one has been able to "cure" schizophrenia, and recognizing levels of achievement points the way towards further research. Care and treatment of schizophrenic and psychotic patients on a twenty-four-hour, continuous care basis is possible and necessary in our society. Where there has been severe damage to the organizing capacity of the individual, atrophy of innate capacity, or absence of innate capacity at birth, such continuous care by society may be required.

Three years of attuned therapy, using the relationship, inter-pretations, and reconstruction of the preverbal state broke through a paranoid affective state. Mr. Bryson came to trust the therapist and, through the therapist others at the center. He came to have a home away from home.

CASE STUDY 4

Combinations of Subphase Inadequacies and the Effect on Structure

The Rogers case was selected for its importance in illustrating the effect that the absence of the capacity to delay gratification has on adult behavior, and for its importance in illuminating how some preverbal and preoedipal experiences are connected to the faulty development of the capacity to delay gratification. This absence of frustration tolerance is a central factor in addictions of all kinds—drugs, alcohol, gambling, and overeating. As psychotherapists, we are challenged to develop efficient programs to help such sufferers find a way to move into the mainstream of life. Understanding the complexity of the causes of addiction will help clinicians address themselves fully to the issues involved, whether in institutional program development or in treatment.

In this case, inadequacies in the symbiotic phase, combined with problems during the rapprochement subphase, interfered with the development of frustration tolerance. Mr. Rogers' overeating, compulsive spending, impulsive sexual acts, repeated school failure, and frequent job changes are all examples of behavior that is, in part, the result of poor frustration tolerance. Mr. Rogers had good endowment, underdeveloped ego functions, and in the course of five years of treatment, he achieved considerable change in functioning and gained access to an enriched life. The case content in sessions focused on understanding the past, especially the preoedipal childhood, and the changes came about for him as he could come to understand his motivations. The key to the resolution of the problems was not manipulation of the environment, e.g., debt or diet counseling, but the development of inner structure and ego functioning.

177

In the Rogers case, we illustrate therapeutic reconstructions of the symbiotic period and rapprochement phase that are guided by Mahler's theories. We discuss the subject of preverbal and pre-oedipal reconstruction. Coenesthetic empathy, (one aspect of the tools used in treatment that Mahler and her coworkers used in arriving at their findings) is defined and related to its role in the technique of preverbal reconstruction.

Mr. Rogers was unable to date or woo. We discuss some of the dynamics of wooing, for it is a problem for many people who come for help today.

PRESENTING PROBLEMS

Mr. Rogers, at 26, after two previous unsuccessful experiences in therapy, arrived for another try with a third therapist. He was depleted of funds because of previous compulsive spending, and had outstanding debts to creditors and could obtain no more credit. He was depressed because of a girl friend's rejection. He felt frenzied and in a panic that he had lost his girl friend and had tried to get her back by telling her he would "blow his brains out in front of her" if she did not return to him. He was miserable in his current job as a bookkeeper. For all his efforts in attempting night courses at college over the past eight years, he had managed to complete only two years of college. He could think of nothing hopeful. He felt he had not made it, and never would make it.

BACKGROUND HISTORY

When he first presented his thoughts, Mr. Rogers had only a vague sense that something from his childhood had created the handicaps that had produced this miserable state. He thought that his parents' failure to provide him with a stimulating, culturally enriched childhood was the cause of his problems. If they had attended operas and read books, he would have made it. If his father had only taken him to sports games, he would have made it. His picture of his parents' life together was a view of them sitting together in front of the television set, holding hands. When the family went out together, they would walk "in a unit of four."

In the initial sessions, Mr. Rogers reported that two months after graduating from high school, he ran away from home and got a job in a resort establishment. His parents did not know where he was and he was listed as a missing person for several months. He returned home and took a bank job, but suddenly quit to join the Navy. He hated the Navy and its oppression of his will. He went AWOL but managed to arrange a medical discharge.

As his story unfolded, his need for adventure became apparent, as well as the problems this adventure-seeking had created for him. The keen intelligence that helped him to recover from the scrapes he created was also noted. In fact, he knew from testing in high school he had a high Intelligence Quotient. Beginning in high school, he experimented with many kinds of sexual adventure. He once forced a girl to have sexual relations with him, resulting in a series of legal problems. All these exploits had taken up time and energy but had not helped him to feel better. He had been trying for success but did not have any.

INITIAL TREATMENT

During the initial stage of therapy, Mr. Rogers' depression remained acute and, shortly after treatment began, he was laid off from his work. He lost his car, too, for the old car "died," and he could not afford the repair bills. He trekked from his home to his therapy, hitching rides to get there. He arrived unshaven and in bedraggled clothes. He spent the hours at home sitting in his room, occasionally listening to music, but mainly just sitting in despair. He felt as if the world had fallen out beneath him. His normal energy supply was depleted because the hopefulness that provides the energy for the intrapsychic system and enables the individual to plan and think about tomorrow was gone.

As is true in many cases of depression, the therapist carries the hope and the vision of a brighter future for the patient in the initial phases. Bearing in mind those aspects of Mahler's work that illuminate nodal points at which depressive states are experienced, the worker listened for clues of early depression in the explanation Mr. Rogers gave of his life experiences. These clues, together with his upset at his girl friend's rejection, made it possible for the worker to envision that Mr. Rogers' feeling that "the rug had been pulled from under him" was repetitive of earlier subphase loss. He was not in a hopeless position, he just felt that way.

Mr. Rogers' associations affirmed that in some way his current experiences revived the pain and disappointment associated with the birth of his brother and the return of his father. These two events occurred within a short space of time, and deprived him of the previously privileged position he had enjoyed. That such a situation can be experienced as a form of accidental trauma has been affirmed by Mahler, who notes the important impact of the birth of closely spaced siblings. With this in mind the therapist sought to provide empathy for this affront that had occurred during the development of his sense of self. It would now be up to the therapist to find a way to clarify the exactness of the early traumas, explain it to him, and help him back on his feet. It is not unlike what the mother of the practicing and rapprochement child must do when the child has taken off in the elated grandiose state in which "all is possible"— the love-affair-with-the-world phase—and has fallen down with a bad cut and bruise, and feels suddenly terribly despairing, hopeless, and frightened. The mother says, in essence, "You had a terrible fall, you feel awful, but you are all right. You are not permanently lost or injured. This is not irreparable."

Mahler and those who have elaborated upon her work have provided us with significant conceptualization of those early life experiences that can deplete the inner reservoir of self and, once depleted, inhibit later growth. These insights provide the therapist with tools for locating the earliest deprivations in the client's experience and early developing structure, and enable us to begin with the client where it hurts him most—where the initial loss began. The therapist's empathy for his pain in having fallen, and the emphatic belief that he could recover, provided an external stimulus and energy source that he could latch onto. His good feeling in the session came from his libidinal quest to be connected and loved. His longing to be loved had not atrophied. So, in the initial phase of treatment, Mr. Rogers placed all his energy into connecting with the therapist. The therapist accepted this connection and encouraged his interest in the libidinal search for attachment and communication with the gratifying environmental human resource—the therapist-client dyad.

In the early phase of the work, Mr. Rogers attended one session a week and was encouraged to call the therapist when he felt acutely depressed between sessions. He was encouraged to talk. He rather quickly began to find great value in talking, and wished to prolong the session beyond the working hour. This was explained to him as his long-standing wish to get to the bottom of things, and the wish to extend the good feeling he was having in being understood in the session itself. The client's attempts to extend sessions have usually been understood as a form of resistance or hostility. But where there has been subphase loss, and an insufficient or poorly matched supply of needed nutrients in the early dyad, the patient will act in ways that seek repair via the therapeutic relationship.

The good experience with the therapist is emphasized so that the client can use the meaning of the relationship as a tool in self-awareness. With our increased understanding of object-related libidinal needs, we can help clients use their positive feelings for the worker as growth forces within themselves.

MIDDLE PHASE OF TREATMENT

Following the establishment of the initial relationship and the therapeutic alliance, a deeper exploration began. A glimpse of the early feeding problem and a loss in the early symbiotic phase was postulated when he spoke of his present 2:00 A.M. forays to the refrigerator for ice cream. He knew that he wasn't hungry, but he could not resist eating the ice cream. He became worried about his weight. He was encouraged to examine further his thoughts, feelings, and ideas about food. Mr. Rogers explained that he always ate alone and never spoke when eating, rather he gulped his food down. His family never spoke at meals. They ate together, but he remembered eating in a quick mechanical way and leaving the table without conversation. His mother had told him he was a "good baby" who had always slept through the night from the time he was brought home from the hospital. Further examination of his first year of life revealed mixed patterns in the feeding schedules. His father had been in the service from his birth through the twenty-third month of his life. During this time, his mother lived with her mother and sister, who doted on him. He was not a neglected or abused baby. From what could be reconstructed of the probable attitudes of the women feeding him, it was assumed that he would have been fed rapidly and frequently, and not permitted to cry. The background of the women in his family suggested overindulgence in feeding practices. He was an overfed, overgratified baby during the daytime, and an underfed, untended baby at night who was expected to sleep throughout the night.

But what did these feeding experiences mean for him in the early symbiotic phase, and what did they mean for the inadequate person that he felt today? Again, Mahler's theories served as guidelines for understanding. Optimal frustration is required in the feeding experience to provide the infant with a personal sensation of a self, especially a body-self. Deprivation of any feeling of hunger robs the infant of experiencing himself. To know the feeling of hunger is a motivating force impelling the infant to seek for, and take some form of action that will bring relief. When action is taken by the infant and the goal, the reduction of unpleasure, is attained, a personal sense of entity, a sense of efficacy and personal satisfaction is gained (Winnicott, 1953). Broucek (1979) reports that infants as young as 4 months of age are observed to experience joy when they realize that they themselves have been the cause, or agent, of obtaining gratification. She cites Bibring, who in his classic paper on depression asserted that "any condition which forces a feeling of helplessness upon the infantile ego may create a predisposition to depression" (Broucek, 1979, p. 311, 314).

Thus, it was inferred that Mr. Rogers did not experience joy or the enrichment of the sense of self-pleasure from his capacity to connect with the world during the daytime feeding experiences. But, in addition, further information suggested that he was not held, comforted, or fed at night. It is not physiologically possible for a newborn infant to sleep through the night in the first few weeks of life. The therapist's knowledge of infant needs helped to sort out what the real need would have been, and what was, in fact, available from the environment.

Towards the end of this period of exploration of the early feeding patterns, Mr. Rogers presented a problem he experienced in studying a current physics course. He found that he had great difficulty, at certain times, in grasping the concepts; it became too much for him to abstract and he described it the following way: "You know those games where you have to put your hand in a covered box and figure out what you are touching without looking? Well, that's how I feel about physics. I feel all in the dark."

A preverbal reconstruction explanation was offered over a three-month period:

> This must have been how you felt as an infant at night. Infants truly cannot sleep comfortably through the night—they awaken. We are getting a look at how it might have felt when you awakened, let's say at 2:00 A.M., and were hungry or were uncomfortable in some other way. You must have grasped and foraged about in your crib in the dark, to touch something familiar and comforting, but you did not find it. You were left wishing and longing for comfort for your body. You were also left feeling you really could not get what you needed by your own ef-

forts. In addition, by not experiencing some frustration of your daytime feelings, you did not have a chance to feel your own power, which is experienced in the sensation of hunger, and in the vigorous crying and effort that brings the food. So, during the day you did not have enough experience in stretching yourself and experiencing that your own efforts brought results, and during the night you didn't find what you needed.

Following this reconstruction-explanation, he recalled a scene from age 2. His crib was placed in one corner of the room, far from the door. When the door was closed, he could stand up and by grasping both sides of the crib he could rock the crib across the room. A return of a memory can be regarded as confirmation of the correctness of an interpretation—a picture of a vigorous, physically very active infant emerged. He was once told that at 9 months he climbed out on the apartment building ledge. We never found evidence that his exceptionally aggressive physical actions were organized by the family's wishes for an active baby, as may be the case in cueing by mother. The opposite, "good babies are quiet babies," seemed to be true. Rather, he had developed an excessive reliance on what was probably an innately active body to help overcome emptiness and loss. The combination of deprivation and body physiology, was, perhaps, one strand that accounted for the adventuresome, impulsive actions in his current life.

Mr. Rogers' response to explanations and reconstructions was always quite calm and unexcited. He could not show much in the way of the affect of excitement or elation. However, he examined, digested, and integrated the content, and began to pass all of his courses with very high grades. In the third year of therapy, he one day mentioned that he had received his B.S. degree in the mail. This was stated in his usual, low-keyed, sober, matter-of-fact tone and he quickly passed onto other matters. He was stopped, asked to think why he had not paused over this announcement, asked whether he wished to be congratulated and whether he thought this deserved congratulations. He had never celebrated anything. He followed up this examination of his low-keyed affect by planning and giving a party for his graduation. The affect of elation was catalyzed by bringing attention to his accomplishment, and stimulating his ego to think of the meaning of the accomplishment. This intervention helped him consider that he could do more to give himself pleasure.

Where there has been little experience with pleasure in the client's past, the adult is restricted in understanding the nature of pleasure and is unable to even consider the right to pleasure. Furthermore, he or she often longs for a nonspecific vague rescue, or

help to obtain pleasure, and looks for outside sources for that pleasure. By bringing to the observing ego's attention the highlight of an
accomplishment, and turning it to look at its own capacity for self-
appreciation, we enable the client to use his inner mental resources,
and increase his capacity for self-evaluation, self-soothing, and self-
pleasure.

We are reminded of how often clients complain that a birthday
or an accomplishment has been overlooked by others, often resulting
in their feeling terrible rage toward the others in their life for this
neglect. As they are helped towards self-appreciation, they can orga-
nize pleasure systems in their own behalf, or communicate clearly to
others what their needs are, with resulting desired reciprocation
from their friends, relatives, and coworkers. The capacity to enjoy
compliments and congratulations and to enjoy celebrations comes
first from the inner experience of self-pride that has its beginnings
in the symbiotic phase, but has its strongest push in the mother's
pleasure with the child's accomplishments in the rapprochement period. Mr. Rogers' self-organized graduation party was an indicator
that he had grown in his capacity to become active, was experiencing self-pride, and was engaging in the wider world outside of the
therapeutic relationship.

LATER PHASE OF TREATMENT

As Mr. Rogers began to recover from the loss of his girl friend,
he brought to the therapist his fear of meeting new women. He simply could not imagine saying "Hello" to an unfamiliar woman. He
longed for a woman to knock on his door, present herself to him,
and express her interest in him. He wanted assurances, in advance,
that a woman would like him. He was speechless and his mind was
empty as he tried to consider how he might meet a woman. He had
a few female friends from the past who bored him and whom he
didn't like, but out of fear of attempting to meet new women and
out of desperate isolation, he would, from time to time, call one of
them, make a sexual contact, and leave. He tried group sex, and
some quick seductions, but they were all empty. He could not imagine himself as being able to interest a woman of value. He would
frequently start sessions with the comment, "Nothing spectacular to
report today."

The history of the rapprochement period was of great significance in explaining the low self-esteem and impoverished sense of

self that he suffered from. As he experienced some understanding of the meaning to him of his brother's birth, he recalled being told by his parents that, while sleepwalking at age 4, he had entered his brother's room and taken his brother's gun and holster set. He remembered feeling ashamed when he was told of this act. The return of this material in the session reinforced the correctness of the assumption that his brother's birth had been traumatic. We can understand that during the height of his rapprochement crisis, his mother's eyes were on the baby brother, and our client concluded that what was of major interest to her was more important than he was. He concluded that what she gazed at most was what was most valuable. We see, in this conclusion, the enormous power the mother's interest and activity have as forces in determining, for the child, his own self-evaluation. Where there is a lack of responsiveness to the heightened need for recognition in the rapprochement subphase, the child's self-valuation and self-appreciation are depleted.

We can also see, from this example, that subphase experience can color the action and arrangement of later stages of development. By age 4, he had begun the phallic psychosexual stage of development, and his interests turned to phallic subject matter. The gun and holster express such a phallic interest. But, even though he had a gun and holster set for himself, he could not value it fully, nor properly; neither could he feel his own genital equipment was of full value. He felt that what his brother owned was more valuable than what he owned.

We can also note from this act of taking the gun from the brother an attempt to regain the "equipment" and so render his brother less valuable. This would also give him status and control and place him in the limelight of his mother's eyes, thereby eliminating the competitor. Taking the brother's "equipment" is an attempt to gain equilibrium, and secure a place and opportunity for the expression of his own normal phallic exhibitionistic needs. Four-year-old boys often begin to express this with gun play. His shame at being exposed in the act of taking the gun indicates the beginnings of superego formation. His rapprochement period was explained to him as a period of excessive frustration. A reconstruction explanation of his rapprochement subphase was given:

> Just as you were beginning to feel your own separateness with its resulting anxiety and excitement, and just as you needed your mother's attention, you lost her to the other "man." It is no wonder that you think you cannot interest a woman in yourself, and that you think you cannot compete with the other men. You lost out at a very delicate time in your life, and you continued to remember that loss and feel

that you will always lose. You believe your words and actions are doomed to fail or, at the least, have poor results. It is no wonder you feel so depressed and hopeless about finding a woman who can feel excited about you.

During his latency period, he was frustrated by the family's "togetherness" pattern. He could never get either parent to himself even for a short while. The togetherness mold further inhibited the development of his individuality. A boy does need a father to help him form his separate and individual masculine achievement.

We may wonder, too, if Mr. Rogers' feeling of loss of connection with his father, and his longing for his father to have taken him places, may have started during the absence of father when Mr. Rogers was 18 months old. Abelin's work focuses attention on the 18-month-old child's need for a positive relationship with the father as the "differentiated other" and the "knight in shining armour" who comes home from work and plays games of running and throwing that have a special quality of elation and discovery (Abelin, 1971).

During Mr. Rogers' five years of therapy he completed undergraduate college, then obtained a graduate degree, and he passed an advanced Professional Business State Examination. He was employed as an executive in a large corporation. He found and married a compatible young woman. He was able to settle his debts and did not incur new ones.

DISCUSSION

Frustration Tolerance

The capacity to delay gratification or frustration tolerance is a prerequisite for healthy adult functioning. Each subphase of the separation–individuation process contributes qualitatively to this capacity, which, therefore, takes time to acquire. In developmental theory, the first signs of the infant's beginning capacity to delay is inferred from the observation that the crying infant becomes quiet when he or she hears the sound of mother, or sees her. The infant seems to be understanding, in some way, that relief from distress will be forthcoming. Mahler has described this observation as the indicator that thought and the Mothering Principle have been achieved. The mother, as a part-object of positive experience, has been cathected for the infant who forms an inner perception that pleasure in the future is possible. The ideas of "mother" and "pleasure" result in comforting mental representations and, over time, with accumulating good experiences. These thoughts and representations can sustain good feelings about one's future, despite present unpleasure and deprivation.

A sense of competence is fostered as a result of the child's increased body mastery at the practicing phase. This leads to growing feelings of self-confidence with regard to the child's capacity to "do it" eventually, thus modifying feelings of frustration and extending the capacity to wait.

The idea that help is available, already initiated at symbiosis, increases in response to the mother's assistance and comforting at rapprochment. When the toddler feels frightened by feelings of being small and helpless, mother will tell the child that he or she is all right, and restore the feeling of self-assuredness. The recognition that mother will help provides inner support for an expanding capacity to tolerate disappointment, discomfort, and pain. Unpleasure becomes more manageable with the assuredness that, if necessary, help will be forthcoming. The child also gains confidence in that, through its own efforts, he or she may elicit the aid of the loved one. These experiences contribute to the formation of mental representations that, in turn, facilitate the achievement of self and object constancy, an achievement that further adds to the capability to tolerate frustration.

As Mr. Rogers became familiar with his inner needs and longings, especially those needs that had frustrated and overwhelmed him in the past, he began to comprehend his pain, and recognize how his constant, impulsive searches represented efforts to overcome early loss and depression. As his capacity for accomplishment and pleasure in his current life increased, his impulsive acting-out began to change. Instead of desperately seeking immediate gratification, he was able to delay, in order to secure more meaningful gratification later.

Mr. Rogers' growing ability to delay and his increasing capacity to control his impulses led to a feeling of greater personal growth, and stimulated a more positive sense of himself. His real success at school and in other areas of life, contributed to a growing view of himself as a person who was capable of accomplishing goals. It is an important turning point in any case when clients can anticipate a bright future, for then their ability to ·postpone gratification is strengthened by their capacity to enjoy tomorrow by anticipating it in their thoughts of today. Mr. Rogers was able to obtain pleasure from daydreams, fantasies, and thinking.

The Capacity to Woo

Mr. Rogers' traumatic rapprochement period inhibited the development of the capacity to court and woo, and impaired his social interactive skills. With sexual experiences an open option in today's culture, sexual contacts can often be seen to serve as substitute action for social relations and object-relatedness. The underdeveloped capacity to court and woo is a common problem. Sexual activity becomes the connecting activity. The impulsive action-oriented sexual activity propels the person into quick partnerships. When the initial sexual excitement is over, there is nothing left of substance or quality in the experience with the partner. The pleasure of and need for the body contact has enmeshed the individual in a relationship. Then when the relationship is found to be unsatisfying, a complicated maneuver of leave-taking must be undertaken. These people repeat this painful cycle with many partners. They always leap before they look. Mr. Rogers' forceful seduction of his friend's girl into the act of intercourse can be explained by lack of confidence that he would ever be able to convince a woman that he was interesting or worth enjoying sex with, and by his overreliance on body activity for connection.

With adequate self and object constancy, dating, wooing, and falling in love are adventures that are exciting and exhilarating, if somewhat frightening. Wooing behavior requires a movement to and from—a closeness and distancing—that provides intrigue, mystery, and surprise. Wooing behavior also provides the wooer with time to explore who the other person is, in reality, and allows for a chance to examine the other's qualities and attributes. Wooing requires self-confidence, self-regard, and a sense that the self is worthwhile, both likeable and loveable, and that others, too, are capable of loving and attachment.

As Mr. Rogers moved towards the achievement of object and self constancy, he became more discriminating regarding who and what he liked. As his profound neediness was modified and he felt less desperate, he could take time to think. He could look before he leaped.

Shift in Self-Representations

In treatment Mr. Rogers found the discoveries that he and the therapist drew from his material to be of "spectacular" importance. This was his word for the feelings attendant upon the sense of accomplishment he experienced. As his self-pride and pleasure grew in the therapeutic relationship, through repeated experiences in which he and the therapist shared in appreciating the value of his efforts, Mr. Rogers, over time, came to regard himself more and more as a unique and valuable human being.

Preverbal Reconstructions

Separation–individuation theory guided the therapist in helping Mr. Rogers to comprehend the impact of those unremembered but influential impressions and experiences of the first three years of his life, when verbal expression, in accord with the age-appropriate levels of maturation, was at first nonexistent and later only minimally possible. Important development experiences from that early time remain in the unconscious, not as a result of repression, but because as Freud (1915) pointed out, preverbal memories cannot enter the system conscious because they have been deprived of a linkage with words. The symbiotic exchange is at its height before there is generally any degree of verbalization. Experiences are coenesthetically received, and the language of the body and of the affects prevails. Crucial steps in the separation–individuation sequence generally take place during the period that the toddler, even if he or she is starting to speak, cannot yet express in words the profound affective experiences that accompany those processes. Thus, essential steps in the formation of character and the integration of the personality take place as Kramer (1978) reminds us during what is essentially a preverbal time.

According to Mahler (1974), preverbal memories remain as "unintegrated residue" and do not become internalized into the psychic structure. Under the force of the repetition compulsion, however, such early impressions and experiences generate impulses that may become acted out in everyday life, in dreams, and in the treatment situation.

Reconstructions of distorting developmental experiences and impressions of the preverbal period are aimed at illuminating points of developmental impairment, and at clarifying their impact on current difficulties. The two reconstructive explanations that were worked out with Mr. Rogers in relation to his material and through his efforts, helped to clarify the origin of aspects of his troubled behavior, enabling him to begin to understand that which he had formerly acted out, but not recalled. Ultimately, these efforts led to increased control over his actions, and to modification of those actions or behavior that were inappropriate and maladaptive in the present.

Coenesthetic Empathy

The ability to understand experiences and impressions derived from the preverbal period depends on both detailed knowledge of the developmental phenomena of that time, and on our capacity for coenesthetic empathy. As psychotherapists, we have always employed coenesthetic empathy though we have not always referred to it by that name. We refer to the "tuning-in to" the nonverbal communications of the client, which may include body posture, affects, eye movements, moods, the quality of speech, and so on. Such empathy requires the use of our own inner response to the client, our ability for identification—our capacity to feel with the client, so to speak. We sensitively tune-in to the manifest content of the spoken material, as well as to the metaphors employed by the client to convey both his or her past and present affective states.

In an effort to understand the derivatives of early developmental traumata in the present, the therapist seeks to get a feel for the infant or toddler that the adult once was, a long time ago. Questions may be employed to elicit information about that time. What was it like for you then? How did you feel? What did you do about it? These and other questions are designed to enable the client to reach back for the feel of those difficult experiences in the past that continue to have an impact on the client's contemporary problems. Ultimately, reconstructive explanations may be offered that help to clarify, for the client, the origin of present day difficulties.

Reconstructive efforts may serve to promote increased self-understanding by providing the client with a fuller sense of his or her own history. The opportunity becomes available for the revision of self and object representations when distortion has prevailed. It is therapeutically beneficial, for example, to help a client to recognize that current behavior that may presently produce shame or guilt and that is frequently self-defeating in the present time, may once have represented the creative efforts of a small child to compensate, or adapt, in the face of developmental hurdles. The consequent understanding may then lead to a greater measure of acceptance of the "self of the past" and promote increased acceptance of the "self of the present."

Therapist-Worker Relationship

In Mr. Rogers' treatment, it is clear that the therapist was actively engaged in a partnership with him. Though keeping in mind the difference between the troubled adult of today and the developing child of the past, the therapist, in the therapeutic exchange, was guided by the model, drawn from Mahler, of the "good enough mother's" holding patterns and appropriate responses to the phase-specific needs of the child. She welcomed Mr. Rogers' expression of feelings of closeness with her, drawing attention to the sense of satisfaction that he could now begin to derive from being understood, and from sharing in the therapeutic effort and result. The therapist tried to provide, within the treatment situation, certain experiences to which he had been insufficiently, if at all, exposed in the past. This was done in order to enable Mr. Rogers to move forward developmentally. At times in the treatment a gentle push as at differentiation, was given. At other times, when Mr. Rogers was overwhelmed by panic, the therapist served as a model of soothing, by encouraging him to telephone her. The goal was to help reduce the overwhelming, disorganizing panic to more appropriate and tolerable levels of anxiety. Overgratification was strenuously avoided. Nothing was done for Mr. Rogers that the therapist had reason to believe he could do for himself. The therapist was also on the alert for opportunities to help Mr. Rogers stretch his capacity for the tolerance of unpleasant affects. However, the provision of developmental partnering in the case of a client who has experienced early developmental failures is a necessary step.

SUMMARY

Eissler has proposed that in the case of the more troubled individual, the therapeutic task is the "reconstruction of a viable ego" (Eissler, 1953, p. 153). Mahler's formulations help us to appreciate how, in certain cases, we also have a task of construction of that which has not hertofore been acquired. In the case of Mr. Rogers the promotion of psychic structuralization, particularly the fostering of ego development, was achieved not only by the technique of interpretation or explanation, but also by the provision of a new opportunity within the treatment situation for a relationship in which the acquisition of transmuting internalization and the development of selective identification could ensue.

A Case of Marriage Counseling

This case is presented to illustrate the manner in which separation-individuation theory can be drawn upon to enhance the quality of service provided in marital counseling. It demonstrates the way in which the failure on the part of marital partners to complete developmental tasks may place a heavy burden on a marital relationship, particularly when each seeks to achieve in marriage compensations for earlier unmet needs.

This case actually began as individual treatment with Mrs. Rollo, recounting difficulties with her husband, but focusing on her personal problems. However, after a year of treatment, a period during which Mrs. Rollo made some gains with regard to achieving an improved sense of herself and a greater ability to extricate herself from arguments with her husband, the marital balance shifted in a way that apparently exacerbated Mr. Rollo's personality difficulties. In response to changes in his wife, he became increasingly troubled and questioned whether the marriage should continue.

This brought the marital discord into the forefront. Both out of concern for the welfare of their children and out of religious convictions that made divorce untenable, Mr. and Mrs. Rollo then moved towards seeking marital counseling. Mrs. Rollo wished to continue with the therapist, and her husband expressed his wish to join his wife in the therapeutic effort. Consultations were held with him, and for reasons that will be elaborated upon later, a decision was made to shift from individual treatment of Mrs. Rollo to a marital counseling approach with the same therapist. Individual sessions with each partner and periodic joint sessions were held on a regular basis.

We delineate the difficulties each partner presented, a history of their individual development, and a consideration of the manner in which the marital interaction was handicapped by their attempts to repair earlier deficits through each other. An abbreviated account of the process of treatment is given.

MRS. ROLLO

Presenting Problem

Mrs. Rollo, a 36-year-old woman, came into treatment over her desperation with her terror of physical illness. Although she said that the marriage was not a good one, it was difficult, at first, to get a picture of just what was not good about it. Although it was evident that there was a great deal of quarreling, the reasons for this were unclear. The first year of the twice-weekly treatment was spent in enabling the client to achieve some greater ease of handling her fears about her health.

Developmental History

The eldest of three children, Mrs. Rollo had two brothers, one four years younger and one six years younger. Both her parents were alive. She grew up as part of a large extended family whose members all lived in one neighborhood and spent much time together. They knew every detail of each other's lives and there was marked interdependence. (Mrs. Rollo's mother had never separated from her own mother. This was clearly noted later when Mrs. Rollo's ties to her own parents were under scrutiny. This assumption lent weight to aspects of the diagnostic picture of Mrs. Rollo herself, in that a mother who has never separated emotionally from her own mother is likely to prolong the symbiosis of her child, and to have much difficulty in encouraging independent development.)

Mrs. Rollo was the only female in a large group of children consisting of her cousins. The frequent family gatherings were characterized by loud, vehement "discussions" in which those who could shout loudest were listened to. This was part of a fierce competitiveness which the adults encouraged. In her conscious memory, no one was openly put down or criticized for losing, either in sports, games, or the school work in which excellence was regarded as vital. But there was no comfort for the losers either. What was not forgiven was failure to "play hard." This was so extreme, she recalled, that a cousin once broke a leg rather than miss a ball in a football game. Since no quarter was given for size or age, Mrs. Rollo, smaller and younger than many of her cousins, recalled that she often suffered severe loss of self-esteem, with a sense of failure and inadequacy.

She had no question but that she was loved, although her parents never "said" so, and there was absolutely no physical expression of affection. Her father was compulsive and tried to obtain instant obedience. Things had to be done his way or they were "wrong." If this was not forthcoming, his volatile temper would erupt. We inferred, later, that this behavior was in the service of dealing with his own overwhelming anxiety. We must note here the high degree of tension that may build up in a vulnerable child living under these conditions.

In the process of therapy with the client with this as the focus, further explanatory information was gleaned. Mrs. Rollo recalled that, as a child, she had frequently been very frightened at the thought of dying. These fears always came at night and stopped her from falling asleep. She would eventually tell her parents of her fears and get comfort from her father. The worker questioned why it was the father who had been able to help her with her fears, and, in the course of our exploration, subsequent events shed light on this matter. One day Mrs. Rollo came into her session in distress, and asked the therapist to examine a lesion on her arm, and tell her if it was anything to worry about. Since she knew that the worker was nonmedical, it was not that kind of opinion she was seeking. It was agreed that the request would be explored, rather than acted upon. With relevant questioning, a host of memories emerged and were worked with over several weeks.

During Mrs. Rollo's childhood, her mother had frequently been ill. Indeed, on at least four occasions, Mrs. Rollo had spent the summer vacation with an aunt when mother "disappeared." It was only when she was grown up that she learned that the "disappearances" had occurred because mother went into a hospital for observation of various complaints that usually turned out to have no organic basis. At the time she had not been prepared, nor had she asked any questions. She also recalled that at the age of 10 years, she was taken to a large hospital to have her breasts examined because mother thought there was "something wrong" with her. This was, of course, the normal uneven breast development of puberty. At this point in treatment, Mrs. Rollo began to pay more attention to the exchanges with her mother, either over her own health or that of her children. What became very clear was that she had grown up within a home atmosphere of barely hidden, chronic maternal anxiety over illness and the fear of it. The mother felt herself to be highly vulnerable, and since she was not differentiated from her daughter, assumed that the daughter was similarly vulnerable to physical disability. The overanxiety was continued right to the present day, and Mrs. Rollo became aware that even her mother's tone of voice when illness or potential ill-health was discussed could send her into a paniclike reaction. It is persuasive to think that Mrs. Rollo, as one girl among many boys, was acutely aware of her own genital difference, which was unconsciously equated with loss or injury. However, there was insufficient corroboration from Mrs. Rollo herself for this concept to be of value in the work.

In reconstructing Mrs. Rollo's early history, we knew from available evidence that she had differentiated early. She walked, talked, and was toilet-trained before she was a year old. This may have been due to above-average inborn ego apparatuses, or to escape from a parasitic symbiosis. Thus, the symbiotic phase had been hardly adequate so that she had not been able to share in the omnipotence of the dual-unit sufficiently. As a result, she carried into later developmental subphases earlier unmet needs. She defended against closeness by excessive distancing. The practicing subphase had probably been without the joyful elation that is requisite since it was ushered in prematurely. Her discomfort with body-integration, her lifelong depressive mood, and her fear of meeting new people and having new experiences were evidence of these deficits. All of the above characteristics could have multiple meanings, but these fitted for her when we spoke of their possible significance and genesis. She presumably entered rapprochement with many developmental deficits and did not achieve object constancy.

Marital Interaction

Following the painstaking examination of several episodes of markedly increased fears of illness and anxious depression, it was clear that such episodes frequently followed serious marital discord. The therapist hypothesized that what took place during these episodes presented a serious threat to Mrs. Rollo's self-representation and self-cohesion (Stolorow, 1979). At the same time as the therapist attempted to help Mrs. Rollo understand the dynamics of the quarrelling, and limit the episodes, thereby protecting herself from the emotional toll they took, her motivations for entering the marriage became clearer, and linked up with the developmental deficits. These she was unconsciously attempting to repair via the marriage relationship.

When she first knew her husband-to-be, she said that she knew she was far "smarter" than he, so she would no longer have to face the kind of competition she had dealt with in her family of origin. Since she had grown up feeling that there was always someone around "better" than herself, being superior within the marriage promised to be a relief. Beneath her external self-assurance and confidence, she was frightened and needy, and Mr. Rollo, although not smarter intellectually, seemed able, unlike other men, to put limits on her when she was demanding. She therefore thought he was "strong" and would be a source of support when she was frightened. He would be someone who would be able to say to her, "Relax, I'll help you, don't be frightened." He would also be saying what her parents had never said, or been able to comfort her with, as, for example, "No, of course, you can't win, you are smaller than your 10-year-old cousin." Her self-esteem would be bolstered. Instead, because of his own problems and needs, Mr. Rollo withdrew from her when she was afraid, and said, "You're being ridiculous. I'm disappointed in you." When she was not "omnipotent" and could not hold a job and simultaneously raise a family with ease, her failure to meet his demands, reverberating in her unconscious, was felt as seriously reducing her self-esteem. His outgoing, relaxed demeanor had held for her the promise of helping her with her fear of the "stranger"—she would bathe in his ease and overcome her discomfort. Instead, because of his own problems, he had to be the center of attention, and soon tired of coaxing her to participate when in company, and would go off on his own into the "crowd." She experienced this as, "He has disappeared (as mother once had), he'll never come back. He'll be swallowed up and I'll be alone." As a result, she would often nag to go home long before he was ready to leave, while he was enjoying the stimulation he craved. In these ways, the marriage relationship was compromised by prior developmental failures in both partners. The further growth, which often takes place when a marriage can become a developmental opportunity (Blanck and Blanck, 1968), did not occur. Instead, the frustration and disappointment of not having inappropriate needs fulfilled led to anger and fierce quarreling.

MR. ROLLO

Presenting Problems

When Mr. Rollo asked to be included in treatment his conscious and expressed reason was to help his wife, and to improve, even save, the marriage. He stated that he saw no problem in his own behavior. Although it soon became clear to the therapist that Mr. Rollo was unconsciously threatened by his wife's growing independence, treatment began where he was, only gradually reaching below that surface level.

Developmental History

Mr. Rollo, the older of two boys by five years, was his father's proudest possession until the birth of his brother. He recalled his angry disappointment with his father's interest in the new baby. He recalled that up to that time he had often been coached by his father, a great showman and speech maker, to deliver flamboyant speeches to entertain visiting relatives. This ceased after the brother's birth, and we assume that he suffered too sudden deflation of self-esteem. He remained intensely jealous of his brother. He longed for physical affection from his father but never got it, although his brother did. His highly dictatorial and authoritarian father would give him long lectures if he did something wrong. If he tried to escape the barrage of words, or go to his mother for comfort, his father would order him to remain and face his punishment. At such times, he hated his father and was impotently angry. His mother was equally bullied by the father and Mr. Rollo longed to comfort her but was afraid to do so. Outside of the home, his father was thought of with great awe and respect—a boy's club and community leader. Mr. Rollo's longing for recognition and acceptance took the form of grandiose fantasies, and from an early age on, he daydreamed, in his loneliness, of how perfect his life would be when he had his own wife—someone all for himself.

Marital Interaction

Mr. Rollo met his wife a year after his father's sudden death—a year during which he had felt much guilt, in part because he had refused to follow his father's profession and had, thereby, defied and, he thought, disappointed him. He was aware that he had thought his wife-to-be was the sort of person his father would have approved of; she resembled him in physical build, and was a scientist too, seemingly very definite, independent, and sure of herself. In addition, she appeared to be highly interested in him as an individual, which his father had not been. What he mistook for independence in her was, actually, her defense against the closeness she unconsciously wished for so much. He anticipated getting from her the warmth, love, and emotional holding his father had never been willing to give him and that he refused from his mother because it was intrusive and stifling. He thought that at last he had someone of his own who would make up to him for all he had missed and craved. She was to be his "possession," able to read his mind and meet his every need in loyalty and total agreement.

In some ways, Mr. Rollo "took over" characteristics of his father rather than identifying selectively with him. It was with shock and surprise that, in treatment, he recognized some of his father's characteristics in himself. He would trap his wife with words, as his father, a great debater, had done with him. This was something he had hated and feared because of its sadistic quality. In doing this to his wife he turned passive into active and felt strong. He was sure he had either to be the authority in the home (as his father had been) or the "nothing" his father had made him feel as a youngster. He would never allow this to happen to him in his marriage, he said.

He later said that he learned from the worker's attitude in joint as well as individual sessions that one could relate differently and not lose face. A mistake could be admitted, or an opinion reconsidered, without disgrace or ridicule. His wife, who as a result of her background initially had a similar approach to his, also learned to "give in" graciously, without feeling devastated. The result was that they were gradually able to discuss, rather than debate with a win-or-lose, fight-to-the-death technique. In addition to the therapist's example, increased comprehension of what they had been doing, and why, made the change possible.

In growing up, Mr. Rollo's relationship with his mother had been one in which he had constantly fended off her intrusiveness. She tried to be a part of every facet of his life—what he wore, how he spent his time, and so on came under her scrutiny. He recalled taking great delight in outwitting her by arranging great parties when his parents were away. He would orchestrate events so that they would never have any inkling of this aspect of his life. This need to outwit his parents, especially his mother, was seen as the adaptive effort of an adolescent to feel his own person and escape parental control and intrusion. However, when carried over into his marriage, as it was, such machinations became nonadaptive and led to serious conflict. He tried to avoid repetition of earlier painful feelings by being secretive about his job, his earnings, even his friends. He thereby excluded his wife in many inappropriate ways.

Above all, his great need for closeness, the obverse of his wife's distancing as a defense against the wish for closeness, kept him in a constant state of sparring to maintain this system. If he got close, she was unconsciously threatened by her wish for merger while he, consciously craving closeness, unconsciously also protected himself from this longed-for but threatening gratification by starting a fight. This effectively took care of the unconscious threat posed by a sexual relationship; they seldom had sex.

TREATMENT

Treatment was effected via individual and joint sessions. The individual sessions were regularly scheduled once-a-week meetings with each spouse, which were not changed unless a crisis arose. Joint sessions were held approximately twice a month, more frequently if either spouse requested it, or if the therapist, with their agreement, saw a special need. The latter eventuality arose, for example, when the couple became blocked in their ability to solve a mutual problem and the quarreling became destructive.

As has been noted, Mr. Rollo asked for help when changes in his wife resulted in modification in the marital interaction, and when it was possible, he was seen individually for extra sessions, as his self-understanding lagged behind that of his wife. He had to have acquired a minimal understanding of his conflicts before any joint sessions could be really helpful.

Each spouse was intelligent, quite articulate when listened to as an individual, could make conceptual connections, and worked hard in treatment. Each related positively to the therapist, and was convinced of the therapist's real interest and wish to help. Each had a keen sense of humor, which sometimes rescued them from an impasse. The opportunity to be listened to nonjudgmentally was of special importance to both. Explanations were given to help each understand their developmental histories, and where problems and inadequacies seemed to have occurred. Preverbal reconstructions and interpretation of current anxieties, as these could be understood, were made.

Once the problems in the marriage were identified and could be understood, focus was upon whether the demands each was making of the marriage could possibly be met. The degree to which each had brought unfulfilled childhood needs into the marriage was consistently clarified. Both confused the past with the present and behaved towards the spouse as if he or she was a parental figure. A simple example of this, observed in joint sessions, was Mr. Rollo's reaction when his wife would start to complain about something, or even go into any explanation. He would become visibly agitated, and be unable to hear her out. When questioned by the worker on this matter, he realized that he was feeling like a little boy again, being "talked at" by his father. Mr. Rollo's angry reaction would hurt his wife's feelings, she would withdraw or attack, and a circular negative interaction would take place between them.

It was via joint interviews that this interaction could so clearly be demonstrated. The therapist could point this out, and alternate ways of handling such situations could be discussed. Sometimes a reaction was so complicated that it would be deferred for further consideration in an individual session. The advantage of having one therapist for both individuals offset the disadvantages. Subtle nuances of behavior and feeling could be picked up, and the therapist could observe the clients' interaction at first hand. The disadvantages included the possibility of overidentification with one spouse. The therapist had to be on the alert for this constantly.

In this case, one of the main purposes of joint interviews was to deal with the clients' extreme trouble in communication. Verbalization of feelings allowed for naming and differentiation of affects.

The most complicated area to be reviewed proved to be that which related to the problem each had with finding optimal distance from one another. Sometimes this could be worked upon as seen in the transference to the therapist, sometimes as seen in their behavior in joint sessions where it could be caught in action. This aspect was not resolved to the therapist's satisfaction when treatment ended. There was, however, more directness, less hostility, and more rapid recognition of impending conflict and ability to work together on it. Both acquired the necessary tools for conflict-resolution. They could better understand the tension each lived with sometimes, and by exercising more control, self-discipline, and respect, ensure the survival of the marriage.

References

Abelin, E. L. Role of the Father in the Preoedipal Years. Panel Report by Robert C. Prall. *Journal of the American Psychoanalytic Association,* 1978, *26,* 143.

Azarin, N. and Foxx, R. *Toilet Training in Less Than a Day.* New York: Simon & Schuster, 1974.

Benedek, T. Adaptation to Reality in Early Infancy. *The Psychoanalytic Quarterly,* 1938, *7,* 200–214.

Benedek T. Parenthood as a Developmental Phase. *Journal of the American Psychoanalytic Association,* 1959, *7,* 389–417.

Benedek, T. Parenthood During the Life Cycle. In E. J. Anthony and T. Benedek (Eds.) *Parenthood: Its Psychology and Psychopathology.* Boston: Little, Brown, 1970.

Benjamin, J. D. The Innate and the Experiential in Child Development. In H. Brosin (ed.) *Lectures on Experimental Psychiatry.* Pittsburgh: University of Pittsburgh Press, 1961, 19–42.

Bergmann, M. The Place of Paul Federn's Ego Psychology in Psychoanalytic Metapsychology. *Journal of the American Psychoanalytic Association,* 1963, *11,* 97–116.

Bergmann, M. Psychoanalytic Observations on the Capcity to Love. In J. McDevitt and C. Settlage (Eds.) *Separation–Individuation: Essays in Honor or Margaret Mahler.* New York: International Universities Press, 1971.

Bergmann, M. and Hartman, F. *The Evolution of Psychoanalytic Technique.* New York: Basic Books, 1976.

Blanck, G. Psychoanalytic Developmental Diagnosis, *The Lydia Rapport Lectures.* Northampton, Mass.: Smith College School of Social Work, 1978, pp. 559–598.

Blanck, R. and Blanck, G. *Marriage and Personal Development.* New York: Columbia University Press, 1968.

Blanck, G. and Blanck, R. *Ego Psychology: Theory and Practice.* New York: Columbia University Press, 1974.

Blanck, G. and Blanck, R. *Ego Psychology II.* New York: Columbia University Press, 1979.

Blum, H. Borderline Childhood of the Wolfman. *Journal of the American Psychoanalytic Association,* 1974, *22,* 721–742.

Broucek, F. Efficacy in Infancy: A Review of Some Experimental Studies and their Possible Implications for Clinical Theory. *The International Journal of Psychoanalysis,* 1979, *60,* 311–316.

Burlingham, D. The Preoedipal Infant-Father Relationship. *The Psychoanalytic Study of the Child,* 1973, *28,* 23–47.

Burnham, D., Gladstone, A., and Gibson, R. *Schizophrenia and the Need-Fear Dilemma.* New York: International Universities Press, 1969.

Chodorow, N. *The Reproduction of Mothering.* Berkeley, Los Angeles: University of California Press, 1978.

Deutsch, H. Some Forms of Emotional Disturbance and their Relationship to Schizophrenia. *The Psychoanalytic Quarterly,* 1942, *11,* 301–321.

Eissler, K. R. The Effect of the Structure of the Ego on Psychoanalytic Technique. *Journal of the American Psychoanalytic Association,* 1953, *1,* 104–143.

Erikson, E. H. *Childhood and Society.* New York: Norton, 1950.

Eirkson, E. H. *Insight and Responsibility.* New York: Norton, 1964.

Fleming, J. Some Observations on Object Constancy in the Psychoanalysis of Adults. *Journal of the American Psychoanalytic Association,* 1975, *23,* 743–758.

Fraiberg, S. The Origins of Identity. *Smith College Studies in Social Work,* 1968, *38,* 79–101.

Fraiberg, S. *Insights from the Blind: Comparative Studies of Blind and Sighted Infants.* New York: Basic Books, 1977.

Freud, A. *Normality and Pathology in Childhood.* New York: International Universities Press, 1965.

Freud, A., Nagera, H., and Freud, W. E., Metapsychological Assessment of the Adult Personality: The Adult Profile. *The Psychoanalytic Study of the Child,* 1965, *20,* 9–41.

Freud, A. and Dann, S. An Experiment in Group Upbringing. *The Psychoanalytic Study of the Child,* 1943, *6,* 127–169.

Freud, S. 1905. Three Essays on the Theory of Sexuality. In J. Strachey (Ed.) *Standard Edition,* Vol. 7. London: Hogarth Press, 1953, pp. 135–243.

Freud, S. 1915. The Unconscious, In J. Strachey (Ed.) *Standard Edition,* Vol. 14. London: Hogarth Press, 1967, pp. 159–215.

Freud, S. 1917. Mourning and Melancholia. In J. Strachey (Ed.) *Standard Edition,* Vol 14. London: Hogarth Press, 1957, pp. 237–258.

Freud, S. 1917. The Libido Theory and Narcissism. Lecture XXVI—Introductory Lectures on Psychoanalysis. *Standard Edition,* Vol 16. London: Hogarth Press, 1963, 4–12–30.

Freud, S. 1937. Construction in Analysis. In J. Strachey (Ed.) *Standard Edition,* Vol. 23. London: Hogarth Press, 1964, p. 225.

Furman, E. *A Child's Parent Dies.* New Haven and London: Yale Universities Press, 1974.

Gil, D. *Violence Against Children.* Cambridge: Harvard University Press, 1970.

Goldfarb, W. Psychological Privation in Infancy and Subsequent Adjustment. *The American Journal of Orthopsychiatry,* 1945, *15,* 247–266.

Goldstein, J., Freud, A., Solnit, A. J. *Beyond the Best Interest of the Child.* New York: The Free Press, 1973.

Greenacre, P. The Predisposition to Anxiety. *The Psychoanalytic Quarterly,* 1941, *10,* 66–95, 610–637.

Greenacre, P. The Predisposition to Anxiety. In *Trauma, Growth and Personality.* New York: International Universities Press, 1952, pp. 27–82.

Greenacre, P. The Childhood of the Artist: Libidinal Phase Development and Giftedness. *The Psychoanalytic Study of the Child,* 1957, *12,* 47–72.

Greenacre, P. Early Physical Determinants in the Development of the Sense of Identity. *Journal of the American Psychoanalytic Association,* 1958, *6,* 612–627.

Greenson, R. *The Technique and Practice of Psychoanalysis*, Vol. 1. New York: International Universities Press, 1967.

Hall, E. T. *Beyond Culture*. Garden City, N.Y.: Anchor Press, 1977.

Hartman, H. *Ego Psychology and the Problem of Adaptation*. New York: International Universities Press, 1939–1958.

Hartman, K. E. and Lowenstein, R. M. Comments on the Formation of Psychic Structure. *The Psychoanalytic Study of the Child*. New York: International Universities Press, 1946, pp. 11–38.

Herman, L. and Lane R. C. Cognitive Ego Psychology and the Psychology of Learning Disorders. In D. S. Milman and G. D. Goldman (Eds.) *The Treatment of the Emotionally Disturbed Child*. Kendall-Hunt, in press.

Holley, W. L. and Churchill, J. A. Effects of Rapid Succession of Pregnancy. In J. Smart and R. Smart (Eds.) *Children: Development and Relationships*. New York: Macmillan, 1972.

Jacobson, E. *The Self and the Object World*. New York: International Universities Press, 1964.

James, J. Premature Ego Development: Some Observations on Disturbances in the First Three Months of Life. *The International Journal of Psychoanalysis*, 1960, 41, 288–294.

Kaplan, L. J. *Oneness and Separateness: From Infant to Individual*. New, York: Simon & Schuster, 1978.

Kernberg, O. F. *Instinct, Affects and Object Relations*. Unpublished manuscript, 1974.

Kernberg, O. F. *Borderline Conditions and Pathological Narcissism*. New York: Jason Aronson, 1975.

Knight, R. P. Borderline States. In R. P. Knight and C. Friedman (Eds.) *Psycholanalytic Psychiatry and Psychology*. New York: International Universities Press, 1954, pp. 97–109.

Kohut, H. *The Analysis of the Self*. New York: International Universities Press, 1971.

Kohut, H. *The Restoration of the Self*. New York: International Universities Press, 1977.

Kohut, H. and Wolfe, E. The Disorders of the Self and their Treatment. *International Journal of Psychoanalysis*, 1978, 59, 413–425.

Kramer, S. *Technical Consequences of Object Relations Theory: The Significance and Application of Separation–Individuation Theory*. Paper presented at the Fall Meeting of the American Psychoanalytic Association, New York, 1978.

Kris, E. *Psychoanalytic Exploration in Art*. New York: International Universities Press, 1952.

Lichtenberg, J. The Development of the Sense of Self. *Journal of the American Psychoanalytic Association*, 1975, 23, 453.

Lichtenstein, H. Identity and Sexuality: A Study of their Interrelationship in Man. *Journal of the American Psychoanalytic Association*, 1961, 9, 179–260.

Lichtenstein, H. The Role of Narcissism in the Emergence and Maintenance of a Primary Identity. *The International Journal of Psychoanalysis*. 1964, 45, 49–56.

Lichtenstein, H. *The Dilemma of Human Identity*. New York: Jason Aronson, 1977.

Loewald, H. Freud's Conception of the Negative Therapeutic Reaction, with Comments on Instinct Theory. *Journal of the American Psychoanalytic Association*, 1972, *20*, 246–301.

Mahler, M. S. On Child Psychosis and Schizophrenia: Autistic and Symbiotic Infantile Psychoses. *The Psychoanalytic Study of the Child*, 1952, *7*, 286–305.

Mahler, M. S. On Symbiotic Child Psychosis: Genetic, Dynamic, and Restitutive Aspects. *The Psychoanalytic Study of the Child*, 1955, *10*, 195–212.

Mahler, M. S. Autism and Symbiosis, Two Extreme Disturbances of Identity. *International Journal of Psychoanalysis*, 1958, *39*, 77–83.

Mahler, M. S. On Sadness and Grief in Infancy and Childhood: Loss and Restoration of the Symbiotic Love Object. *The Psychoanalytic Study of the Child*, 1961, *16*, 332–351.

Mahler, M. S. On Early Infantile Psychosis: The Symbiotic and Autistic Syndromes. *Journal of the American Academy of Child Psychiatry*, 1965, *4*, 554–569.

Mahler, M. S. Notes on the Development of Basic Moods: The Depressive Affect. In R. M. Loewenstein, L. M. Newman, M. Schur, and A. J. Solnit (Eds.) *Psychoanalysis, A General Psychology; Essays in Honor of Heinz Hartman*. New York: International Universities Press, 1966, pp. 152–168.

Mahler, M. S. *On Human Symbiosis and the Vicissitudes of Individuation*. New York: International Universities Press, 1968.

Mahler, M. S. *A Study of the Separation-Individuation Process and Its Possible Application to Borderline Phenomena in the Psychoanalytic Situation*. The Psychoanalytic Study of the Child, 1971, *26*, 403–424.

Mahler, M. S. *Rapprochement Subphase of the Separation-Individuation Process*. Psychoanalytic Quarterly, 1972, *41*, 487–506.

Mahler, M. S. 1975. *On the Current Status of the Infantile Neurosis. In The Selected Papers of Margaret Mahler, Vol. 2. New York: Jason Aronson*, 1979.

Mahler, M. S., Furer, M., and Settlage, C. F. *Severe Emotional Disturbances in Childhood Psychosis. In S. Arieti (Ed.) American Handbook of Psychiatry, Vol. 1. New York: Basic Books*, 1959, pp. 816–839.

Mahler, M. S. and Kaplan, L. *Developmental Aspects in the Assessement of Narcissistic and So-called Borderline Personalities. In P. Hartococollis (Ed.) Borderline Personality Disorders. New York: International Personality Disorders*. New York: International Universities Press, 1977.

Mahler, M. S., Pine, F., and Bergman, A. *The Psychological Birth of the Human Infant*. New York: Basic Books, 1975.

Malone, C. Developmental Deviations Considered in the Light of Environmental Forces. In E. Pavenstedt (Ed.) *The Drifters*. Boston: Little, Brown, 1967, pp. 125–161.

Masterson, J. *Psychotherapy of the Borderline Adult*. New York: Brunner/Mazel, 1976.

Meissner, W. W. Theoretical Assumptions of Concepts of the Borderline Personality. *Journal of the American Psychoanalytic Association*, 1978, *26*, 559–598.

Merriam, E. *Mommy's at Work*. New York: Scholastic Book Service, 1971.

Moore, E. B. and Fine, D. *A Glossary of Psychoanalytic Terms and Concepts*. New York: The American Psychoanalytic Association, 1968.

Pao, Ping-Nie. *Schizophrenic Disorders.* New York: International Universities Press, 1979.

Parens, H. *The Development of Aggression in Early Childhood.* New York: Jason Aronson, 1979.

Pharis, M. E. *The Emotional Birth of the Family.* Address to The Hunter School of Social Work, New York, Spring, 1979.

Pine, F. On the Expansion of the Affect Array: A Developmental Description. *Bulletin of the Menninger Clinic: The Early Development of Affects and Moods,* 1979a, *43,* 79–85.

Pine, F. On the Pathology of the Separation–Individuation Process as Manifested in Later Clinical Work: An Attempt at Delineation. *The International Journal of Psychoanalysis,* 1979b, *60,* 225–241.

Prall, R. The Role of the Father in the Preoedipal Years. *Journal of the American Psychoanalytic Association,* 1978, *26,* 143–161.

Rangell, L. Aggression, Oedipus and Historical Perspective. *International Journal of Psychoanalysis,* 1972, *53,* 3–11.

Ribble, M. *The Rights of Infants: Early Psychological Needs and Their Satisfaction.* New York: Columbia University Press, 1943.

Robbins, M. Borderline Personality Organization: The Need for a New Theory. *Journal of the American Psychoanalytic Association,* 1976, *24,* 831–853.

Sandler, J. The Background of Safety. *International Journal of Psychoanalysis,* 1960, *41,* 352–356.

Schur, M. Comments on the Metapsychology of Somatization. *The Psychoanalytic Study of the Child,* 1955, *10,* 119–164.

Schur, M. *The Id and the Regulatory Principles of Mental Functioning.* New York: International Universities Press, 1966.

Settlage, C. Psychology of Women, Late Adolescence and Early Adulthood. *Journal of the American Psychoanalytic Association,* 1976, *24,* 631–645.

Settlage, C. The Psychoanalytic Understanding of Narcissistic and Borderline Personality Disorders: Advances in Developmental Theory. *Journal of the American Psychoanalytic Association,* 1977, *25,* 805–833.

Smart, M. S. and Smart, R. C. *Children: Development and Relationships.* New York: Macmillan, 1967.

Speers, R., McFarland, M., Arnaud, S., and Curry, N. Recapitulation of Separation–Individuation Processes When the Normal Three-Year-Old Enters Nursery School. In J. B. McDevitt and C. F. Settlage (Eds.) *Separation–Individuation: Essays in Honor of Margaret S. Mahler.* New York: International Universities Press, 1971.

Spitz, R. *The First Year of Life.* New York: International Universities Press, 1976.

Stoller, R. J. *Sex and Gender, Vol. 2. The Transsexual Experiment.* New York: Jason Aronson, 1975.

Stoller, R. Primary Femininity. *Journal of the American Psychoanalytic Association, Supplement, Female Psychology,* 1976, *24,* 58–79.

Stolorow, R. D. Defensive and Arrested Developmental Aspects of Death, Anxiety, Hypochondriasis and Depersonalization. *The International Journal of Psychoanalysis,* 1979, *60,* 201.

Stolorow, R. D. and Lachmann, F. The Developmental Prestages of Defenses: Diagnostic and Therpauetic Implications. *Psychoanalytic Quarterly,* 1978, *42,* 73–101.

Thomas, L. *The Lives of a Cell.* New York: Bantam Books, 1974.

Tolpin, M. The Infantile Neurosis: A Metapsychology Concept and Paradigmatic Case History. *The Psychoanalytic Study of the Child*, 1970, *25*, 273–305.

Tolpin, M. On the Beginnings of a Cohesive Self. *The Psychoanalytic Study of the Child*, 1972, *26*, 317–352.

Turrini, P. A Mother's Center: Research, Service, Advocacy. *Social Work* 1977, *22*, 478–483.

Wallerstein, J. and Kelly, J. The Effects of Parental Divorce: Experiences of the Preschool Child. *Journal of Child Psychiatry*, 1975, *14*, 600–616.

Wilson, N. *The Developmental Psychology of the Black Child*. New York: Africana Research Publications, 1978.

Winnicott, D. W. *The Child and the Family*. New York: Basic Books, 1949.

Winnicott, D. W. Transitional Objects and Transitional Phenomena: A Study of the First Not-me Possession. *The International Journal of Psychoanalysis*, 1953, *34*, 89–97.

Winnicott, D. W. The Capacity to be Alone. *International Journal of Psychoanalysis*, 1958, *39*, 416–420.

Winnicott, D.W. *The Maturational Processes and the Facilitating Environment*. New York: International Universities Press, 1965.

Zetzel, E. 1949. Anxiety and the Capacity to Bear It. In *The Capacity for Emotional Growth*. New York: International Universities Press, 1970.

Zinman, D. Women and Smoking: A Deadly Combination. *Newsday*, January 17, 1980, p. 3.

Bibliography

Abelin, E. L. The Role of the Father in the Separation-Individuation Process. In J. B. McDevitt and C. F. Settlage (Eds.) *Separation-Individuation: Essays in Honor of Margaret S. Mahler.* New York: International Universities Press, 1971, pp. 229-253.

Blanck, G. and and Blanck, R. *The Lydia Rapoport Lectures.* Northampton: Smith College School of Social Work, 1978.

Blanck, R. The Case for Individual Treatment. *Social Casework,* 1967, 46, 70-74.

Blanck, R. Marriage as a Phase of Personality Development. *Social Casework,* 1967, 48, 154-160.

Blanck, R. Treatment of the Borderline Structures. *The Lydia Rapoport Lectures.* Northampton:, Mass.: Smith College School of Social Work, 1978, pp. 17-31.

Blum, H. The Prototype of Preoedipal Reconstruction. *Journal of The American Psychoanalytic Association,* 1977, 25, 757-778.

Blum, H. The Maternal Ego Ideal and Regulation of Maternal Qualities, *National Institute of Mental Health, Volume on Human Development,* Washington, D.C.: National Institute of Mental Health, in press.

Edward, J. The Therapist as a Catalyst in Sepration-Individuation. *Clinical Social Work Journal,* 1976, 4, 172-186.

Edward, J. The Use of the Dream in the Promotion of Ego Development. *Clinical Social Work Journal,* 1978, 6, 261-273.

Freud, S. 1900. The Interpretation of Dreams. In J. Strachey (Ed.) *Standard Edition,* Vol. 4/5. London: Hogarth Press, 1953.

Freud, S. 1914. On Narcissism: An Introduction. In J. Strachey (Ed.) *Standard Edition,* Vol. 14. London: Hogarth Press, pp. 67-102.

Freud, S. 1920. Beyond the Pleasure Principle. In J. Strachey (Ed.) *Standard Edition,* Vol. 28. London: Hogarth Press, 1955, pp. 3-64.

Freud, S. 1926. Inhibitions, Symptoms and Anxiety. In J. Strachey (Ed.) *Standard Edition,* Vol. 19. London: Hogarth Press, pp. 77-174.

Golan, N. Crisis Theory. In F. Turner (Ed.) *Social Work Treatment.* New York: Free Press, 1974, pp. 420-456.

Goldberg, A. (Ed.) *The Psychology of the Self, A Casebook.* New York: International Universities Press, 1978.

Hartmann, H. Contribution to the Metapsychology of Schizophrenia. *The Psychoanalytic Study of the Child,* 1954, 9, 31-36.

Hartmann, H. Psychoanalysis and Developmental Psychology. In *Essays on Ego Psychology.* New York: International Universities Press, 1964, pp. 99-112.

Hurley, R. *Poverty and Mental Retardation.* New York: Random House, 1969.

Lohman, R. Dying and the Social Responsibility of Institutions. *Social Casework,* 1977, 58, 538-545.

Modell, A. On Having the Right to a Life: An Aspect of the Superego's Development. *International Journal of Psychoanalysis,* 1965, 46, 321-333.

Murray, J. M. Narcissism and the Ego Ideal. *Journal of the American Psychoanalytic Association,* 1964, *12,* 477–528.

Provence, S. and Lipton, R. C. *Infants in Institutions.* New York: International Universities Press, 1962.

Sandler, J., Holder, A., and Meers, D. R. The Ego Ideal and the Ideal Self. *The Psychoanalytic Study of the Child,* 1963, *18,* 139–158.

Simos, B. Grief Therapy to Facilitate Healthy Restitution. *Social Casework,* 1977, *58,* 337–342.

Smith, L. A. Review of Crisis Intervention Theory. *Social Casework,* 1978, *59,* 396–405.

Spiegel, L. A. The Self, The Sense of Self, and Perception. *The Psychoanalytic Study of the Child,* 1959, *14,* 81–109.

Stoller, R. The Sense of Maleness. *Psychoanalytic Quarterly,* 1965, *34,* 207–218.

Ticho, G. Young Adult Women and Female Autonomy. Panel Reports by E. Galenson. *Journal of the American Psychoanalytic Association,* 1978, *26,* 165.

Zimmerman, H. S. Mothers Center Manual, 1980 The Mothers Center of Family Service Association of Nassau County, Inc. New York.

Glossary of Terms

Abysmal affective panic. A symptom of the psychotic symbiotic child, panic stricken behavior. A severe panic reaction (Mahler, 1968).

Adaptation A concept that Hartmann brought to psychoanalysis in 1939, which draws from biology. The human organism is endowed with innate capacities to fit into his or her environment. Adaptation serves survival.

The infant's inborn ability to be shaped by and to shape himself or herself to his or her environment. The child's facility for conforming to the shape of his or her environment (Mahler, 1975).

Affectomotor storm rage reaction A term, defined by Mahler (1952), describing the distress of the ungratified infant. The term describes a nondifferentiated state involving affect and movement, diffuse organismic distress.

If this state is not relieved, it can result in organismic distress (Blanck, & Blanck, 1979).

Affects Subjectively experienced feeling states (Moore and Fine, 1968).

Affects that Mahler has helped illuminate in her studies are confident expectation, elation, low-keyedness, anxiety, affectomotor storm rage reactions, organismic distress, abysmal affective panic.

Aggression One of the two drives (libido is the other). Mahler has accepted the revised definition of aggression as defined by Blanck and Blanck (1979). The aggressive drive serves as a source of energy that fuels the individuation thrust, that propels the child away from the mother, that serves to sever connections. The two drives are said to operate in concert with one another—libido, the drive to unite, operates simultaneously with the drive to disconnect.

Ambitendency An experience of the toddler in the rapprochement subphase in which the child wants to be united with and at the same time separate from mother. It is a simultaneous presence of two contrasting behaviorally manifest tendencies (Mahler, 1975).

Anxiety "A distressing affect (feeling tone) which is subjectively experienced as worry and similar fear of a real danger or its anticipation. There are typical dangers (conscious in early childhood, unconscious later on) that give rise to fear and to neurotic conflict" (Moore and Fine, 1968, p. 21).

Anxiety states are said to accompany the differing levels of early development and correlate with the psychosexual stages, as well as ob-

211

ject-related stages of development. The following is the list of the levels of anxiety, starting with the earliest and ending with the most advanced form: fear of annihilation (first year of life); fear of loss of the object (second year of life); fear of loss of love of the object (second and third years of life); fear of castration (third, fourth and fifth years of life); fear of the superego (following the consolidation of the functional superego) (Blanck and Blanck, 1974).

Autism (normal)   Describes the inferred psychic state of the newborn from birth through roughly the second month of life. This phase is referred to as objectless, with only fleeting states of alert mental activity (Mahler, 1975).

Autism (infantile)   Refers to a form of psychosis in which the child remains fixated at, or regresses to, the first most primitive phase of life, the autistic phase. The most conspicuous symptom is the child's inability to perceive the mother as representative of the outside world. Mahler considers infantile autism to be the result of an inborn, constitutional defect, or one acquired as early as within the first days of extrauterine life.

Autism (secondary)   A term that denotes the symbiotic psychotic child's retreat into autism. (Mahler, 1968).

Autisticlike withdrawl   A temporary defense. A temporary or partial fusion of the self and object representation. A form of behavior that seems to be in the service of rest and recuperation of the ego (Mahler, 1968).

Autistic shell   The quasisolid stimulus barrier available to the infant through roughly the first 4 to 6 weeks of life, that protects the infant from an excess of distress from outside sources. This shell is said to "crack" at about 4 to 6 weeks (Mahler, 1975).

Autoerotic resources   The infant's use of his or her own body to provide pleasure, self-comforting, and soothing to relieve tension; for example, thumbsucking, or rocking.

Auxiliary ego   The external caretaker's action of taking over for the infantile ego; the action of the mother to protect the child from stimuli. When the child does not yet have the capacity to do so, the mother provides a buffering and protective shield.

Average expectable environment   A concept designated by Hartmann that refers to the environment into which the child is born. First is the mother and the maternal care she gives the infant. Behind the mother is the father, the concept of the family, the entire social structure, and the generational cultural continuity. The infant born with innate potentials transacts with the average expectable environment. Development is charted by observations of the good enough infant in the average expectable environment (Hartmann, 1939).

Bad Introject   The taking into the self representation of a perception of a negative or bad part of the object (mother). A bad introject would be one that would not meet essential soothing needs of the infant. A taking in of the retaliation of the mother. The opposite of a supporting, encouraging introject.

Basic depressive affect   A feeling of despair, designated as arising in the rapprochement period as a result of insufficient response of the environment that leaves a proclivity to depressive illness.

Basic mistrust   A term defined by Erickson (1968) as the counterpart of trust in the first of life cycle stages. Basic mistrust forms as a result of frustration. It is considered necessary and part of healthy development to have developed the capacity to mistrust.

Basic trust   A term proposed by Erickson, to describe a state of relationship in which the child has learned to "rely on the sameness and continuity of the outer providers." (1968, 248)

Basic mood   In accord with Edith Jacobson, defined as the habitual mode or response to inner and outer stimulations with positive or negative affects (Mahler, 1975).

The basic mood is an individually characteristic affective response based on the child's early experiences (Mahler, 1966).

Body image   Demarcations (mental perceptions) of the body-ego are deposited in the mind. The body-ego contains two kinds of self images, or representations: an inner core and an outer core. These images form in the symbiotic period and are the core of the self around which identity develops (Mahler, 1974, 1975).

Borderline pathology   Pathology defined, by most authors, as a nonpsychotic state but also a nonneurotic state. It includes those persons who have attained incomplete structure. These people preserve reality testing but have problems in interpersonal relations and productivity. They usually have multiple symptoms. In the borderline condition, whole fused self and object representations are not attained. Included in this category are the severe character pathologies, addictions, narcissistic personalities, infantile personalities, antisocial personalities. (Blanck and Blanck, 1974).

Castration anxiety   Fear of loss or damage to the genitals (castration complex) that arises within the child (Moore and Fine, 1968).

Castration anxiety previously observed only in the phallic phase was found by Mahler in the rapprochement subphase.

Cathectically stable sense of identity   Identity is defined as "the experience of the self as a unique coherent entity which is continuous and remains the same despite inner psychic and outside environmental changes. The sense of identity begins with the child's awareness that he exists as an individual in a world with outer objects, and that he has his own wishes, thoughts, and memories, and his own distinctive appearance" (Moore and Fine, 1968, p. 50). Mahler believes that the formation of a stable sense of identity is dependent on an optimal human symbiosis. The use of the word "cathexis" denotes a concentration of drive energy in the self-identity.

Cathexis   Denotes the investment of the psychic energy of a drive in a mental representation (Moore and Fine, 1968).

Checking back to mother   A visual pattern, observed in the infant in the differentiation period, of comparing mother with the other; the familiar and the unfamiliar. This pursuit serves to form discrimination between mother and all that is different. Also called **custom's inspection.**

Coenesthetic empathy   The clinical worker's use of his or her inner sensations, intuitions, guesses, and identification in understanding the client's affective and bodily state and motor behavior.

Coenesthetic organization   A system of sensing and experiencing, primarily visceral (of the inside of the body), centered in the autonomic nervous system. The infant's system is said to obey the rules of coenesthetic organization. Proprioceptive and enteroceptive processes are part of the coenesthetic organization.

Confident expectation   A mood state of confidence in the self and object that arises out of an optimal experience in the symbiotic phase; similar to basic trust.

Conflict-free ego sphere   Ego functioning that remains autonomous and free of inhibition and impediment. Hartmann (1939) proposed inborn ego apparatus of primary autonomy that can develop outside of conflict with the drives and, in fact, can provide for the direction and development of the drives.

Darting away   A characteristic behavior of the toddler especially noticeable in the rapprochement subphase. Darting away is the act of quick running away from the mother with the expectation of being chased and swept into her arms (Mahler, 1975).

Deanimation   A defensive maneuver of the psychotic child. The child withdraws from reality, especially from the animate, human external involvement with a human object (Mahler, 1968).

Defenses   Mechanisms employed by the ego to force out of awareness impulses, basically sexual and aggressive, that would arouse anxiety in the individual (Moore and Fine, 1968).

Development   A term defined by Hartmann that includes the processes of both biological and psychological growth. Ego developmental theorists trace the unfolding of the developmental processes.

Diacritic perception   Perception takes place in the sensorium (mind); its manifestations are cognitive processes, among them conscious thought (Spitz, 1965).

Diacritic perception begins in the first year of life and follows coenesthetic reception.

Differentiation   "The first subphase of the separation–individuation process manifested from 5 to 9 months of age. Total bodily dependence on mother begins to decrease as the maturation of locomotor partial functions brings about the first tentative moving away from her .... differentiation of a primitive, but distinct, body image [in the mind] seems to occur" (Mahler, 1975, p. 289).

Differentiation (premature)   A psychic experience in which the self representation becomes too distinct too soon from the object representation. That is, the infant experiences a loss of the mother-self membrane before he or she is capable of tolerating the experience of separateness. Brought on by innate precocious ego potentials, overstimulated aggression, or maternal unattunement, the infant has moved out of the safe anchorage.

Distance contact   The toddler's visual or auditory experience of being in contact with the mother when at a physical distance from her. A term used to describe the experience of the practicing subphase toddler who hears the mother when she is in the next room, or sees her from across the room.

Ego   One part of the three parts of the psychic system; the other two are the id and the superego. Apparatus of inborn ego potentials are postulated that aid in the development of an ego and id and, ultimately, the superego. The ego is defined by its functions: reality testing, thought frustration tolerance, anticipation, object relations, regulation of drives, mediation between the superego and the id, to name a few. Part of the ego is unconscious.

Ego, apparatus of primary autonomy   The infant's inborn ego potentials and equipment such as motility, intelligence, recall capacity intention, perception, object comprehension capacity (Hartmann, 1939; Mahler, 1975). This inborn apparatus may be unique, insufficient, or absent and have a bearing on the infant's interaction and capacity to adapt to the environment.

Ego functions (autonomous)   Those ego functions that are originally con-flict-free, that is, develop outside of conflict. The inborn ego appa-ratus is said to be resistant to being overrun by instinctual forces. These are perception, motility, intention, intelligence, speech, lan-guage, etc. The primary autonomous ego functions develop at a cer-tain pace, relatively independently of the drives (Moore and Fine, 1968).

Ego ideal   One part of the superego. The ego ideal holds up ideal stand-ards; the model of who the person should become. Formed from frag-ments and experiences in the subphases, the ego ideal takes a firm shape through the identifications in the oedipal complex. It is formed from both positive experiences and disappointments in the parents. There is always a tension between the ego ideal and the ego.

Ego (observing)   A specific function of the ego that permits the ego to look at itself. Part of the self can observe the other parts; for example, a person can examine and notice his or her thinking processes. Self-awareness, the capacity for self-scrutiny, the capacity for self-examina-tion, and the development of the capacity for self-analysis are related to the functioning of the observing ego.

Ego (precocious)   The inborn potential of a given infant may contain a unique ego apparatus such as a hypersensitivity of visual alertness, touch or taste alertness, an excessive startle reaction, or unusual mo-tility. Because this inborn equipment functions for the infant, it can lead to a premature awareness of self and object. The functioning of the inborn apparatus may serve to create an imbalance within the psychic system.

Elation   The affect of joy and glee observable in the toddler of the prac-ticing subphase, the result of experiencing escape from the mother of engulfment; pleasureable feelings that accompany accomplishments; pleasure experiencing mastery of motoric activities. The affect of the love-affair-with-the-world phase.

Enteroceptive system   The sensing and experiencing capacities of the in-ner organs, for example, the stomach's experience of hunger and satis-faction when hunger is relieved. Part of the coenesthetic system (Mahler, 1958).

Failure to thrive syndrome   The child seems to be adequately provided with food but fails to gain weight, creating severe risk to survival. When these children are placed in a more favorable environment, they are able to gain weight.

False self   A pathological personality constellation in the adult. Also referred to as the "as if" personality." The core of a solid self does not develop, rather the person imitates those around him or her in order to acquire an identity (James, 1960).

Fear of merger; fear of engulfment   An anxiety feeling that accompanies either the toddler's wish to become one again (return to the fused state with the mother of symbiosis), or the anxiety feeling stimulated by the parent's effort to engulf the child in a merger.

Fourth psychological organizer   The oedipus complex may be regarded as the fourth psychological organizer. It transforms the previous mainly external regulation of narcissism into internal self-esteem regulation by the superego (Mahler and Kaplan, 1977).

Gender identity   A psychic sense of maleness or femaleness; the sense of "I am male," or "I am female," observed to crystallize in the rapprochement subphase.

Gentle push   The mother's emotional willingness to let go of her toddler, to encourage the child towards independence that may be a sine qua non of normal healthy individuation.

Good enough mother   A term first designated by Winnicott (1953) defined by him as a necessary facilitator for the child's growth, making it possible for the child to progress from the pleasure principle to the reality principle. The good enough mother is one who makes an active adaptation to the infant's needs. This gradually diminishes according to the infant's growing ability to tolerate frustration.

The good enough mother forgoes her exercise of intuitive understanding for the sake of furthering development (Blanck and Blanck, 1974).

Hatching   "The process of emerging from the symbiotic state from which the toddler has only recently individuated (emerged). It is the 'second,' the psychological, birth experience—the process by which the 'other-than-mother' world begins to be cathected" (Mahler, 1975, p. 290).

"A new look of alertness" is observed in the infant's behavior. The hatched infant has become more permanently alert and perceptive to the stimuli in the environment.

Holding behavior   The primary maternal preoccupation. The kind of physical care provided by the caretaker, which includes cradling, patting, closeness, rocking, firmness, bodily support, and eye contact. Optimal holding patterns provide a feeling of warmth and well-being, "a safe anchorage."

Considered the symbiotic organizer of psychological birth (Mahler, 1975).

Homeostasis   A state of well-being experienced as a feeling of internal stability.

Idealizing transference   A term developed by Kohut (1971) that refers to the transferences that arise from the therapeutic mobilization of the idealized parental image in narcissistic pathology.

Imaging   The inferred activity of the mental work of the child who in the absence of the mother turns his psychic energy inward in search of an inner world that will bring back the perfect state of self that was lost when the mother left. The child is holding onto the sensations of well-being and safety that come from communing with the inner world (Kaplan, 1978).

Inborn signal equipment   The crying of the infant serves to signal the mother who brings help.

Individuation   One of the two tracks of the separation–individuation process; individuation is the development of the child's own individual characteristics (Mahler, 1975).

Infantile neurosis   "The psychological symptomatic manifestation of the universal developmental conflict taking place at the phallic-oedipal phase of development" (Moore and Fine, 1968, p. 53). Freud stressed it as the common fate of all human beings. How the oedipus complex is resolved is part of the description of the infantile neurosis. An adult neurosis may or may not show a close correspondence to the infantile neurosis.

Internalization   "In its broadest aspect, a progressive process by which external interactions between the organism and the outer world are replaced by inner representations of these interactions and their end results. Incorporation, introjection and identification are object-related mechanisms used for this purpose" Moore and Fine, 1968).

Intersystemic conflict   Opposing forces of the mind. In structural theory, this refers to conflicts between the three psychic institutions, the id, ego, and superego.

In contrast to intrasystemic conflict, which refers to opposing forces within one of the institutions, as within the ego.

Intrasystemic conflict   Opposing forces within one psychic system; as an intrasystem conflict in the ego. For example, the wished for self image of the ego propels one set of goals for the ego, while the body representation propels another set of goals. There also can be conflict within the id and the superego.

Libido   A quantitative concept that refers to a measure of the drive energy of the sexual instinct. The term is used to represent sexual drive energy. The libido can cathect (be invested in) the intrapsychic representations of objects (object libido) or the self (narcissism) (Moore and Fine, 1968).

Defined by Blanck and Blanck (1979) libido is the drive that serves to unite, as distinguished from the aggressive drive, which serves to severe connections. Mahler supports the new definition of the drives.

Low-keyedness   A noticeable change in behavior of the practicing subphase child to the mother's absence; the child's toned-down state. Gestural and performance motility slows down, interest in the surroundings is diminished, and the child appears to be preoccupied with inwardly concentrating attention on imaging the mother (Mahler, 1975).

Making it   A term used to denote either the mother or child's perception of the child's capacity to survive and to be able to grow up into an adult, with sufficient mastery over life's events. A positive perception encourages positive self-regard and self-esteem. A negative perception encourages anxiety.

Maturation   The term that refers to biological developing processes. It refers to an inner timetable of physical and physiological events, as distinguished from development, which is reserved for psychological and biological processes in development (Hartmann, Kris and Lowenstein, 1946).

Mirroring frame of reference   The mother's responses, conscious and unconscious, of her perceptions of the infant, which she conveys to the infant about himself or herself. The infant then adjusts to this mirror—a kind of echo phenomenon (Mahler, 1968).

Mirroring admiration   the mother's admiration of the child's accomplishments.

Mirror transference   A term developed by Kohut (1971, p. 28) which refers to transferences that arise from the therapeutic mobilization of the grandiose self.

Mother after separation   A concept that suggests that the toddler who has begun to establish personal autonomy and a degree of separateness, and is therefore discovering the helplessness of the separate self, will find himself or herself torn between the wish to face the anxiety of the continued separated state, and the wish to return to what can seem like a better state—oneness and symbiosis. The mother of symbiosis is a perceived threat to the developing self.

Mothering principle   Stands for the infant's perception and assumed acceptance that relieving ministrations are coming from the human partner. The idea of a mother who satisfies and gratifies is experienced in the mind of the infant. This phenomenon is observed to begin in the later part of the symbiotic phase (Mahler, 1975).

Mutual cueing   A circular process of interaction established very early between mother and infant by which they "emphathetically" read each other's signs and signals and react to each other. Out of the complexity of signs and signals the infant sends to mother, the mother responds to certain of these signals. A selectivity on the mother's part; then the infant adjusts to her cues. The result in the infant is considered one strand of beginning identity formation (Mahler, 1968, 1975).

Narcissism (a) absolute primary narcissism   The state of the mind of the infant in the normal autistic period described as primitive hallucinatory disorientation; absolute infantile omnipotence; no object or self exists in this inferred state (Mahler, 1975).

(b) primary narcissism   The state of the mind of the infant in the early symbiotic period wherein the state of self-absorption still exists, but because there is now a dim awareness of an outside world, the "absoluteness" of nonawareness of a world of self or other is no longer as absolute as in the first six weeks of life. In this stage, there is a beginning of a feeling of a self (Mahler, 1975).

Narcissism, normal   Defined as cathexis of the self-object unit with positive affective value: this has its inception in the symbiotic phase (Blanck and Blanck, 1979).

Narcissism (secondary)   Denotes a state of mind of the infant in the later part of the symbiosis in which the infant has incorporated the mother into his or her personal experiences and inner perceptions. Secondary narcissism is the optimal symbiotic experience; a self-mother experience. A state of oneness; a state of omnipotence (Mahler and Kaplan, 1977; Mahler, 1975).

Narcissism (sound secondary)   The acquisition of healthy self-regard. It is an affective state in which the self representations are cathected with value (Blanck and Blanck, 1979).

Narcissistic compensation   A defensive and adaptive process in which the infant or toddler takes over a function that is not being provided by the mother; that attempts to serve in the development of normal narcissism.

Narcissistic defects   The inability to adjust omnipotent self and object images to reality. Narcissistic defects include tendencies to idealization and devaluation of self and object; a sense of emptiness and worthlessness go along together with feelings of grandiosity and entitlement (Meissner, 1978).

Nodal points   A point of concentration, a central point. Mahler refers to crossroads of the separation–individuation as nodal points in structuralization, maturation, and development, at which certain events are particularly traumatic (Mahler, 1975).

Object   a term connoting the inner mental representation of a person. The term "object" is often regarded as unacceptable, in that it sounds mechanistic. However, it has come into usage in order to distinguish the fact that the internal representation of a person is not necessarily the same as the actual, real person.

Object constancy   A mental representation of a positive libidinally cathected inner image of the mother, implying maintenance of that mental representation regardless of the presence or absence of the love object (mother), and despite internal stress or need. It also implies the unification of the good and bad object into one whole representation; it fosters fusion of the drives and tempers hatred for the object (Mahler, 1975).

Object representations   "An enduring schema of a particular person other than the self modelled by the ego from a multitude of impressions, images and experiences with that person. A person recognized only because of his capacity to gratify instinctual needs is referred to as a need-satisfying object" (Moore and Fine, 1968, p. 64).

Oedipus complex   "A characteristic grouping of instinctual drives, aims, object relations and fears universally found at the height of the phallic phase (3–6 years)" (Moore and Fine, 1968, p. 66).

Mahler, in keeping with Rangell (1972) refers to the oedipus complex as the fourth psychological organizer (Mahler and Kaplan, 1978).

On-the-way-to libidinal object constancy   The fourth of the subphases of the separation–individuation process. The establishment of both individuality (self constancy and self-identity) and object constancy are the central issues of this subphase. The process is also referred to as "the beginning of consolidation of identity and the attainment of a degree of object constancy" (Mahler, 1974, p. 40). This process is an ongoing life process.

Omnipotence   A normal view of the self that forms first in the fused "not I" and "I" unit of symbiosis; gains strength through the practicing subphase, based on the continued belief in the psychic fusion with mother; then is gradually deflated in the rapprochement period, ultimately leading to a normal reality-oriented view of self and object capacities.

Optimal closeness (optimal gratification) optimally available   Refers to the position of the mother in regard to attunement with the infant and, later, the toddler's needs, that provides the best atmosphere and environment to promote the growth of the child. In symbiosis, certain firm supporting holding behaviors of the mother and eye contact with the infant were found to be best for provision of optimal closeness. The mother's availability to express pleasure in the rapprochement child's feats is a provision of optimal availability.

Optimal distance   A description of the toddler's choice of that distance from the mother (in this case physical distance) from which that child could function best (Mahler, 1975).

As the rapprochement toddler experiences the sense of the separate self, that child will be physically close to mother, or separate from her, depending on which location provides inner pleasure, anxiety, or equilibrium of the feeling of safety.

This term is also used to understand defensive behaviors in which persons with borderline organization, fearing merger yet needing the object, arrange conditions that attempt to achieve self-stabilization.

Optimal frustration   The amount of anxiety or stress or frustration the infant or toddler can tolerate without undue strain on the state of ego at a specific phase of development. This concept carries connotations of a span of time, or a level of intensity of the stress. Optimal frustration promotes growth, as in alertness to an inside self in the symbiotic phase during a period of hunger. Too much frustration will cause regression to an earlier level, or, if prolonged, malformation in the development ego.

Organismic distress   A global diffuse internally painful sensation of physiological distress experienced within the interior of the infant's body, considered the forerunner of anxiety (Mahler, 1968).

Penis envy   A mental attitude and feeling of discontent with one's own genital equipment; discovered by Mahler as occurring during the rapprochement subphase, and creating hostility to the mother in the female child but also creating a dynamic in fostering identification with the mother.

Pleasurable inspective behavior   The infant's activity of looking at the other-than-mother people in the environment with confident expectation, curiosity, wonderment, and pleasure, as distinct from stranger anxiety as a response to the other-than-mother.

Polymorphous perverse   A term used to describe pathology in which actions and/or thought processes are chaotic, and multiple perverse sexual fantasies dominate action and thought (Kernberg, 1975).

Practicing   "The second subphase of the separation–individuation, lasting from about 9 months to about 14 months of age" (Mahler, 1975, p. 291). The infant can crawl away and attain upright locomotion in this period. Space is explored.

Preverbal reconstruction   A description of the state of the ego in the infant or toddler in interaction with his or her environment at a given sector or nodal point in his or her early development that represents as accurate a duplication of the experience and process of that psychic state and interaction as is possible. The preverbal reconstruction is given to the client in an explanatory form.

Primal identification   The first inferred psychic state; the absolute infantile projected omnipotence ascribed to the sensorium of the infant in the autistic period (Mahler, 1975).

Projection   A defense of the ego, "a process whereby a painful impulse or idea is attributed to the external world. The ideas or feelings which the person cannot tolerate in himself or herself may undergo a transformation before they are projected (Moore and Fine, 1968).

Projective identification   A primitive defense mechanism found in borderline structure. The purpose of the projection is to externalize the all bad, aggressive self, and object images. Then the problem for the person becomes defending the self from these dangerous retaliatory external objects. There are insufficient ego boundaries in these persons. Therefore, they feel they must identify themselves with the object onto whom the aggression has been projected, and then ongoing "empathy" with the now external threatening object maintains and increases the fear of their own projected aggression (Kernberg, 1975).

Proprioceptive system   The sensing capacities of the outer organs and areas of the body, for example, the ear's capacity to hear inner and outer stimuli; the skin's sensing warmth or cold. Part of the coenesthetic system (Mahler, 1958).

Psychological birth   The attainment of unified whole self and object representations occurring at about 3 years of age.

Psychological birth of the individual is referred to as the separation-individuation process: the establishment of a sense of separateness particularly in regard to one's own body, and the principal representation of the primary love object. The principal achievements of this process take place from the fourth to fifth month to the thirtysixth month (Mahler, 1968).

Rapprochement   The third phase of separation-individuation, lasting from 14 or 15 months to about 24 months of age or beyond. It is characterized by a rediscovery of mother, now a separate individual, and a returning to her after the obligatory forays of the practicing period. The toddler loves to share his or her experiences and possessions with mother, who is now more clearly perceived as separate and outside. The narcissistic inflation of the practicing subphase is slowly replaced by a growing realization of separateness and, with it, vulnerability. Adverse reactions to brief separations are common, and mother can no longer be easily substituted for, even by familiar adults. It often culminates in a more or less transient rapprochement crisis (Mahler, 1975).

Rapprochement crisis   A period during the rapprochement subphase occurring in all children, but with great intensity in some, during which the realization of separateness is acute. The toddler's belief in his or her omnipotence is severely threatened and the environment is coerced as the toddler tries to restore the status quo. The child wants to separate from, but be united with, the mother (ambitendency). Temper tantrums, whining, sad moods, and intense separation reactions are at their height (Mahler, 1975).

Reflex equipment   Inborn physiological mechanisms, such as sucking, rooting, grasping, clinging, the Moro reflex (startle reaction), which serve tension discharge and gain homeostasis (Mahler, 1968).

Refueling, or "libidinal refueling"   During the practicing subphase, the infant forays away from the mother, but when he or she becomes fatigued and depleted of energy, the toddler seeks to reestablish bodily contact with mother. "This 'refueling' perks [the child] up and restores the previous momentum to practice and explore" (Mahler, 1975, p. 290).

Repetition phenomenon   Refers to a repetition of experiences. This term is drawn from Freud's description of the repetition compulsion. "The phenomenon represents a general tendency in all human behavior to repeat painful experiences. The repetition act in adult experience is self-defeating, but the underlying motive is assumed to be that the action seeks to redo the original trauma in hopes it will be mastered" (Moore and Fine, 1968, p. 87).

Representation   A mental picture of the self or object, as distinguished from self or object (person) in reality.

Safe anchorage   A word used to denote the mother's provision of a firm, attuned holding pattern for the infant of symbiosis. It promotes a feeling of well-being and safety in the symbiotic infant.

Secondary process thinking   "Predominately logical, controlled thinking characterized economically by the use of minimal amounts of neutralized psychic energy as opposed to free fantasies and massive discharges of unbound energy involved in the primary process.

"Secondary process also characteristically introduces the concept of delay, or postponement of immediate discharge, as contrasted with primary process which strives for immediate discharge" (Moore and Fine, 1968, p. 88).

Selective response   The mother's response to only certain of the innumerable signals from the infant. These selected responses arise out of the mother's conscious and unconscious ideas of who she would like her baby to become. Her cues to the infant leave an indelible imprinted configuration on the infant (Mahler, 1968).

Self   The totality of the psychic and bodily person (Jacobson, 1964).

Self constancy   An enduring individuality, including the awareness of being a separate and individual entity, and a gender-defined self (Mahler, 1975).

Self images   Part pictures of the self, as a body image; a "wished-for-self image." The totality of the self images make up the self representation.

Self image (grandiose)   An age-appropriate self image of the practicing subphase in which the child thinks of himself or herself as omnipotent and invincible, brought about by the feelings of exaltation and pleasure in body mastery of that subphase, and as a result of the idea of being still in the self-mother psychic orbit. Also used to denote a pathological self image if still operant in the adult.

Self-representations   "A more enduring schema than the self-image constructed by the ego out of the multitude of realistic and distorted self-images which the individual has had at different times. It represents the person as he consciously and unconsciously perceives himself. It includes enduring representations of all the experienced body states, and all the experienced drives and affects which the individual has consciously or unconsciously perceived in himself at different times in reaction to himself and to the outer world" (Moore and Fine, 1968, p. 88).

"The unconscious, preconscious, and conscious endopsychic representations of the bodily and mental self in the system ego" (Jacobson, 1964, p. 19).

Self-Soothing   The act of relieving inner tension, developed over time, brought about by the internalization by the child of the mother's action of soothing him or her.

The capacity for self-soothing is significantly linked to the development of signal anxiety and regulation of anxiety in adults.

Sending power   The infant's innate ability to evoke the kind of mothering he or she needs (Mahler, 1975).

Separation   One of the two tracks of the separation–individuation process. Separation refers to the child's emergence from symbiotic fusion with the mother, to boundary formation and disengagement. Separation is a psychological mental state pertaining to the separation of self and object; it never refers to physical separation.

Separation anxiety   "A descriptive term which refers to the painful affect of anxiety engendered by the threat of, or actual physical separation from a loved one." Separation anxiety is a normal reaction, if not excessive, in the first years of life (Moore and Fine, 1968, p. 89).

The normal anxiety accompanying the rapprochement crisis.

Shadowing   Characteristic behavior of the toddler especially noticeable in the rapprochement subphase. It is defined as the child's incessant watching of and following every move of the mother (Mahler, 1975).

Signal anxiety   Is a part of normal ego functioning, and serves the purpose of alerting the individual to a danger, the result of unconscious conflict (Moore and Fine, 1968).

The capacity to regard anxiety as a signal has its inception somewhere in the second year of life (Blanck and Blanck, 1974).

Splitting   Normal splitting. Memory islands of good and bad self images, and memory islands of good and bad object images form vaguely in the latter half of the symbiotic phase. There are four sets of images: good self, bad self, good object, bad object (Mahler, 1968; Blanck and Blanck, 1979).

The child, in order to preserve the good self images, will separate the longed-for image of the love object from the hated image of the love object. A common experience in the rapprochement subphase (Mahler, 1968).

As a defense: Kernberg introduced the term "splitting," defining it as an active defensive separation of the "all good" images from the "all bad" images. This mechanism is said to be the major defense in borderline states (Blanck and Blanck, 1974).

Stimulus barrier   An inborn shield that protects the infant from external stimuli.

Stranger reactions   "A variety of reactions to people other than mother, particularly pronounced during the differentiation subphase . . . . Stranger reactions include curiosity and interest, as well as wariness and mild or even severe anxiety" (Mahler, 1975, p. 293).

Structure   According to structural theory, the mind is divided into three functional groups, called ego, id, and superego. These are called structures because of the realtive constancy of their objectives and consistency in modes of operation (Moore and Fine, 1968).

Superego   In structural theory, one part of the three part system; the id and the ego are the other two. The superego represents moral attitudes and standards. It has several functions: critical and punishing functions, mood regulation, reward functions, protective functions, maintenance of gender (Moore and Fine, 1968).

Symbiosis   The term used to designate the inferred second stage in the mental development of the infant, occurring roughly between the ages of 6 weeks and 5 months. Symbiosis refers to a fused mother-self experience where the "I" is not yet differentiated from the "not I."

Symbiosis (parasitic)   A condition in the mother-infant relationship in which the mother experiences the child as part of herself. The mother's ministrations to the infant discount the infant's needs and care is provided by what the mother needs. The mother contains the infant in the symbiotic orbit.

Symbiotic psychosis   A childhood psychosis indicating a fixation at or regression to the stage of the need-satisfying part object. It is characterized by catatoniclike temper tantrums and panic-stricken behavior. The symbiotic psychotic child is unable to use the mother as a real external object as a base for developing a stable sense of separateness (Mahler, 1974).

Symbiotic psychotic child   A psychotic condition of childhood in which the infant, or the child at a later age, shows the inability to move out of the symbiotic orbit. The clinical picture includes abysmal affective panic, somatic delusions, hallucinations, and agitated temper tantrums.

Transitional object   A Winnicott (1978) concept defined as the infant's first recognition of and choice of a not-me possession. The object is usually a piece of cloth, a blanket, or a teddy bear. The object always soothes and facilitates the infant's recognition of reality, and soothes the child in the experience of becoming self-sufficient.

Transitional phenomenon   Coping mechanisms used by the child to manage anxiety generated by separation. Examples: bursts of physical activity, imaging, transitional objects.

Transmuting internalizations   Kohut's (1971) concept, elaborated by Tolpin (1972), with application to developmental theory. It describes the process by which the infant acquires the ability to soothe and calm himself or herself and deal with experiences of anxiety through the slow internalizations of those maternal functions that originally the mother used to soothe, calm, and regulate the infant's anxiety.

Triangulation   The growing recognition of the child in the rapprochement subphase that mother and father have a special relationship to one another, and that the child has a relationship with the parents as a couple different from the earlier relationship of the child to each separate parent. (Abelin, 1971).

Wished-for self representation   A term explicated by Jacobson that defines an image residing in the ego containing the ego's aspirational model for the self. It is different from the ego ideal that resides in the superego.

Wooing   The rapprochement toddler's efforts to interest the mother in his or her feats of accomplishment. The beginning capacity to woo indicates the beginnings of self-pride and self-pleasure. A positive response to the child's wooing by the mother is essential in order for the elation of this phase to be carried forward. Paucity of maternal interest, or inability to share some elation, will cause subphase inadequacy in the development of sound secondary narcissism (Blanck and Blanck, 1979).

Working alliance   Also called the therapeutic alliance. A relatively non-neurotic, rational rapport that the patient has with the analyst. It is the reasonable and purposeful part of the feelings the patient has for the analyst, indicating the patient's ability to work in the analytic situation (Greenson, 1967).

"Where there has been subphase inadequacies, the therapist uses himself or herself within the therapeutic alliance" (Blanck, 1978, p. 160).

"A conscious aspect of the relationship between analyst and patient. In this, each implicitly agrees and understands their working together to help the analysand mature through insight, progressive understanding and control. It involves a therapeutic split in the patient's ego, with one area of ego functioning cooperating with the analyst by observing the other experiencing part of the ego" (Moore and Fine, 1968, p. 93).

Zonal maturation   The development of psychic interest in the psychosexual zones: oral, anal, and phallic-urethal.

Author Index

Subject Index